"I can still remember the first time I heard Martin Shaw tell a story. The tale that emerged was like a living thing, bounding around, throwing itself at all of us there listening. I had never heard anything like it before. Shaw is a one-off, his work is urgent and necessary, and *Scatterlings* is his testament. *Scatterlings* is told in a way that makes it unlike any other book I have read."

–Paul Kingsnorth, author of *The Wake*

"One of our most gifted oral tellers is paying necessary homage, offering his attention and capacious intelligence to the Devonshire land of his begetting . . . quietly tracking earth's own imagination, the dreaming of the high moor and the meandering river, the edge where the cliffs meet the strand and both are washed clean by the tides."

–David Abram, author of *Becoming Animal: An Earthly Cosmology*

"I will say this about Dr. Martin Shaw: I wish him protection from the saints and something like a pardon from the Lucid Gods. He is now as much and as good a teller as there probably is among those of us adorned and afflicted by the English tongue, and he has lingered a while in the old caves, as he says.

He knows that things can happen when the word is nailed to a tree, to be read. Things do happen.

And yet he's done it, and done it so very well, and so much in thrall to the chant that you can hear him. It may be wisdom he's done here. It may be something wiser.

I know that if I had to choose kinship, Dr. Shaw the dowser and scribe on my left or the Old Gods of Song who have granted me my tongue and my days on my right, I'd be pressed. Hard pressed. Probably I am.

So hail this *Scatterlings*, this treasure. Barley and love for its burdened, heathen son, the one who's come down from the hills with this Relic From the World Tree and from it has carved his plume and a way home. Would that this plea for a better day and its maker be granted not the cliff face but the long road, and peace for his earned, learned days. Now, homeward."

–Stephen Jenkinson, author of *Die Wise*

"Shaw has a poet's sensibility and a poet's voice."

–Ann Skea, author of *Ted Hughes: The Poetic Quest*

"*Scatterlings* connects us with the land under our feet, and stories to take us to the home we have forgotten about. It is time to remember where we have come from, where we belong, and these words speak the spirit of place. Listen to them, hear the call to remember, to come home, back to the soil, back to soul. Allow the magic of Martin's words to reach deep into you, into your gut and your heart."
—Llewellyn Vaughan-Lee, Sufi teacher and author of
Spiritual Ecology: The Cry of the Earth

"This book will tear away the veil that has separated us from our past and our future. It will rekindle hope and an infinite trust in our being and becoming."
—Anne Bearing, author of *The Dream of the Cosmos: A Quest for Soul*

"With great skill, agility and elegance Martin Shaw takes us deeply to the mythic life-blood of his beloved Dartmoor — *Scatterlings* word-magic will embed you ever more powerfully in the soul of your own land, wherever on Earth you happen to be."
—Dr. Stephan Harding, author of *Animate Earth.*

"A great work of imagination: *Scatterlings* will nourish the soul of those who read it. Shaw's wonderful book weaves together the history, mystery and mythology of Dartmoor. The magic of the moor and spell-binding stories told from the heart is a delightful combination."
—Satish Kumar, Editor-in-chief, *Resurgence*, and author of *Earth Pilgrim*

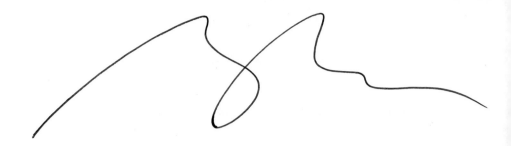

SCATTERLINGS
Getting Claimed in the Age of Amnesia

MARTIN SHAW
Foreword by David Abram

White Cloud Press
Ashland, Oregon

To the woman who walks the moor with me.

White Cloud Press titles may be purchased for educational, business, or sales promotional use. For information, please write:

White Cloud Press
PO Box 3400
Ashland, OR 97520
www.whitecloudpress.com

Cover and interior design by Christy Collins, C Book Services

First printing: 2016
16 17 18 19 20   10 9 8 7 6 5 4 3 2 1

Library of Congress Cataloging-in-Publication Data
Names: Shaw, Martin, author.
Title: Scatterlings : getting claimed in the age of amnesia / by Martin Shaw.
Description: First edition. | Ashland, Oregon : White Cloud Press, [2016] |
  Includes bibliographical references.
Identifiers: LCCN 2016035690 | ISBN 9781940468501 (paperback)
Subjects: LCSH: Folklore--England--Dartmoor.
Classification: LCC GR142.D25 S53 2016 | DDC 398.209423/53--dc23
LC record available at https://lccn.loc.gov/2016035690

Contents

FOREWORD

Well, the fact is, I pleaded with Martin Shaw not to write this book. A few years ago I had come upon Shaw's first published work, *A Branch from the Lightning Tree: Ecstatic Myth and the Grace of Wildness*, while I was browsing in a bookstore. That title and the starkly beautiful cover were enough to win me over; I took the book home. I figured it'd be good to read some mythic tales from around the world, tales that maybe I'd not heard before, and was curious to see what this author would do with them. But once I opened the book and began reading—man, oh man, this was something new!

I was already well acquainted with that lineage of psychological writers, fed by Carl Jung's imaginative work, who scavenge carefully among mythic and folk traditions, drawing fresh water from old faerie tales and folktales. These mythologists lean deep into the stories to discern archetypal patterns, listening closely to various characters and following the dream logic of their magic adventures, harvesting from such stories uncanny insight regarding the workings of the human soul. The lustrous craft of such writers—from Joseph Campbell to Marie-Louise von Franz, from the visionary psychologist James Hillman to Shaw's early mentor, the poet-bard Robert Bly—had brought a nourishing wildness into contemporary psychology, a sense that even today the human mind is secretly and steadily fed by a clamor of conflicting energies, daimonic powers seething in the inexhaustible deep of our collective psyche. Yet there was the rub; most all of these writers assumed that the tumult of forces revealed in the old, oral stories resided somewhere *inside* us—that the gods, goddesses, demons, and spirits afoot in the tales could be traced to powers that lurk within the largely unconscious depth of the collective human interior, and hence that the tales had real relevance only to human persons and not to the spider weaving its web in the near corner of the room, or to the raucous crows hollering outside the window, much less to the hordes of salmon that once muscled their way upstream, or clear-cut mountainsides and dripping glaciers, or the thunderclouds now massing on the horizon.

That's why Shaw's writing, in *A Branch from the Lightning Tree*, struck me as something fresh. Here at last was someone reflecting on old peasant folktales who wasn't just psychologising the stories, someone who had spent gobs of time living in and learning from the wild backcountry, and who consequently knew something of dank woodlands and drenching storms and the ways of self-willed creatures—and who let this savvy bleed into his unfurling of the old tales. Finally! At some point I went hunting for some more info on this author and learned that he lived on Dartmoor: a vast and boggy highland punctuated by numerous *tors*—hills topped with dramatic granite outcrops that look like ruined temples or tumbled fortresses, an impression that's difficult to shake, given that the moor is also riddled with megaliths, stone circles, and other traces of human practice dating back some five thousand years. I learned, too, that Shaw was the founder of something called the Westcountry School of Myth up there on Dartmoor, that an upcoming project of his was a book-length recounting and exploration of the Parzival stories, and that he was also gathering a clutch of local folktales and legends—stories endemic to Devon and the Dartmoor highlands—which he was hoping to publish in book form, as well.

This last made me sit up. From my own scattered fieldwork as a cultural ecologist, and the familiarity it's given me with a small handful of traditional, oral cultures indigenous to southeast Asia and North America, I'd come to feel that writing down old oral-tradition tales was not something to do lightly. Indeed, in many cases was not a particularly helpful thing to do at all. Why? Well, oral culture is often remarkably place-based, attuned in countless subtle and complex ways to the specific topography, textures, tones, and rhythms of the local earth. Moreover, traditionally oral tales commonly hold, in their layered adventures, specific information regarding local animals and plants (how best to hunt particular creatures and how to prepare their skins for clothing or shelter; which plants are good for treating particular ailments; how to prepare them in poultices, or as potions . . .), as well as particular instructions regarding the forms of ritual blessing necessary to ensure a livable life in that region.

And why is oral culture so deeply place-based? Well, because there's simply no way to *remember* many of the stories of a nonwriting, oral culture without now and then encountering the sites—the waterholes, forested mountainsides, clustered boulders, and tight river bends where those storied events once happened or are felt to have happened.

For most us today, born of a highly literate civilization, printed books are the primary *mnemonic*—the primary memory-trigger—for activating the accumulated knowledge that's been stored up by our ancestors over the generations. We turn to books, like this one, when we wish to recall some of the old stories or to access the practical knowledge those stories hold. Yet for communities without any highly formalised system of writing—for cultures without books—the animate, expressive landscape *itself* carries the stories. Only by encountering over and again those clustered boulders, the mouth of that deep cave, this cliff-edge vista or wooded peninsula or mist-covered swamp, are we continually brought to recall the storied events that happened there and the detailed ancestral knowledge stored in those stories. Similarly, when we hear the yip-yipping of coyotes or come upon the tracks of a grizzly by the half-eaten carcass of a spawned-out salmon, we can't help but recall yet another tale in which that bushy-tailed trickster, or Old Honey-Paws, or perhaps even the Salmon of Wisdom figures as a central character. For *in the absence of books, the animate, expressive terrain itself is the necessary mnemonic, or memory-trigger, for remembering the oral tales.*

For this reason, the old, oral-tradition stories tend to be deeply entangled with the rhythm and pulse of particular places. Although it's sometimes hard for highly literate folks to sense, there's an indissoluble rapport between an indigenous storyteller and the lilt of the local land; he may feel that, by intoning a tale, he is translating secret or sacred matters *overheard* from the speaking earth. That is how Sean Kane puts it, in his wonderful book *Wisdom of the Mythtellers:* "Myth, in its most ecologically discreet form, among people who live by hunting and fishing and gathering, seems to be the song of the place to itself, which humans overhear." Or as Martin Shaw insightfully frames it herein: a really fine storyteller, by the eloquent practice of her art, is carefully echoing signals emanating from the expressive terrain around her; the teller is participant in a subtle process of *echolocation*, by which the deep earth speaks, and listens, and returns to itself, nourished.

Moreover, in the absence of books, stories are far less portable than they have become for us today. If they are not written down, tales cannot travel so easily from the places that body them forth, and hence the tales can't so readily forfeit, or lose, the intricate place-specific knowledge that they still hold and transmit for those who live in that region. If the strongest oral tales are best understood as the place itself speaking through the teller, well, writing down those tales would seem to interrupt this direct transmission.

For the written stories can now be carried elsewhere, and within a short time they can be read—by multiple others—in distant cities and even on distant continents. Since the story no longer neatly matches the contour of the strange new terrain where it's being read (since it cannot aptly echo, or invoke, the many-voiced landscape that surrounds the reader wherever she finds herself) the tale now seems to float free of the ground. Soon enough, all of the place-specific savvy contained in that tale, regarding the precise song for calling a particular creature or the precise technique for harvesting certain vision-inducing herbs, is forgotten.

Back in the tale's home terrain, we might hope, people are also reading the published story, although for them it's now the page, rather than the living land, that carries and transmits the tale. People no longer need to step outside; they no longer need to hear the gurgling speech of the river or to gaze the jumbled stones on that hillside in order to recall the old stories. The palpable land, with its creaturely denizens, has become superfluous to the remembrance of ancestral knowledge. Since the tales have been uprooted from those sites and replanted on the printed page, we no longer need the sight of those distant cliffs or the scent of those cottonwoods in order to think clearly. Or rather, we no longer *think* that we need them.

Stripped of its stories, the land is beginning to fall mute. No longer an expressive, animate power, the local earth soon comes to be seen as a purely passive background or backdrop against which human life unfolds.

It's for this reason that I had the gall and the gumption to phone up Martin Shaw, an author I'd never met or spoken to, and ask him *not* to publish the old oral tales that he'd gathered from his corner of Britain. I wanted him to tell the stories and to get others telling the tales, out loud, there in that land, but not to publish them in a book and so strip them from the local earth. Speak the stories, by all means! Sing them out on the high moor, gesturing towards that circle of half-fallen standing stones as you do so. Gather people for the telling; let them imbibe the air of that place and lend their ears to the speech of the River Dart gushing over the guttural stones as the story stutters through their bodies. Let them gaze into the morning mist to see the spirits rising from the boggy fields as they hear the chanted words!

The stranger on the other end of the line listened patiently to what I had to say and then replied, with a most openhearted and musical voice, beard-thick with roots and mossy tones: "Too late." He'd been gathering these tales for a long time already, letting them simmer in his body (and maybe tossing in a few herbs) while they worked their way into his own idiom; he'd been walking the terrain of the tales and watching to see what sprang up as he muttered and uttered them forth.

Huh ... Crestfallen that my telephonic intervention had failed in its intent, I nevertheless found myself intrigued, and somewhat pleased, to make this first acquaintance with a voice so thoroughly infused with the singsong tones of that place. We kept on talking for a long while and soon found ourselves laughing, as well. Before I knew it, we'd arranged to teach together at Schumacher College, a wonderful place where I'd already taught many times, a sort of Hogwarts for grown-ups there in Devon, not far from Dartmoor and just a few long meanders downriver from where Martin lived.

And it was there, during that fine first stint of teaching together, that Martin startled me one morning with a query. Seeing as I'd had the audacity to phone him up, outa' the blue, and ask him *not* to write his book of land-based tales, he now had the *utter chutzpah* to invite me to write a foreword for the very same book I'd pressed him not to write! The sheer gall of the man ...

But there was method in his madness. For while the book you now hold in your hands is, indeed, a confluence of curious tales heard, gleaned, and gathered by Martin Shaw from that corner of the earth where he himself was born and raised—the very land where he gradually grew into his craft as a mythteller—it is also much more than that. This book is a compendium of discoveries, hard-won insights, and practical teachings for any who aspire to the bardic craft of the storyteller. And for others, too, who seek simply to apprentice themselves to a place. *Any* place.

For what better way to become native to a terrain than to open one's senses to the innumerable tales secretly unfolding themselves under the hill, emptying one's ears toward the fluid articulations of the burbling stream and the quiet laughter of the jackdaws? By leaning into and listening close to Martin Shaw's tellings of these various stories and to the way these stories came to claim him and made a home in his own vernacular, we can't help but glean precious clues regarding the way English roots itself in particular soils, regarding the way stories sprout and proliferate, the manner in which different species of tales inhabit the woods, the winds, or the waters of a place. And so, inadvertently, we find ourselves becoming more attentive to the weirdness of our own home terrain, to the human and more-than-human happenings out and about in our locale.

So the ancestral affinity between story and earthly place is a key theme in this work—the way some tales are so deeply rooted in the soil that they can often be heard as an upsurge of eloquence from the unseen depths underfoot. Yet that melody is neatly counterbalanced herein by another, apparently contrary, theme: the propensity of certain stories to *migrate* from one region to another.

Long before written records, deep into prehistory, many human groups were nomadic in their ways. But also in more recent times, right up until today, even the most long-settled communities are sometimes forced—whether by human hostilities or by a deepening drought, by spasms of "ethnic cleansing" or by slowly rising seas—to pull up roots and traverse strange territories before settling and sinking tendrils into the soil of a new land. And the stories valued by those communities also travel, mingling with other tales and sometimes migrating huge distances, sounding themselves out in strange contexts, striving to plant themselves in various dry and inhospitable soils before finding a topography conducive to the twists and turns those stories hold. If and when a story does take root in new ground, the altered creatures and climate and culture of that realm will inevitably twist and torque the tale afresh.

And therein lies Martin Shaw's implicit corrective to my phoned-in objection, the strongest possible response to my plea that he not publish these Devonshire stories and so sunder them further from the land that once held them. For even the most deeply place-based tales inevitably have elements—at the least, particular words—that at some point arrived from elsewhere, while some spoken stories in their entirety have been forced by circumstances to wander, to migrate, to change their residence. And thus *the recent displacement and dissemination of stories via the printed page (and now via the internet) is only the most up-to-date form of an exuberant waywardness that's always been integral to spoken stories, a vagrant or vagabondish quality that's long been a part of the mythteller's craft.* (I am not certain that I completely agree with that, but it's a splendid contention, and one that's got me steadily pondering. I mean, really, *who knew* that the Arthurian legends—tales that seem so close to the heart and soul of Britain—may have originated, as I learned in these pages, among nomadic tribespeople on the Iranian steppes?)

Moreover, Shaw suggests that as we now plunge headlong into what I call "the age of consequences"—into an age when so many of our civilisation's reckless choices are now circling back to bite us, when seasonal cycles are abruptly

going haywire and anciently established patterns of life no longer match the
swerving circumstances—the new intercultural exchange and crossfertilization
between stories may simply be necessary for survival. After reflecting on the
many migratory creatures now forced by the changing climate to alter ancient
navigational routes and so to find new habitat for themselves, Shaw writes:

> It may be that stories are being forced to move from their old geographi-
> cal habitations because they have something important to say about this
> wider crisis. As the crane settles in a new and unfamiliar German forest
> while snow falls, so a Seneca shaman story is told in the tentative sur-
> roundings of a Plymouth pub. I believe the two emerging migrations are
> connected. They are speaking over the frontier divides—crow to myth, to
> waterfall, to folktale.

It's a potent, if painful, thought.

Nevertheless, and despite the wide-ranging and galloping forays on which
he takes his readers, Shaw is thoroughly given, heart and soul, to the intimate
particulars of his home terrain. He pours libations to the unseen elementals,
to the small ones and the huge ones, tuned as he is to the other-than-human
powers that feed the local vernacular—lending their specific languor to the
local pubs, offering their shapes and shadows to the many rites and ritual gestures that characterise life in that region. He has lingered over countless pints
with many an old farmer, wringing forth a newfound verse to some centuries'
old song; he's listened close to the counting rhyme of the local shepherds as
they tally their sheep: "*Hant, tant, toghery, forthery, fant, sahny, dahny, downy,
dominy, dik . . .*"

And so the imagination, or psyche, that powers these curious tales belongs
not to anyone's private "inner world" nor to the collective unconscious of any
single species; Martin Shaw is quietly tracking earth's own imagination, the
dreaming of the high moor and the meandering river, the edge where the cliffs
meet the strand and both are washed clean by the tides. His craft is different
from that of those who see stories as entirely human creations and who mine
them for insights into the confused psyche of our species. His tellings are
constrained less by the befuddlements of contemporary humankind and more
by the life of the land itself. Despite appearances, the magic afoot in these
tales is rarely of a supernatural variety; it does not arrive from some other
dimension, but percolates up from under the ground or alights like a cloud of
swallows newly arrived from North Africa—their spring migration.

With this book, then, one of our most gifted oral tellers is paying necessary homage, offering his attention and capacious intelligence to the Devonshire land of his begetting and of his voice's begetting—reciprocating the favour, returning and thereby replenishing the gifts instilled in him by the dreaming land and its denizens, human and otherwise. Listen close.

DAVID ABRAM

Hare

Who is queen of Dartmoor?
how does the salmon or white doe fare?
Who is the one to ask for?
Lay your gifts at solitary Hare.

I'd glimpsed her first from the shepherds' hut. And then sometimes outside, throwing coffee granules into the rain.

Late autumn, frost, and bold as brass, Hare in the long grasses. Bounding, darting, lying low like a small, earthy tump. Hairy, toothy, wet backed, utterly wild. An emissary from an entirely different century, or even outside time altogether.

By spring there'd be rabbits on the grass, and she'd be gone. But, for a little while, Hare was in my life. Come March, I'd search but wouldn't spot those long ears in the scrub, those great jugs of sound. But I remember her jubilance in the rain. I remember.

January. It's a mild afternoon, the very first snowdrops flower by my boots, the sun like a dulled bronze coin behind a glowing flank of gray cloud. I enter the wood behind the hut. I bow under the first gateway of holly, then oak, then into that always unexpected grove of redwood trees. I never quite get used to them.

Today the wind is like foam breakers crashing on a distant beach: immense, protracted roars up in those scoured branches. I stretch my neck to see if there're any fishing boats wrapped round the timber. I pass a smearing of bloody magpie feathers enmeshed in wire fencing. There's been a scrap of some kind. Magpie did not dust itself off. Crow continues to drill the road overhead, and underneath there are little clusters of songbirds.

Today I love Hare like I love pirate ships, old maps of Scotland, and pipe smoke in autumn. A kind of love without thought. Just a great, affectionate lurch of the body towards what claims it. So in the absence of my teacher, I give praise to air that it may carry these words to those vast, twitching ears.

HARE

Taken into battle and used as divination by Queen Boudicca. As it erupted from the folds of her skirt, the way it leapt gave sacred information to the Iceni. It takes a woman to understand Hare's powers. As long as you expect it to behave as a swaggering hero you will be disappointed, but let it be its nature and you are in the presence of wisdom.

HARE

A body suffused unusually and liberally with blood. A royal dish. The people of the fields prefer rabbit to the bucket-blood, dark flesh and strong stink of Hare's meat. For the rich this can all be negotiated by servants in faraway kitchens. Then, magically, it becomes highly desirable. But Robert Burton in *Anatomy of Melancholy* warns against it: "Hare is a black meat, melancholy and hard of digestion; it breeds *Incubus* often eaten, and causeth fearful dreams" (Evans 1972, 92).

HARE

The leaper. The hare-brained swift whose time is spring: of buddings and sudden emergings; there's no plod with this one. The Algonquin have knowledge for us moor people: they say Hare is Michabo, Great Hare, maker of sun, moon, and earth. Hare is ruler of the winds; the reason Dartmoor is so filled with chills is because of the daily comings and goings of those laying tribute at Hare's feet.

Hare: Here are some of your faraway names:

Lord Hare, Lord of the Day, Manabozho, Hiawatha, Manabosho, Manabush, Manibozho, Nanabozho, Winabozho, Great Hare, Minabozha, Nanaboojoo, Nanabush, Abnaki Gluskap, Iroquois Ioskeha, Menominee Manabush, Montagnais Messou, Messibizi, Messon, Missabos, Missiwabun, Wan.

Hare: Here are some of your close-up names. These I whisper:

Old Turpin, Puss, Light Bringer, Hidden Quiet of the Byre, Long-Flank, Tremble Heart, The One They Track With Silver, The Way-Beater, The Stag of the Stubble, Get-Up-Quickly, Flincher, Dew-Beater, The Furze-Cat, Lurker, Squatter in the Hedge, The Swift as Wind, Shagger, The Fellow in the Rain, Wide-Eyed One that Lurks in Broom, The Low Creeper, One Who Turns to the Hills.

Dartmoor Hare:

Here is a story about you and your people.

INTRODUCTION
Getting Claimed

Whatever the colour of Englishman you scratch
you come to some sort of crow.
TED HUGHES
(in a letter to Alan Bold)

Scatterlings is about holding up the corner of the earth that has claimed you. It's messy and opinionated and asks more of you than you will likely want to give.

It's the tale of a mythteller making a circle round his den and bedding in. No tales of flapping Tibetan prayer flags, no wandering the deserts of North Africa. Over five years I've worked the crooked lanes of local story until I could go no further. Till I walked straight out of this century altogether.

This tale comes with a price attached. It's recklessly insistent on the urge to kick your boots off, get down on your knees and kiss rough soil, crawl under barbed wire fences and touch the bark of holy trees, hoot and strut and weep and let the wild darkness get its beautiful paws on you once again. Hurl whisky on the grave of Joe Strummer; kiss the wounded; spend a night in a hollow tree. Taste the golden milk from the teat of a rain bear. Unrefine yourself. Uncivilise yourself. It's about the hundred secret things. For all its bookishness, for all its insistence on study, make no mistake, what this tale desires most is to get you out where the buses don't park. What it calls for is a kind of elegant disintegration. What follows is a different kind of activism, a different kind of thinking.

This book is a kind of incomplete but sincere attempt to steward just a fraction of the culture so speedily disappearing from my stretch of the earth. The old notion of a storyteller was a hefty one—of *a cultural historian of place*. So the weight of the vocation is implicit. It's a straight trade of growth for depth.

I

Scatterlings takes a while to get where it needs to go, and that's proper.

It winds and backtracks, catches the fragile scent of a wildflower meadow, scratches its fur on a robust oak, boxes the dew with a mountain hare, occasionally admires its rooster feathers in the melancholy reflection of an ancient lake, makes love in apple orchards, sleeps late, gets lost, swims with a dagger between its teeth, eats too much rich food, staggers on. Its loyalty is to weather patterns, not sound bites.

We hear it everywhere these days: time for a new story—some enthusiastic sweep of narrative that becomes, overnight, the myth of our times. A container for all this ecological trouble, this peak-oil business, this malaise of numbness that seems to shroud even the most privileged. A new story. Just the one. That simple. Painless. Everything solved. Lovely and neat.

So, here's my first moment of rashness: I suggest that the stories we need turned up, right on time, about five thousand years ago. But they're not simple, neat, or painless. I also think this urge for a new story is the tourniquet for a less articulated desire: to behold the earth actually speaking through words again, more than some shiny, new, never-considered thought. We won't get a story worth hearing until we witness a culture broken open by its own consequence.

No matter how unique we may think our own era, I believe that these old tales—faerie tales, folktales, and myths—contain much of the paradox we face in these storm-jagged times. And what's more, they have no distinct author, are not wiggled from the penned agenda of one brain-rattled individual, but have passed through the breath of a countless number of oral storytellers.

Second thought: The reason for the purchase of these tales is that the deepest of them contain not just—as is widely purported—the most succulent portions of the human imagination, but a moment when our innate capacity to consume (lovers, forests, oceans, animals, ideas) was drawn into the immense thinking of the earth itself, what aboriginal teachers call "Wild Land Dreaming." We met something mighty. We didn't just dream our carefully individuated thoughts: We. Got. Dreamt. We let go of the reins.

Any old Gaelic storyteller would roll his eyes, stomp his boot, and vigorously jab a tobacco-browned finger toward the soil if there was a moment's question of a story's origination.

In a time when the land and sea suffer by our very directive, could it not be that the stories we need contain not just reflection *on*, but the dreaming *of* a sensual, powerful, reflective earth?

It is an insult to archaic cultures to suggest that myth is a construct of humans shivering fearfully under a lightning storm or gazing at corpse and reasoning a supernatural narrative. To make such a suggestion implies a baseline of anxiety, not relationship. Or that anxiety *is* the primary relationship. It places full creative impetus on the human, not on the sensate energies that surround and move through them. It shuts down the notion of a dialogue worth happening; it shuts down that big old word *animism*. Maybe the ancient storytellers knew something we have forgotten.

Two routes towards the cultivation of that very dreaming were through wilderness initiation and, by its illumination, a crafting into stories for the waiting community. Deeply ingrained in old village life was the knowledge that the quickest way to a deep societal crack-up was to ignore relationship to what stood outside its gates.

Storytellers weren't always cosy figures, dumping allegories into children's mouths; they were edge characters, prophetic emissaries. They had more in common with magicians, as loose with the tongue of a wolf as with a twinkly fireside anecdote. Many nights spent under the twisting autumn oaks banged their eloquence up against a wider canopy of sound, something still visible on the shaggy flank of their language.

Part of a storyteller's very apprenticeship was to be caught up in a vaster scrum of interaction, not just to attempt to squat atop the denizens of the woods. To this day, wilderness fasting disables our capacity to devour in the way the West seems so fond of; in the most wonderful way I can describe, *we* get devoured.

The big, unpalatable issue is the fact that these kinds of initiations have always involved submission. For a while you are not the sole master of your destiny but in the unruly presence of something vaster. You may have to get used to spending a little time on one knee; you may have to bend your head.

Without a degree of submission, healing, ironically, cannot enter. It is not we in our rather lonesome, individuated state that engender true health, but the act of soberly labouring towards a purpose and stance in the world that is far more than our own ambitions, even our fervent desire to "feel better."

So, I suggest that the stories are here. And they include all these difficult conditions. That's the price tag. This is not in any way to claim redundancy to modern literature but simply to hold up the notion of living myth.

So the stories are here, but *are we?*

I think we are losing the capacity to behold them. We *see* them for sure—our eyes scan the computer screen for the bones of the tale, we audition them for whatever our polemic is, and then we impatiently move on. It is not hard then to suggest that we are fundamentally askew in our approach: we are simply not up to the intelligence of what the story is offering. Our so-called sophistication has our sensual intelligence in a headlock and is literally squeezing the life out of it. When we *see* something, we have stayed pretty firmly in devouring mode; when we *behold* it, we are in a lively conversation. This is a move this book will come back to many times.

But these stories I speak of are not being brought slowly into our bodies or wrought deep by oral repetition. We have lost a lot of the fundamental house-making skills needed to welcome a story.

TURNING OUR HEAD FROM THE PELT

Once upon a time there was a lonely hunter. One evening, returning to his hut over the snow, he saw smoke coming from his chimney. When he entered the shack, he found a warm fire, a hot meal on the table, and his threadbare clothes washed and dried. There was no one to be found.

The next day, he doubled back early from hunting. Sure enough, there was again smoke from the chimney, and he caught the scent of cooking. When he cautiously opened the door, he found a fox pelt hanging from a peg, and a woman with long red hair and green eyes adding herbs to a pot of meat. He knew in the way that hunters know that she was Fox-Woman-Dreaming, that she had walked clean out of the Otherworld. "I am going to be the woman of this house," she told him.

The hunter's life changed. There was laughter in the hut, someone to share in the labour of crafting a life, and, in the warm dark when they made love, it seemed the edges of the hut dissolved in the vast green acres of the forest and the stars.

Over time, the pelt started to give off its wild, pungent scent. A small price, you would think, but the hunter started to complain. The hunter could detect the scent on his pillow, his clothes, even his own skin. His complaints grew in number until one night the woman nodded, just once, her eyes glittering. In the morning she, and the pelt, and the scent were gone. It is said that to this day the hunter waits by the door of his hut, gazing over snow, lonely for even a glimpse of his old love.

We are that hunter, societally and, most likely, personally. The smell of the pelt is the price of real relationship to wild nature: its sharp, regal, undomesticated scent. While that scent is in our hut there can be no Hadrian's Wall between us and the living world.

Somewhere back down the line, the West woke up to the fox-woman gone. And when she left she took many stories with her. And, when the day is dimming and our great successes have been bragged to exhaustion, the West sits, lonely in its whole body for her. For stories that are more than just a dagger between our teeth. More than just a bellow of conquest. We have turned our face away from the pelt. Underneath our wealth, the West is a lonely hunter.

Around halfway through the last century, something wonderful happened. Mythology and faerie tales regained a legitimacy amongst adults as a viable medium for understanding the workings of their own psychological lives. By use of metaphor, tales of sealskins and witches' huts became the most astonishing language for what seemed to lurk underneath people's everyday encounters. The use of metaphor granted greater dignity and heightened poetics to the shape of their years.

What was the glitch that lurched alongside? A little too much emphasis on these stories as entirely interior dramas that, clumsily handled, became something that removed, rather than forged, relationship to the earth. The inner seemed more interesting than anything going on "out there." We and our feelings still squatted pretty happily at the centre of the action. There was not always that sharp tang of fox.

When the Grimms and others collected folktales, they effectively reported back the skeletons of the stories; the local intonation of the teller and some regional sketching out was often missing. Ironically, this stripped-back form of telling has been adopted into the canon as a kind of traditional style that many imitate when telling stories—a kind of "everywhere and nowhere" style.

Now, whilst it's certainly true that there are stories designed for travel, for thousands of years even a story arriving in an entirely new landscape would be swiftly curated into the landscape of its new home. It would shake down its feathers and shape-leap a little or grow silent and soon cease to be told. No teller worth his or her salt would just stumble through the outline and think it was enough; the vital organs would be, in part, the mnemonic triggers of the valley or desert in which the story now abided. This process was a protracted courtship to the story itself. It was the business of manners.

Oral culture has always been about local embedding, despite the big human dilemmas that cannot help but sweep up between cultures. This may seem an unimportant detail when you are seeking only to poke around your childhood memories in a therapist's office, but it falls woefully short when this older awareness is reignited—the absence of wider nature becomes acute, the tale flat and self-centred.

I don't think we have the stories; these stories have us. They charge vividly through our betrayals, illicit passions, triumphs, and generosities. Psyche is not neatly contained in our chest as we scuttle between appointments; we dwell within psyche: gregarious, up close, chaotic, astonishing, sometimes tragic, often magical.

Well, something piratical is happening. It is time to rescue the stories, rehydrate the language, scatter dialectical inflection amongst the blunt lines of anthropological scribbles, and muck up the typewriter with the indigo surge of whale ink. We're singing over the snow to the fox-woman.

The wind that moves the barley

I was alone when the phone call came. Mid evening, the house quiet. My father was sick, properly sick. From out of nowhere. Months of treatment ahead, uncertain outcome, family plunged into worry and high alert. Many now reading will have taken a call like this. I sat in the half dark of my living room, cradling the phone.

It was this, rather than any academic or theoretical interest, that got me walking. I did it for my own sanity, my own grounding, I did it for information. I needed a wider cradle for the melancholy that would move through me in the coming months. To stew in my own juices, locked away in the house would have been unfitting. There is an old place in us that understands that deep feeling is not entirely confined to our body, that there are a thousand murmuring layers between us and a dark pool of water. Grief called me to take a bigger shape. It always did.

Walking is a big thing for me and my dad. Without exception, the significant conversations between us in my childhood were not in the house but out on the lanes somewhere, I padding faithfully alongside him.

So, as a man entering midlife I chose the old way to bear witness to this turn of fortune. I walked. It would not be to the wider feast of faerie tales or myths I'd turn; it was to be something tangible to my muscles, scent, and vision. It would be local story. I'd stomp its unfoldings into my bones. Get claimed by it. I'm not sure I knew what I was getting into.

What does it mean to be claimed? Well, it means giving up the landlord's portion. Adherence to study. Getting so smoked, so weathered by a tuft of ground, that maybe, just occasionally, you become its eyes.

You should be relieved, I'd imagine, to hear that there won't be some systematising of three easy steps to "encountering the wild"; that kind of so-called coherence will most likely strangle the thing it claims to love. Unfashionably, this is a call to reflection as much as to action. About paying deep attention to where you find yourself and elevating that attention into the high ground that we sometimes call a craft.

These are local stories, based on and around Dartmoor. You should know right now they don't do what the epics do; their wingspan is simply not as broad, their feathers maybe not as startling, their genius less heroic. There are no firebirds, no dragons, no weddings—at least not in the grand sense. There we have it.

This is a wintering book, no doubt. The stories were walked, often more than once, over a passage of four winters. We will be walking that deep scattering of story—starting where the Dart arrives into Old Totnes and ending on a Twelfth Night, in Scoriton, the hamlet where we first started the raising of Dulcie, our daughter.

As an adorable little nipper, almond-eyed Dulcie would often be carried in the folds of my battered leather jacket into the fiery warmth of our local pub, The Tradesman's Arms. We would eat vinegary chips whilst she slept, wrapped in the coat, us listening to folks play music and to swap stories awhile before stepping out into crisp Dartmoor air. Stand with me at the pub door a moment.

To the south is Torbay graveyard, and Ezra, Hilda, Leonard, Monica, and Lee—great-grandparents, grandparents, and aunt—away down the crow road. We've been here a few hundred years now: sailors, preachers, hoteliers, brewery men, storytellers, headmasters, painters—back when we were the Brays and the Thackerys as well as the Shaws.

To the north, up Tony the farmer's track, is a treasury of Dartmoor story, drifting down in the sharp air and just tickling the tip of the baby's nose. We catch the scent of fresh manure and diesel oil as we pick our way carefully over the cobbles of Rosemary Lane with our precious bundle and all pile into bed. And around us the great ship Dartmoor creaks and groans under the indigo heavens, and the unattached stars drift like long-distance runners above our small cottage.

The stories coming are not ones that I tell when travelling; in fact, the condition for their being here at all is their being told in the setting—the estuaries, standing stones, gullies, and copses where the tales unfold. There is something quieter about them.

I tell them to sing them back to themselves; let your and my imagination be a gifting back to these places. They are the primary clientele. I have deliberately let what transpired be visible: there are concrete, coffee shops, passing joggers, and television aerials occasionally dotted throughout. That's part of our landscape these days. To deftly airbrush them out would be a move from imagination to fantasy, and I'm not prepared to do that. It won't serve us.

Many stories are recently experiencing huge migrations; just check out the mythology section of a decent bookstore. Many are entering what I would call *A Commons of the Imagination*. These aren't that; we could call them *slow ground stories*—almost all are specific to a particular stretch of land. As we place renewed importance on local food and local business, we would do well to value the high nutritional value and hedgerow education of local story. This wider move seems healthy, a questioning of the endemic of eternal progress. What have we been sold, exactly? Why do we sense a betrayal somewhere in the background?

A figure that will arise again and again in *Scatterlings* is the nomad. The nomad is the one who holds the local and the commons in either hand. The nomad holds great clues for working the tension between these seeming opposites.

A significant portion of commentary comes not from scholarly sources, but from walking the land itself over a hard winter, mapless, just following the directions embedded in the stories. The companions of gurgling gray stream and bog, barn owl and peat fire led directly into the erupting responses to the stories that I experienced. There were surprises, much eeriness, and a humbling waiting. I was walking out of Devon as I knew it altogether.

Surrounding this setting is the wider ground that is England (and a few lingering references to the Welsh and the Irish). England—home of translucent shopping malls, dished-out violence on Friday nights, then over to the last, wheezing vestiges of a constipated aristocracy. There are plenty of writings on that particular malaise. I want to dig around in the scrub a little. Get underneath the paint job.

I remember the old villages and hamlets—Buckland, Painswick, Ryhall, Ponsworthy. Names with stories attached. We remember the rebel spirit of

Robin Hood, Emily Pankhurst, Bert Jancsh—feisty souled but also noble spirited—rather than the bilious kings and feudal lords that fill our history books.

Three chapters engage what I call liminal culture: points in the history of this country when a lively orality, or nomadism, or magical intelligence, or relationship to the wild places had been maintained. Woven in is the way I was trained by stories in the first place and then maintained that relationship, and the understanding that my way of communicating myth got rendered by the temperament of the land.

One of the clearest imprints in these stories is an emphasis on service and the idea that the bigger the trouble, the greater the expectancy that the trouble is actually wrestled into a gift for a wider circle. Not just a human one. Victory is not the aim; beauty is the aim.

For many of us, wound means truth. In a sugared world, holding your gaze to something broken, bereft, or damaged seems like the deepest position we can take. We see this way of thinking move all the way through the modern arts. It's what gets the big grants. Myths say no, that the deepest position is the taking of that underworld information and allowing it to gestate into a lived wisdom that, by its expression, contains something generative.

The wound is part of a passage, not the end in itself. It can rattle, scream, and shout, but there has to be a tacit blessing at its core.

Many stories we are holding close right now have the scream but not the gift. It is an enormous seduction on the part of the West to suggest that jabbing your pen around in the debris of your pain is enough. It's not. It's a trick to keep you from doing something more useful. That's uninitiated behaviour masquerading as wisdom. Lead is not gold, no matter how many times you shake it at the sun.

So, I come for tuition, to walk a myth line out of my own seductions.

The stories the West tells in private

Connection to where we come from is starting to matter. I guess it always did. I started to notice it about a decade ago. At the end of an evening of teaching they would appear, the weight of the West on their shoulders: beautiful folks, usually, who would patiently stand in line till it was their turn, and then, shuddering with emotion, speak vividly about their experiences in the Amazon with visionary plants, their apprenticeship to a Vietnamese medicine woman, their pilgrimage to Tibet, or their name change from Bert to "Dragon-Bull-Rainbow Man." With absolute sincerity in their Scots-Irish, Polish, Norwegian, or Welsh eyes, they relaid their tale and then expected me to be approving of it. By now you will be getting the emphasis—I'm not. Maybe I was for the first hundred times.

Now, to be clear: these people are signposts to becoming real human beings. In a numbed-out, glow-screen world, this is a vivid attempt to wake up, to feel something real for once, to take up a little more space in neurotic and numbing times. I've stood in line just like them, twisting my braids and trying hard to think nonattached thoughts. It's a step to sanity when the cards are stacked so horribly against the psyche.

But why the impulse to be anywhere but here? I think it's the stories the West tells itself in private. Because when the taxes have been paid, Siberia has been Google Earthed to the last inch, and the last sinew of oil has been drained from the North Sea, I think the stories we secretly tell ourselves are little more than nightmares. The West's esteem is far lower than we expect.

Our bones know the cost of what we're harnessing; our bellies are acid-strewn with the price. Hobbling alongside this hero myth is the Banshee of the Blood Pool; it is she that claims the storyteller's chair when we rest. It can be no other way. So where else can we go but out of where we come from? How could we stay in the madness? Well, I'm proposing we don't let ourselves off the hook so easily. We shouldn't be feeling so groovy.

Let's squat down in the gunk.

So what happens if we try to root? Rather ironically, the latest addition to hipspeak is a desire to be indigenous. No work history required. Well, *indigenous* is a complicated word. I've seen whole gatherings grind to an irksome halt as growingly more red-faced speakers try to get clear about what the word could mean. Funnily enough, I've never heard anyone who could qualify for the description *indigenous* actually use it. But Western people seem to love it at the moment. We turn up at the gate of the Crow reservation with our arms open and expect to get a warm reception.

So how do we work with this longing? Let's perhaps dial it down a little. I won't be so inflammatory as to make an offer to suddenly becoming indigenous. But I will gamble a little, throw my hat in the ring, and say that I think coming "from" somewhere can be highly overrated. I'm slightly crazed by the whole conversation.

I can't tell you much about being "from" a place—I meet people who are so "from" a place that they are bigoted, numb, and miserable. They see it, but, by God, they don't behold a shred of it. Now, please remember this perspective is not someone speaking for an indigenous tribe of painted people in the lower Amazon; this is a Brit reflecting on his part of the west of England.

I also suggest that if you don't have the bones of loved ones in the ground of that land, then you have no legitimate aboriginal claim for from-ness. Until the wiggling denizens of the soil have a good chew on the composting lump of Aunt Agatha or Grandpa Terry, any sense of from-ness is pretty abstract.

I know this stuff can make your head spin, feel impossible to calibrate and not worth the time—something long gone in the trade for better coffee and a swifter wi-fi connection.

Well, I offer a retuning of intention, a slightly more sober directive—to be *of* a place, to labour under a related indebtedness to a stretch of earth that you have not claimed but which has claimed *you*.

To be *of* is to hunker down as a servant to the ruminations of the specific valley, little gritty vegetable patch, or swampy acre of abandoned field that has laid its breath on the back of your neck. Maybe it's a thin crest of swaying weeds between broken-down sheds. As David Abram's work reminds us, earth is air too; the myriad of wind tongues, the regal pummelling of the clouds—regardless of being in a city, hamlet, or tent on a Norfolk beach. Remember to look *up*.

To be *of* means to listen. To commit to *being around*. It's participation, not as a conqueror, not in the spirit of devouring, but in the spirit of relatedness. I think this takes a great deal of practice. It doesn't mean you never take a life, live on apples and peas, or forget that any stretch of earth holds menace and teeth just as it does the rippling buds of April. You learn from the grandeur of its menace as much as from the blessings.

To be *of* means to be *in*. To have traded endless possibility for something specific. It means that, over the slow recess of time, you become that part of the land that temporarily abides in human form. That your curvature and di-alectical brogue is hewn deep, wrought tough by the diligence of your service to the earthy tangle in which you find yourself.

To be *of* means talking, not about a place but with a place—and that's not a relationship available indiscriminately, wherever you travel, but something that may claim you once or twice in a lifetime. It means staying when you don't feel like staying. Cracking the ice on the water butt, climbing into your mud-encrusted boots, and walking out into the freezing dark with a bale of hay. It has very little to do with how you feel, because guess what? Feelings change.

All of this relates entirely to the practice of mythtelling: It's this kind of *of* that I've tried to adopt in the gathering of these Dartmoor stories. Knowing the stories of a place is bending your ear to its neighbourly gossip. Like anything worth the salt, a place can't reveal itself in a soundbite or a glimpse; the soundscape of the skylark has to settle deep into the curl of our ear, the hundred ways the elm bends its head to autumn. The nature of these things requires proper time; there's no way round it, nor should there be.

Maybe we started turning our head from the fox pelt early on: in the very origination story of the naming of Britain. When Brutus of Troy arrived in Albion he arrived with a sword, not a blessing. What he encountered, as have the heroes of so many Western myths since, was conflict with giants. The giants are the people of the deep history of the island. Some used to call them the small gods.

Brutus, through force, pushes them to the recesses of the land, to the high places of Dartmoor, to the bony ridge of the lizard of Cornwall—far from the cultural life of this emerging nation.

Whilst to the wary eyes of the warriors those giants may seem terrible, nothing much is said about their age-old relationship to the land in which they dwell. How can Brutus behold that relationship when the sword turns nervously in his hand and he seeks to claim a prophesied dominion?

And so it is for us: we sweep out these Grendels, these Sidhes and Goemagogs; we hold our bright torch to the back of the cave and claim the One over the Horde.

We don't have the time to learn the language of the giants, so we, in turn, become them. A kind of mimicry. What we exile, we become.

We got it wrong from the start. Brutus has not been to the Underworld. He is brilliant but not initiated; he does not know what he is looking at. And so it has gone ever since.

But some of us are trying to reenter the countries of our birth in a different way. To walk the shores not with a shield but with speech, with seeds rather than slaughter. To open a dimension of this country that is not just Britain but Albion. Not Devon but *Dumnonia*, or *Defenascir*, or somewhere else again.

I think it's time we went looking for the small gods again.

Moon milk cave

The cave glows like a child loose with glitter, scattering the limestone. I bend my head and enter. There it is. Before my eyes adjust to the dark, I can see luminous hurls of algae flecking the mottled browns and grays of the cave wall. Moon milk they call it.

I'm inside the south moor by just a few feet. The Buckfastleigh ridge. Underneath. Underworld. The air is chilled, sour, and as I gingerly move forward into cramped space I can sense the capacity for disorientation. The old man gestures to various sandy lumps and asks us to guess what they may be. Well, I know they are going to be old. Deer scat, possibly bear, or even wolf?

The guide's eyes briefly flare with triumph. Hyena. The hound of Africa seems to have once had residence in cosy old Devon. It doesn't stop there. In the half light, his hands point out other clusters—not just scat this time but bone. He gives a roll call of the animal remains collected in the cave: rhinoceros, straight-tusked elephant, bison, cave lion.

Seeing his cue, the guide moves into proper storytelling mode; his arms curve up into the moist air and he expounds on the mutable nature of something as seemingly permanent as Dartmoor and informs us that the caves were formed under the immense weight of the Dart River, that the moors themselves were once a vast crust of mountains, that what we consider Dartmoor is merely the gums of the proud ridge of gray teeth that jutted towards the sky. That these bone piles tell us of a once balmy climate where the hippopotamus and wild boar thrived.

Just as my mind scrambles to keep up with this steaming tropical underbelly, the old man delivers his coup de grâce. Descending just a few more steps into the cave, he turns and, with a grave expression, notes: "We are entering a dead zone now, no bones, no life of any kind here." This is an even older layer, long before curious wolves would have found themselves trapped in this fusty holt. This passage belongs to the river goddess—dark with iron and manganese, uneasy cold, just as the first cave was curator of warm bones. Almost within arm stretch of each other are the two worlds of ice and heat. The great flowing crush of time, unimaginable prehistory, bears down on my peering skull. I am already dust.

These are tomb animals; this is not a den but a cemetery of beings that fell or wandered into the small opening and never got out. There is no human imprint, no owl-man scratched, blown, or ochred on the rib-curved walls, no wide-eyed boys squatting on fur, no torchlight beckoning us into yet deeper tunnels, just the immense stillness of a realm that never expected our company.

This is a place of deep time intelligence; I recognise it straightaway. Why? Because a mythteller knows that the most impactful dimensions of a story are always underneath, chthonic, their creaking bucket carrying us down to where alligator skulls and stored honey reside. They do emergency surgery down there that can take us weeks to catch up with.

The emotive connections we make with myths are rather like the entrance to this cave—a way in—and then our imaginations crash through the yellow bracken, tumble into the hard cut of limestone, and we find ourselves in another world, a realm we may not escape from. Day intelligence; the place of lists, process work, and schedules is not the deepest home for story. Elevate stories there too often, and they grow pasty, truculent, and finally sick. They are not to dance for us like disgruntled bears.

As I gaze up at the glistening crust of ceiling I see the glittering moon milk in a new way: as *language*, not just human, dripping down through these slurried layers of time, back into the keeping of this womb of prehistory.

This is not one of the great initiation pits, those places of unshackling into the dreaming of rock and fur and salt wave, those places where the tribe that was the hill and the bird and the river carved its heart-boggling manifesto into your fledgling imagination; it is older even than that. And my own thinking seems to have run aground, can go no further back; the tart air is sharp clumps of sacred breath. I make my speechless gestures of prayer and leave. As I come blinking out into drizzly pale light, I have just glimpsed a far older, toothier, stranger world. A world turned upside down.

I walk awhile and enter the convivial atmosphere of the riverside Abby Inn, amazingly just a short walk from this underworld. Pint gathered in, I take my seat on a wooden bench and enjoy the brew, chewy with plenty of malt. I lose myself watching the rapid scatter of the Dart River over the stones. Despite the knackered chatter of local builders over my shoulder, the aura of the cave still has me, leaves me blurry with questions as I sip the brew.

There's a lot going on. I can't quite get a hold back on the world upstairs just yet. I'm sick of things making sense. I thought I knew the moor, but down there, in the brown light flickering on an elephant's tooth, I wasn't so sure. The long-departed cave lion is more indigenous to the moor than I will ever be.

Old time, deep time

I am in my writing hut now. Very late summer, the cusp. There is a shake of the frame every few minutes as it totters on its wheels. I can hear the drone of the last harvesting going on in a nearby field, but today the winds dictate primacy, ushering in the change from corn time to dying time.

Somewhere the Holly King is sharpening his blade for his soon-to-come meeting with the Oak King and his long wintering reign.

But I'm not in the hut. Even now that cave still has me. I open up the wood burner, chuck in the kindling, settle under my furs, and step out of my usualness. I walk through the wall at the back of the cave, through the limestone, through the tuff.

A fire is a road to
prehistoric mind.

Into the immensities of deep time.
Flames make nonsense crumble and we are gone:

We are 4,600 million years ago.
In vast space itself, where we
hang in the firm claws
of the Hawk of the Well,
watching.

Earth is a humming chunk of rock, thrashed by meteorites and hurtling comets, a sublime attack, laden with gifts we cannot yet see.

Story churns and gargles
bellows its dramas.

Already the mythos: without chaos there will be no eros—no succulent, vital, devouring, troublesome life. Earth absorbs the carving, accommodating the rupture. But this dance is but a parade of minnows when a vast lump collides like a drunk at a wedding with this baby planet. Their great impact causes both a melting heat and shards of debris to hurl out into the inky blackness— shards that over time twist and bind into the elegant breast of the moon.

Snow Palace.
Dream Guardian.
Vast White Belly.
Tide Keeper.

Our scrying shifts to five hundred million years. The rocky animals that are continents, blissful in their solitudes for so long, come to seek a herding warmth and start a slow cluster together, though the proud cloak of vegetation is still to spread their bony shoulders. The continents share gossip in the way that they do. Shallow seas hold life in its gurgling waters: sea scorpion, well-armored trilobite, starfish. The thin waters are not like ink but luminous with sun, a glowing churn.

Glow-Gold-Wave
Salty Ale of Scales
The Glittering Beginning
The Sewing Needle of the Moon.

Two hundred fifty million years. We behold one vast stretch of land now, its face lush and hairy with plant deities. The continent confidently stretches its wingspan between high latitudes either side of the equator; the horsetail stretches its roots into succulent swamp, and palm trees catch the breeze as dragonflies claim residence in the hot air. Scaled beings—amphibians—lay their eggs in crusts of river beach.

Verdant Lushness
Gray Ladies of the Bank
Sweet Flurry of the Dragon's Wings
Damn Handsome Rock.

One hundred million years. It is the time of snapping jaw and the belly scrape of the sandy places, of the broad and wide-ranging dinosaur. Round their claws scuttles a red sea of termites and, skirting their shoulders, that great survivor, the dragonfly. The continents continue their archaic shoulder rub, and their vivid dreaming continues—the moon milk of the earth's braided intelligence, bestowing on us its intricate and delighted diversity, crowned with silver and white clouds, a-flower with elk and butterfly, whittle-tipped mountains of snow, brown-leafed copse, and urging flanks of red sand.

Deep time. Old time.

Boulder slow, loosened underworld immensity, grinding forever chords of glacial singing, bedazzled green sizzle of the jungle-rump summer lands. We are the bone pile, the swan road, the bitter, dark berries in the belly of the wolf.

And on.

And on.

And somewhere, just a minute ago really, something opened its eyes that looked a little like you or me. And what we heard were the stories. The ancestors were diligent in this regard. Dragonfly would not hesitate to grace us with its buzzing saga of the wind road; Bear would dictate the terms of how we padded the snowy forest. *These* are the stories our bodies were tuned for, which still grind quietly away in our bones as we peer at the computer screen.

And for a long, long time we listened.

As the rain slapped the moss-strewn roof of an Orkney shelter, we listened; as the dream rattle of the cicada poured through the dark, we listened; as our lungs ripped a blood flurry in our chest, as we leapt over boulder and decaying brush pursued by boar, still we listened.

We listened to the Old Time, and knew our brief, majestic, terrible place in it. We were just the latest in a long, long line of storytellers.

Come Ice Giants, and Eight-Legged Horses, come Blodeuwedd of the Flowers, come Fenryr, Cinderbiter, Bertilak, Gringolet, Ossian, Scathach, Gwynn Ap Nudd. The land shudders and births you, as the sea erupts lava that becomes mountains, forests, graves. Come Psyche.

Come Goemagog, Wayland Smithy, Rhiannon of the Mares, Chaw Gully Raven, Robin of Loxley and all the laughing boys of the Greenwood.
Let your names be called, as precious as meat.

And one day, just a moment ago, an old woman came from her place at the edge of the village, her ears replete with listening, a mouth of fresh-cut meadow flowers, and told us to light the kindling.

Once it was dark and the little ones were drifting under the antelope robes, the strange one loped forward into the light of the flames and stood in front of the village.

She said:

Once upon a time.

Once upon a time.
Once upon a time.
So she said.
And she told us the story of ourselves back to ourselves.

CHAPTER ONE

The Aisling

Back in the last century

The timber heaved with orange slashes of flame then crashed down around the rocks. All afternoon a small band of us had laboured under uncertain Welsh skies to build a fire keen enough to heat to a red glow the rocks required for the sweat lodge later that night. The lodge is a small structure, close to the ground, just enough to squeeze in about twenty-five folks, made from hazel, its roof at about chest height. It's heavily covered to block out any light. At its centre is a small fire pit. The real hot spot is opposite the door. It's a place of singing, prayers, story, and healing.

So, the fire is cooking the stones well—"cherry reds" is what the medicine man wants—and it looks like he's going to get them. Our small crew are blearily proud of ourselves and then stop short. The sky is changing. This is not the usual uncertain scudding of a British sky; this is a coal-black entourage of alpha clouds, ready to emphatically sluice our blaze. We won't stand a chance against this billowing ensemble of soon-to-chuck rain gods. I see the first drop drip from the trilby rim of a startled workmate. "Bugger."

Through the dusking comes the old man, ceremony man, braids to his waist, a head taller than anyone, immeasurably ancient, from some other place: Turtle Island. He's over here teaching. Everybody stiffens, grows alert, and dives more fervently into the work of keeping the flames in excitement. There's the first peal of thunder.

Old man pulls me away from the fire a moment and glances up through the strangely glittering light. "Have you told them a story yet?" he croaks in that otherworldly badlands drawl. I don't understand. Who? The crew? I haven't told stories since I was a kid. "Sorry, Grandpa, what do you mean?" I think I blushed as I spoke, wriggling with ignorance.

He points upwards to the dark wings of the air. "Them beings. That's what they're here for. Charm 'em. Barter for us." With that he hurled some language into the fast-coming night—elegant language, a storied tongue, using the currency of his jaw to claim relationship to raindrops, weather patterns, and the old and secretive desire of a darkening sky to be held for a moment in the fragility of the human imagination. I'd never seen an adult doing anything remotely like it. I just did not know such a thing existed. It moved me more deeply than all of Shakespeare. I'd never seen someone so alive. A real human being.

Then he stopped. "You come from here. You have to continue. Keep talking to them." He turned, kneeled, and inspected the antlers we would soon be carrying the rocks in with. Oh, no. So I squinted upwards to the assembled gallery of deities and began. My words were pitiful, bereft of any remote shred of courtship, just my stumbling pony of words, making it quite clear that any significant vocabulary I possessed had long since been shuffled off to the abattoir. It was kind of heartbreaking—lots of unearned confidence with nothing beneath it. I mean zero. All hat and no cows.

For a couple of weeks I travelled on and off with the old man—nothing special, just part of his ensemble. Lots of carrying water, chopping wood, building sweat lodges, and witnessing ceremonies so archaic, so vivid, so extraordinary it was like watching a cave painting peel itself off the wall and dance in lightning strikes right through the soul-black dark of the lodge.

So my time is up. The old man is going back across the waters and I'm carrying my sore little heart back to the rinky-dink caravan that I call home. It's gently mooted by the few pennies I had saved; enough to cross the pond and properly apprentice. As you can probably imagine, that's a dizzying proposition. Like getting airlifted out of hell into a place where real live human beings exist and remember the old arrangement we used to have with the earth. The old man's people need a response, so I take a few hours to go mull in a nearby copse, after we've prepared the final sweat.

I'm just struck dumb with it all. Can't go. Just can't. Want to. Want to so badly my shoulders are shaking as I make the decision and my throat is hurting with all the tears I can't quite get out. I come from somewhere else. This place. The country we used to call Clas Merlin—Merlin's Enclosure, goddamnit, to bring in the big speech—*Albion*. I can't go the road of the Red Man; it's simply not mine. My bones stay here.

It's getting dark again, and the old man comes through the glimmer to hear what's what. I tell him. He's not happy or sad or anything, he just is. Final words: "Keep talking to your bush friends, and don't expect your teachers to be human." That night he sang the old songs in the lodge and I felt very foolish. I never saw him again.

Being in the presence of something great provokes a feeling of dismay in me. I'm not that evolved. Big news is sobering. And when the ceremony man departed I was left bereft, diminutive, and absolutely adrift. My jaw was not a mead hall, my tongue not even a hermit's shack, more a dustbowl concrete cell where words went to die. And the man was telling me to tell stories?

Some time before, I'd gone up to a hill in Snowdonia and sat for four days. Without food, tent, company, watch. I call it a wilderness vigil, but you may know it as a vision quest. And if you know it at all, it's probably due in large part to the incredible work of Stephen Foster and Meredith Little. It was they, and the school they founded, the School of Lost Borders, that reintroduced the practice back into a nonnative climate in the early seventies. Without them, this book would not exist.

I'd gone up there ready for certain things. Some time of deep reflection. Enjoying the beauty of the Welsh wilderness. Maybe a little ceremony, a little marking of life's stages. A psychological spring clean. Things that, although edgy, felt explicable to a Western person—elements of a rite of passage. All I heard about was the *universality* of the experience, every culture seeking the same thing. What I had not expected and could not really have been prepared for was what transpired. What was waiting was powerfully *local*, powerfully specific.

By the end of the time on the hill, I was so far past my own sense of myself and my issues that the experience is almost impossible to write about. In my common parlance, I got dreamt. My own dreaming took a hike. I got taken to a place that almost every sinew of my being would cry out was impossible. Where my nature got humbled, wrenched, wilded, and finally scattered over an area of about three miles.

I beheld things out on the hill. Impossible things. The kind of things you read about in far-distant anthropological journals on initiation and put the book down, shaking your head. Well, I'd had one. An ancient place choosing a particular style to communicate itself. This isn't bragging: it was a messy, exacting, beautiful ordeal that did not leave me with much in the way of wisdom at the time. I just didn't think this kind of thing went down in Britain any more.

Twenty years on, I still have my journal from those days and a couple of years that followed. There is little in the way of a considered therapeutic process about it, few insights that have even the merest whiff of profundity about them. What they do seem to have is the taste of someone slowly being devoured by a place, touching the aboriginal.

As the days deepened, something else entirely gripped me. Something that, by its very nature, would not be confirming the "me" that had turned up to do a little soul searching. That something kicked the shit out of that me.

Most of the experience is not of value here; the fruits are in what followed, not this planting. But a few lines here and there remind me, as well as you, a little of how this all began. Like tree bark, this is an outer layer; the inner layers don't live in everyday language, and remain safe.

FOUR DAYS ON THE HILL
1. Bones
I'm in the old gully. I'm scared of it. Steep banks of oak and holly. I spend the day collecting dead wood into piles. But no fire for me; it's not allowed. Just a tarp, a sleeping bag, and some water. An enclosed world, always in greenish shade. A terrible night: I'm dragged through hard dreams, awful dreams, and woken in half dark. Nine Scottish cattle stand just below my makeshift bed on their way to the creek. Steam from nostrils.

2. Orphan
Already hungry, already lonely. A calf gets separated from the herd and keeps coming back to the gully. I shepherd it out, but it keeps returning. I panic at dusk when it's still not found its people. It won't live. The gully is noisy at night. I have my hat over my face and my blanket round my shoulders.

skull of horse is here   *skull of ram is here*   *a plait of hair under rock*

3. Consequence
I'm woken at dawn by two foals at the end of my blankets. They slip away. I'm weak as a kitten; I keep hearing music. Great swoops of an owl as it gets dark. Terrible dreaming. My life is a huge gift. I just want this to stop.

4. Relatives
There's singing with voices that I can't see. I gather gifts for those I will return to and make a big circle for a last night vigil. It takes hours; I've got no energy, none. I'm all cried out.

In the dark, three turquoise lights come, then two of a dark orange, then many of a golden colour. Over several hours they glide closer in stately fashion. A turquoise ball of light approaches and then suddenly flies into my ear. Into my body. There's a whirring sound. And I am gone somewhere else. Not here anymore. I'm into the hill. This kind of time goes on and on and on. Years pass.

I stay in the other place till there is a roaring of cattle, and everything I have beheld just splits in two—like the curtains of a play—and I'm back. The nine cattle are bellowing in early daylight and surrounding the circle. I've been missing most of the night. I hurl up something solid and black from the back of my throat. A dark lump. I am frightened and break my circle, stagger past the cattle and collapse in the scrub.

Some time later I revive enough to pack my camp and leave the hill. I will not be the same again.

❋ ❋ ❋

And then before I knew it I was standing at Birmingham New Street station in blistering heat, trying to navigate a change of trains back to South London, where variants on this kind of opening continued in their startling, life-will-never-be-the-same fullness. Now, a mountaintop in Wales I could almost comprehend, but it appeared I had arrived back in London with a slippery trajectory in and out of regions that were unutterably mapless to a white kid. This is the reason I'd ended up in the company of the medicine man.

The experience was clearly not typically "inspirational," not something to be quoted on a CV or to gain government funding for a wilderness program for at-risk youth. But Christ, it mattered to me. I was the one who had to sit in its consequence; it was I who had to sweat it out, and ultimately I who had to forge some kind of gift from it. A message through the dark, from way back. It was my life now. So, as I sat in the lodge with the medicine man and told him the full, halting story, I really didn't know what he'd make it of it. Well, he didn't think it strange in the least. He just played with one of those great braids and started to talk about the powers of a place. Turned out, there are stretches of the world where such experiences are not so unusual. He got me working. It was long medicine, that first fast: years of brooding as it slowly, properly, revealed its hand. Most everything that I initially tried to make of it fell away.

There's an old Irish word, *aisling*, often translated as "dream vision," which touches on something of the experience. You go to the mountain and are led to a powerful place. The spirit of the place will arrive—often in the shape of a woman—and for a period of time will reveal something of the nature of the land. When you return to your village you, usually through poetry, reveal your instruction. It's a job for life.

As it goes, my experience, though having a kind of intensity to it, has proved no more extraordinary than any of the fasts I have supported for others. The gradient of so-called otherworldliness can oscillate, but that's really not the point. The point is becoming a true human being. Many get there in subtler, more elegant ways. Whilst it's important for me to state pretty baldly some of my own story I ask you not to fetishise it or start a game of comparisons. The aisling will arrive for anyone who learns to listen long term in the wild places. I just needed more of a kick up the arse than most. I was always a slow learner.

Some of this story is told in other books. I ended up leaving London, returning a large record contract, and heading out to the woods, my only offering a cradled grief manifesting as a battered heart after the end of a youthful marriage. Looking back, I realise I took a lot of hits in fairly close succession.

This story is useful to tell, I suppose, because it's the story of someone experiencing big, old-time instruction and then being set adrift in a society of deep forgetting, amnesia, and hostility. That's a hard gig. But it's also the root of almost every story worth telling.

I'm just a kid from a Torquay estate; I don't have a name like Wolf-Bites-Owl or Tracker-in-the-Snow. I come from a place that in part is very brilliant, very sick, and very lost. I come from the West. And my task these few years has been to abide in exactly that. To not lose the scent of it. To find what is still regal and mystical and generative in it. Twenty years ago its land claimed me, and I will not refuse it.

It's also important for me to state publicly that old powers still reside meshed in the hills and cliff faces and the streams of England. It is an entirely understandable misunderstanding when eco folks insist this could not possibly be the case, that there has been too much industrial damage. That the land is simply too angry, too exhausted. Well, I carry a simple message: it's not so. Test my statement.

My time in the tent was just before the emergence of the pulse of a cell phone in your pocket or the omnipresent, luminous squat of your laptop on the table, so when the tent flaps were sealed against the March squalls and the oak gave itself to flame, you could claim a resolute, triumphal aloneness.

I never gave a damn about being an obscure poster boy for alternative living; I eat vegetables because people I love tell me I have too. But I'm a straight-up, unredeemed, never-quitting pagan romantic—that's one of the few things of which I'm certain. So when I decided to live outdoors, well, man, Genghis Khan himself was going to be envious of my tent. A trellis of thick ash; ornate, steam-bent roof poles; canvas as black as the ace of spades; a floor of fur laid three skins deep; and books: gorgeous, obscure, fiery, heart-breaking and -making books. Books everywhere in wobbly Camelot towers. You'd have loved it.

Cut wood from the lightning tree without the farmer noticing, crawl twice daily under a barbed-wire fence, continually stretch stew to last a week, live in a circle, get buffeted by weather, hit the books, and spend lots of time out in the crow dark of an English copse—that was the drill. I drifted into a prophetic frequency.

So there I stayed, out on the edge. I visited people, maintained friend-ships, earned a crust when I had to, but my real focus was elsewhere. A ruddy-cheeked apprentice to barbarous weather, medieval texts, a hurting loneliness, edgy dreams, animal tracks in dewy grasses and frosty mud, I would sleep in the winter months with batteries under my clothes, under my sheep, goat, and deerskin covers. In the morning there would be enough body heat to get about ten minutes of a tape recorder working before the batteries succumbed to the icy cold again. The sound of the sitar or a genius poet or Mongolian horse music would charge through the yurt as I coaxed the burner, drank my coffee, and peered through the felted opening at sloughing sheets of gray rain moving steadily over the valley's oak garland.

Dragging bashfully behind, though, was speech. Story. That thing that happened with the medicine man as we peered up to a story-starved thunder being and began to use the dusty old language of praise. That's the thing that will go with me into the ground.

So I was gone for good, punch-drunk in love with the sound of brave, fragile language. So I went to see storytellers. Surely that was the place to go. Here's the thing: I'd really experienced story only as the moment in a ritual when your tongue became the antler tip of the collective happening. Speech was exquisitely tied up with the temperament of the grasses shuddering under your feet, the strut-caw of the distant cockerel, the moment when you glance into the shadows and realise your ancestors have strolled up and are leaning on their staffs, not quite cheering you on but not telling you to stop either.

So, peering over a cup of weak tea in a black-box theatre as a recital wended its script-inflected anecdotal way through a tiny crowd failed to convince, I'm afraid. In fact, it evoked a little more than that. I thought it was absolute, unutterable bullshit.

The notion that supposedly full-grown adults engaged in this activity provoked in me a whirling sea of suspicions about mental health issues and hurt teenagers who never quite made it into drama school. I'm not proud of this attitude, but that was the business end of my thoughts at the time. Had I encountered the likes of Hugh Lupton, Jan Blake, Ben Haggarty, and actually *many* other tellers, I would have reworked that opinion.

So, as you may be sensing, I wasn't quite cooked. Still not quite ready to place a hoof back in the market square. Well, it's one thing to cock-a-snoot, but what can you deliver, oh mighty one? So, in the end, I realised I had to learn a story and tell it myself.

The night came at the black tent. Old friends rolled in for whisky, Guinness, and song, not realising under my host's grimace that there was the quaking reality that at some point I was going to attempt this thing called telling a story. I waited. I'd clear my throat. Bottle it. The party would continue. I think there were bagpipes. I'd wait.

By around three in the morning, the tent was just a pile of bodies snoozing under goatskins, the burner was now so roasting hot that the door flap was open on a freezing February night, the moon was out and glinting on the empty bottles, and I was finally ready for my story. Pretty sure I was speaking to no one, I began. Now, remember, this wasn't speech procured from deep inside the sweat lodge or hurled into the irritable gullet of Welsh rivers, this was me speaking to a human audience. Well, an audience working on their dreams, at least.

So by lantern I warbled. Like a toddler leaping from wet rock to wet rock across a stream, it would have been an alarming proposition had anyone witnessed it. A crazed prisoner amok in the word labyrinth. Ums and ahhs, overwrought phrases squatting self-consciously in a muddy sludge of half-memorised images. I sat stock still, probably with my eyes closed, till I showed mercy to the story, took it out to the pasture, and ended it. Finished. Then, out of the darkness, from one of the slumbering lumps: "That was . . . eh . . . quite good."

God almighty. Gavin was awake. It was the voice of the village speaking back to me. You see, sincerely pitiful though it was, this was the first time I had been able to offer anything that remotely resembled a gift to other people since I'd left the city. Ceremonial work was not really about humans so much; it was a daily, unremarkable, labor-intensive maintenance programme for the unbearable wonder of all things. How you "felt about it" was not a going concern for me; attending to that just seemed to perpetuate the tyranny of our own fluctuating feelings.

But this odd little story was different. It seemed to be a crossroads between the out-in-the-woods space I'd been abiding in and my friends, good natured, slumped and snoring in the dark. It seemed generous. I loved that. Stories seemed generous. And they looked both ways. It was tacit ritual. I saw for the first time a track back to the village. Another kind of work had begun. And during it, I would take on a great deal more respect for the art of storytelling.

THE MANY WAYS THINGS HAVE OF BEING WHAT THEY ARE

It was a labour born and rooted entirely in my openings in the wilds. There were no courses to attend, no elocution lessons, no lines of ink to memorise till I could scattergun the first row with my literary recital of the oral tradition. It just wasn't going to come from there. At least not at first. It had to come from the source: the living world.

I've always loved copses and defiant little grubs of hedge and tree that sprout unbidden from the backs of council estates. I grew up playing in one, and it had been there that, as a kid, I had first heard the sound of ghosts. That low sound in beech trees, when an elegant, late-summer wind moves through the slender branches. You just know that's the sound of the dead. I knew, even as a five-year-old, that some part of my story was being told through that sound. That I'd hear it again someday.

Later, a little older, I would gaze at the dark bow of trees leaning over our brick wall at the back of the house, dropping succulent-looking, possibly dangerous red berries onto the uncut grass. It wasn't exactly sinister, it was magnificent. I knew every berry was a story from the forest.

So, as a young man, I took myself out to a little stretch of old-growth wood, mostly oak and elder, and dug in. If myth really was the power of a place speaking, then I had to bend my head daily to its murmurs.

The vast majority of time I spent over those years outdoors was not in full voice but in listening. A kind of tenderising of the heart. A shaggy equilibrium painfully wrought, where I felt and could maintain the sensation of being flooded by a place. Not an emptying but a filling.

And as weeks would unfold, this roving ecosystem gradually settled its shape somewhat; out of the ravenous floods cascading through my frame, things calmed, and the few same birds, animals, and insects as well as, occasionally, certain regal energies that stand alongside them, started to show up.

The time for this work was usually dusk. I would wait for a frittering of delicate lights to lace the air; they would denote whether it was time to settle back on my goatskins or to cross the rickety bridge and make my way back up the hill to my tent. This kind of vagabond sit took place hundreds of times over those years. I was in the presence of mighty things, and, in their way, they presented me with the big thoughts, over and over again.

This is weft and the weave of story for me. The endless lyrical emerging of the earth's tremendous thinking and the humbling required to simply bear witness to it. And the extraordinary day, when for an hour or so you realise that you too are being witnessed. You are part of the big sound. You have pushed the coats aside and walked through the back of the wardrobe.

When my mouth had chewed on enough silence and my body had located its fragility in the face of winter, when darkness and sorrow had bruised up against solitude, I began to taste, fully, the price of my labour, and slowly I began to speak. And what came was praise.

Inventive speech appears to be a kind of catnip to the living world. Especially prized has been the capacity to name, abundantly and gracefully, dozens or even hundreds of secret names for beings you had spent your whole life strutting past, and muttering: *willow, holly, bat, dog-rose.* They are not their names. Not really.

So the first big move was not one of taking anything at all—I'd done that quite successfully my whole life—but of actually reorganising the detritus of my speech to formulate clear and subtle praise for the denizen I beheld in front of me. Not "the Goddess of the River" but "River Goddess." The moment I squeezed "of the" into the mix, thereby hovered an abstraction, and the fox-woman fled the hunter's hut.

Green Curve
Udder of the Silver Waters

The Hundred Glittering Teeth
Small Sister, Dawning Foam
On the Old Lime Bank.

This wasn't even particularly imaginative. It wasn't flattery. And most of all, it wasn't for me. I wasn't comparing myself. It was simply describing, acutely, what I witnessed in front of me. Some things I realised I was never going to behold clearly. I wouldn't have language for *butterfly, birch, ivy,* and *clay.* There it is; they remained indistinct. Admired, but indistinct. But, grindingly slowly, some beings made themselves known to me, became a lintel overhead, a den in which I could claim a degree of kinship. Not what I would choose, but what chose me.

So the first part of my apprenticeship to story began in a tiny stretch of woodland glade—a corral of about twenty feet—tenderising my own nature until the beings that wished stepped forward, and gave me the slow and halting opportunity to name just a few of the hundred secret ways they have of being themselves. Maybe four thousand years ago they weren't so secret.

It was apprenticeship to the swaying unfolding of the earth's imagination, an endless permutation of Psyche touching the fire tips of Eros's fingers and creating life. The interior was everywhere! Concerned friends would worry that I had travelled too deep into the tangles of myself, that I wouldn't find a way out. I would laugh and gesture out towards the valley. That was where I was. I was already *out.*

I went looking for stories in dark places. In caves, hundreds of feet into the base of Welsh hills, the immensity of tree root and stone suspended above my fragile head. I learnt to slow words down there. Words flushed deep with water and boulder vast. I took myself to dreaming places, forgotten places, places deserving of shrines. I built small shelters in ancient, solitary haunts and sealed myself into the dark for days and nights. It was in those places I learnt many holy names for time. Time as malleable as a concertina, as robust as Irish cattle, as slippery as the trout escaping the hook. Each of the secret words was true wealth for my parched tongue. They required payment in full and I was not sad to give it.

It was in the ebony world that luminosity came. Great stretches of images from a future I was yet to have: of people and estuary maps and animals; of beings we rarely have the names for anymore. It was in that place that I was shown a discarded set of antlers, which I was soon to find in clock time at a local rubbish dump. Those bone wands were a big story for me and formed the centre of many negotiations and ceremonies with the soulful world. And yet, one day I would have to give them away.

I went looking for stories in the palace of the birds: the pastoral murmur of the wood pigeon, the thrilling blue call of the tawny owls in their midnight kingdoms. I learnt feathered words up there, sounds that whittled a new and fragrant shape to my jaw. For a little while, I was a boy of the moonlight, cloaked and rooted by the base of great trees. It is no great brag to say that a part of me is still there.

If I'd believed the propaganda of our times, I would have seen England as too farmed, too crushed-tight with humans and their history, soil too poisoned, forest too hurt and impoverished for such an education—better to turn to the vastness of Siberia or some other pristine wilderness. Thank God I didn't. The eye of the needle is everywhere, abiding patiently for you to quilt your life to the Otherworld, which is really our deeply natural function anyway. Small pockets of absolute aliveness, greenness, riven-deep mystery are all over our strange and bullishly magnificent isle.

So my first move towards story was to give one up, beginning the slow move from a society of taking to a culture of giving. The living world was not there for my temporary edification or a transitory backdrop for my "healing"; it was home. A home that scared me, rattled me, soothed me, shaped me. Without the investment of time and focus, the words I longed to speak would simply be phony on my tongue. The worst aspect of storytelling is when you hear the words spoken but know the teller never took the journey to get them. The teller just squatted by the well and stole the words when one who had made the journey crawled out of the Underworld. Well, I sure wasn't much of a teller at that point, but I knew I had river mud on my boots and green vines in the wine of my blood.

Later in this book we will touch upon just how a storyteller might sift through the unbridled rawness of such experiences and find stories both broad and wily enough to carry them. If you try them too often as "I" statements, they will, in the end, get just too straight-up lonesome and wander off to die somewhere. There's a greater vehicle waiting for them. They need those ancestors peering in, leaning on their staffs, not quite cheering you on, not quite telling you to stop.

CHAPTER TWO

Brutus

It is fitting to begin our stories with a pilgrimage. To break bread with the
dead, to bring sustenance to a ghost, to sit in the shivering dark of a cave
with an ancestor. So let us begin our wander, you and I, towards the home of
the last great wild man of the moors. It is through his mouth we will hear our
first story.

MOO ROA MAN

You would glimpse him when my father was a boy—they called him Moo Roa
Man. It is very early morning, and there he is, striding briskly in a tattered tweed,
gripping a staff. He is on the stomp from his shanty digs high up at Huntingdon
Warren on Dartmoor. Through bog and over stream he weaves, eager for the
bacon, eggs, buttered toast, and tea he will wolf down in Buckfastleigh. On his
return from the long romp he will be spotted wielding enormous branches for
his fire. Berry-bright eyes and a snowy clump of hair sit above that shabby coat,
mulched with rain and belted with a cord of rope, his boots so scuffed some say
they have become hooves. A piper at the gates of dawn.

His appearance could spook you. Seen shuffling just within the tree line,
he has local folk claiming he is a wild man—that the moors once again have a
Wudu-Wasa, a lord of misrule. His stroll through the hamlets has the kiddies
burying their heads in their mothers' fragrant aprons.

Wild man? *Wodwo?* Has he walked into our time from the very back
of the cave? I say the opposite: he is walking *from* our time into limestone
dreaming, into granite dreaming, into aurochs dreaming. He had a history
we could comprehend. The son of a Methodist preacher, he served time as a
popular schoolteacher, but on retirement turned his head away from a life of
civic duty, went to lodge in a deep remoteness, befriended the rabbit warrens
and the hidden trout pools that were once plentiful, extended his soul to a
more natural weight in the world.

When the snow got deep he would look for lodgings in Buckfastleigh; he was not above advertising in the *Western Morning News*. In kinder weather, those who visited him described his dwellings as "indescribably derelict"—a kind of two-roomed cave, decorated liberally with the rusting remains of an aircraft that had crashed outside. Still, his fire was merry enough, where he would endlessly place toast onto the glowing peat and deftly remove it at just the right moment, or slurp a constant supply of industrial-strength orange tea thickened with oatmeal. He was known to be immensely strong. Not strong like an athlete filled with steroids, but strong like the bull-wolf, strong like a confluence of mountains.

Not just content with early morning wanders, he often went farther at night. He liked gossip by lantern and the warm, boozy humour of the barmaid. With bone-white stars just surfacing, he would canter down to the pubs of Ivybridge and South Brent. His scarecrow shape was known in the ale halls and fondly tolerated. There was absolute silence when he told his stories. When enough rough beer had settled his belly, and with a bag of vinegary chips stuffed deep in a pocket, he would wend his shaggy way home via the disused railway track from Cantrell to Redlake.

Such was his fierce intelligence, such was his desire for company, that he would write letters to himself to ensure a visit from the postman, who now visited the lonesome settlement twice a week. We can see the startled expression of the postie leaning on the gate as this fox-stack of a man speaks earnestly about Greek philosophy, a folktale, or the movement of bats or gently turns over the meaning of the book of Luke. "One of the roughs," he is loved, cherished, by those who know him. He is a slow earth man, his wisdoms of the region thorough, his relationship to it visceral and immediate.

This man who made his way through life as storyteller—a preacher and a teacher—withdrew into the curly folds of the moors for his final years. But we know he yearns for company, loves it, even as he walks to the back of the cave. He found it with starling and thrush, badger and salmon, wind and bush, but I think it is we too that should go to him, this lonely Wudu-Wasa. We go for ourselves and for our culture.

For one last telling from Frederick William Symes.

The telling that never was and always is.

As we hike to the wild upland we gather kindling, strong beer, a rabbit from a Scoriton farmer. We stomp a mile of firm track and then into fast-rising moorland, that familiar bounce underfoot. The view opens, mighty in all directions; for a while we can see the scattered orange glow of distant coastal towns, and then we are enclosed in the brown shoulder of the moor. It is dusk, and the last of the summering heat is leaving the soil. In the half light he will be waiting to meet us, the dead man, ready to walk us clear out of our century. He squats, raggle-taggle, in the shadows of a dry stone wall, his bag and stick with him. The old farm is once again behind him.

We see lingering smoke from the fire, but he's not taking us inside. He turns and we glance up the hill, to the cairn, the "Heap O' Sinners," a place he cherished. The rock in his powerful fists, he has been waywardly adding to the prehistoric mound every time he's seen fit. He urges us on, seems to be looking for something. He halts, gestures; his face crumples. He's found his old chapel.

It's rough hewn into the bowls of the soil, a potato cave. A place to store the vegetables safe from the winter frosts. There was always gossip in the villages that he had fashioned a primal chapel up here.

He produces a few glowing embers of peat from his pocket and places them in the centre of his hand. He settles us by the entrance to his place of prayer. Encouraged to take our ease, we settle our tired backs onto the lichen-strewn lumps of granite.

This Green Knight, Bertilak of the Warren, takes his blade to our necks and loosens us from straight time altogether. The embers glow in his paw, and as we sit huddled, the bull-wolf starts to speak with an Underworld tongue come of fifty-three years under west-country soil.

> *I am older than*
> *this body, dust-boned*
> *in the clay of an*
> *Albaston graveyard.*
>
> *I'm salted with the memory*
> *of a fish that crawled onto mud,*
> *of tracking the hooves of the*
> *elephant, day after day,*
> *across the fragrant jungle of*
> *Dartmoor.*

I have cut the worshipful
throat for Belus,
I sorrowed to my boots
when I smelt the wild fragrance
of Gethsemane.

I watched Lancelot walk
clean out of a Welsh lake,
dry as a bone.

Roadkill told me things:
the crushed head of a rabbit
whispered the Epic of Gilgamesh
to me on the back lanes from
Hexworthy one night.

Best I ever heard. Masterclass.

I swam London's
buried rivers:

Tyburn
Warble
Peck
Effort
Falconbrook
Quarry

I broke bread with ghosts
down there.

I have tales for the lonely road,
lost amongst the cabbage fields
of Lincolnshire,
tales to jade an enemy—
tales for love in a hay barn,

Tales for rooks
over a Pondsworthy copse—
so sweet it'll turn their dark capes
to settle by my feet.

Tales that'll dump
terror in your saddlebags:
you'll give me coin and wine
just to halt the bleakness of my words.

Stories told on the
dark hills of Ceredigion,
with burning bushes
and the lord of the fairies
listening in.

When I was finished
I was laid under
the fur of a wolf-skin,
suckled nine-days
on the teat of a rain-bear
to gather my strength.

Know this: there is a storm
coming to this world.

Disappointment so
deep in the guts of us,
that good people
won't search
when their children
wander into the forest.

Turns the heart
to a lump of coal,
we will sing
our blue-dream

over this dying world
and call it poetry.

Story is all we have left.

The last piece of courtship
to the denizens that flood us
every time we
fight and love and screw.

They are the ones
that make it beautiful.

Speech is how we
taste our ancestors.

He gestures to the entrance and we crawl in. It's large enough to stretch out. From his embers we can see the scarring where a pick axe dug for tin; there are bat droppings heaped at the back. But our attention is on the man.

He will bind us through the age-old night with his words, throw the bones of sound to clatter on the lime of our old mind, coax a myth line from prehistory to the very edge of our own brief years, right here in this mud cathedral. Moo Roa Man points a finger to the ancient murk and begins:

The generous dead are speaking
Enter the green chapel of language

❀ ❀ ❀

Brutus

The court magician was clear. He'd divined—peered for image in the embers, gazed on the movement of penned horses; all sent the same message. The child that the King's wife was expecting would be the death of both his mother and his father. The stars jeered it; the sea waves cawed its hard, green truth.

First death. It occurred in childbirth, when his mother died in the labour of the raw-boned boy's arrival. Even as a cherub, the lad felt hot eyes of blame on him. He lived to appease the vastness of his mother's absence. Fifteen years of this passed.

Over time he had fashioned his own bow, winged his own arrows, and was determined to join his father in the hunt. His father loved the hunt; it was the only time the boy had seen him smile. One morning he, his father, and a small entourage set out into the emerald depths of the Royal Forest.

A mean wind caught the boy's first arrow. It changed direction utterly and struck his father full in the chest. In the heart. Without one word of goodbye, he passed. Second death. The boy carries the red hands now, his small family dead. Clouds scud the sun.

After this, too much prophecy hung around his shoulders to ensure a peaceful existence. In the eyes of the court his seed was crooked, he lived with snakes. He had to strike out. Leave. Never return. Although raised in Italy, his mother was Trojan, and it was Trojan men he surrounded himself with when he sailed out on his grief winds. His name? Brutus.

Many seas came to meet him—the salt wall of the storm, the flat blue when no breeze crept the sail, the jaunty push of the curling wave. All was an education in water. Silence, he knew about. The ship was magnificent, two sheaves of oars on either side that skimmed the waves. A hundred men, fifty on each side, rowed hard. Their boy leader always gazed ahead, mesmeric in focus, golden in aura. Inside is a storm, inside is a storm.

Crusting the tides,
the young crow
who claims
the eagle's meat.

The hundred strive for him:
sea-bulls, fathers of
the whale-wave,
strong as Suns.

They outpace prophecy,
salt-stiff beards, made wise
by the storm dark news
of a thousand sunken ships.

A drift of seal's spray
bone combs of foam,
swift rimmed with shark
and herring,
a cracked green skull,
sloshing under
the timbered bow.

After a time they found themselves led by a swift wind to a deserted island. The men contented themselves with feasting and resting on pearl-white beaches, whilst Brutus wandered in past the tree line.

He came to the ruins of an old temple. It could have been a temple for Artemis or Diana or some great mistress of the hunt whose name is kept safe by badgers. Steeped in ritual etiquette, Brutus wasted no time. At the ivy-clad entrance he lit three fires, then caught and sacrificed a white hart. Mingling its blood with wine, he poured his offering onto the broken altar. The glade protected Brutus from the harsh sun as he muttered his heartfelt prayers for guidance. Afterwards, he skinned the deer, lay on its white skin, and fell into a visionary rest.

A sweet breeze came through the boughs of the green wood. A young woman stood before him; small birds of dazzling colour hummed around her shoulders, the new moon was in her hair, and she carried a scepter with the morning star glimmering at its very point. On her back were an ornate bow and a quiver of ebony-coloured arrows, each with a differing star constellation carved delicately onto its stem.

When she spoke, her breath was of honeysuckle and her tone strong. She told him of an island, far to the west, over nine waves. She spoke of it as a place where he would reign and establish a culture.

She is in
her speaking:

Of boar and bee,
towered flanks of oak,
western tip surged with apples,
the north blue with
remote and lonely mountains.

Always ancient,
a mossy drum-thump
of a roving god,
a moist lump of earth
for lovers to get lost in.

Its rain water
booms goodness
into the Queen's cup.

Through the piling snow
comes a golden cow
to lay cream-udder milk
in the Kings bowl.

Boy.

In your hunting,
with your
hawk
horse
hound

A thousand years could pass,
and you could not dint
this simmering harvest.

The stag will cross deep water
for one who sings at dusk.

Your herds
will be as grains
of sands on the shore.

In winter,

When ghosts stalk
your grey fields,
and frost stiffens
your cloak,
the forest will gift
its vast trunks
to the mead-hall fire,
your glinting plate
will groan with meat.

There will be coin and furs
for the tellers: feed well
their florid jaws,
keep the keg by their arm
and their bed accommodating—
they can bind the weather,
keep your thatch dry with praise,
scythe the very sun from heaven
with the bounty of their sagas.

Your companion in the north
is the old man in the fur coat—

The Bear
red berries pour from his mouth.

Leave him alone.

The fallow deer will take
the ash, elm and hawthorn,
the roe the succulent tip of hazel.

Even the rook sings of love
to the worm in its beak.

I call on my fair distant sister,

Arianrhod of the Owl-Face,
ghoul-black skin,
hair of threaded corn.

Spiderwebs lace her hands,
ivy the ghostly acres of her rump.

She can forgive,
she can be holy terror.

I call on my fair distant brother,

Cernunnos of the bone grove,
seed-bearer, lover of the screech-moon.

He can bless,
or he can bring the dark trouble.

My northern siblings,
see this crow-boy-coming.

Give stretch to wingspan,
king-energy to his wine,
hot sap between his hips,

Let his eye behold.

Brutus woke, deeply moved. The strange young woman had gone. As soon as they boarded the ship, good winds caught their billowing sails. The bows were a blur of foam, and their track was as milk in the ocean behind them. They pushed on through the Straits of Gibraltar, they risked deadly storms on the Cape of Finisterre, but their way stayed fair, they were sweet cargo to the gods.

Eventually, before them rose high cliffs and forest behind them. Even through the trees they could see it was a land of deep valleys. Mist shrouded the green, but they could make out the movement of animals in the verdant shrubbery.

They followed the route of a river inland, and Brutus was struck with
the knowing that this was the very place that the goddess had spoken of.
Wild grass meadows ran to the water's edge, buzzards caught the inebriated
breeze and glided above the sails a-bliss. The soil on the bank loafed in great
humps, ruddy shanks of wealth for those seed throwers. The shallows were
ridged thick with herons gazing on their arriving. All felt the wealth. And
at that place where the glittering tide meets the dappled surge, there Brutus
leapt from his boat and swore this would be his vision-resting, his home.

His dreaming came with a price. The island's inhabitants. Giants who
dwarfed the Trojans. They had been the loudest sound on the island since
it became one. However, the nimble horde found their way through and underneath the grunting swings of the giants' weapons and slowly accomplished
themselves as the superior force. In time, the giants retreated from the Dart
estuary and up onto Dartmoor. There they stayed, in remote caves and deer-
thick forest, scheming through the white flakes of winter.

These Grendels of the hidden.
Spun loose from their proud ground.

What powers retreat?
Do the lion and the nightingale
mourn this fanfare?

Swan skulls mud-crushed
under the wheels of wagons,

The sound of the chapel bell
makes the otter twist
in his green currents.

These Grendels
of the blue swamps,
they bob in the drudge-mud,
one slow eye
on the hero ships.

There was a great champion amongst the big people. Goemagog would not languish in the caves and bellowed for combat. A wrestling match was arranged between him and Brutus's greatest warrior, Corineus. The fight was on what we now call Plymouth Hoe. The giant was three times the size of Corineus, and the few giants who made the trip—cautiously—from the moor to the scrap were optimistic.

Corineus made play with his skill, but the brutal grunt strength of Goemagog kept him from taking the advantage. After a vicious bear hug by the giant (which broke several ribs of the Trojan), the smaller man gained a hallucinatory strength and grabbed, bit, butted, and smote the giant to the very edge of the cliff. A fragile edge is not a good place for a giant, and surely he fell.

Goemagog's body was split-mangled on the razor teeth of the rocks. The sea grew drunk with blood, chanting a salty roar. The red cliffs of Devon's south coast came that way by taking such a deep drenching in the giant's blood. His allies fled, their great feet booming the woods—some across the Tamar river and others back to their lonely byres on the high moor.

And so it is when you follow a vision: you invoke giants. Over time, Brutus became the leader of all of Albion, which became named after him, *Britain*, and his worthy wrestler Corineus had the land Cornwall named in his honour. And across the gray waves, a woman watches from a temple doorway.

❀ ❀ ❀

Dartmoor is three hundred sixty-five square miles of wilderness in the far southwest of Great Britain, the last county before you get to Cornwall. It's rugged, with vast granite tors, mires, seemingly endless stone circles and tribal remnants, sudden mists, and small ponies that are mad for roaming. Our waters are usually flowing, not still, rivers heading green and silver to the ocean. It's still easy to die up here.

Dartmoor has its cromlech tombs, corn-drying barns, longhouses, and a medieval clapper bridge. It holds the Widdicombe Fair, so beloved of folk song, and the Tavistock Goose Fair. Every inch has a name and some curious tale attached, but you may have to buy an old man a pint in the Rugglestone Arms rather than hope to find the story on a computer.

Dartmoor has genuine faerie lore, not the tourist variety, and most of us understand that the vast majority of tors are really ancestors who wandered too far from the path on an unfortunate turn of the moon's cycle. Our antlered lord of the hunt, Dyer, has been residing over in Wistman's Wood these many millennia, with his pack, the Hounds of Yeth. Dartmoor is a great mythteller. My father broke bread with his father up on these green banks; my daughter has been raised entirely within the bounds of the moor.

It emerged way back, about two hundred ninety-five million years ago; it's an old fella. Magma burst through the Earth's crust, cooling over time to become granite. Already present on the surface (in what we now call Devon and Cornwall) were "country rocks": sandstone, limestone, and carboniferous shale. As the granite cooled, hydrothermal movement caused an intense concentration of minerals to form—minerals that resulted in rich veins of tin, copper, arsenic, and lead ores. The same movement caused the formation, very deep down, of china clay. The clay has been quarried over the years, as have the tin and its sister veins.

Before this emergence there had been a tropical sea, hundreds of miles wide. The floor of this ocean is what became the ridges and tors of Dartmoor as this aquatic sculpture took place, the molten granite both baking and pushing up the sediment.

Time passes and it becomes sea again, then sixty-five million years later the waters retreat. A soft chalk left on the ridges is worn away to reveal the granite patiently waiting beneath. There are now flowering plants, evergreen forests, and insects, much of what you would expect of a tropical ecosystem. But coming down onto the north coast of Devon are ice sheets—part of the four great ice ages. The land alternately freezes and thaws, freezes and thaws—in and out like a sighing tide. The ice gods got their sharp teeth into the moor, leaving patterned ground features that can be seen clearly today up by Merrivale Quarry and Cox Tor.

After an immense passage of years almost impossible to contemplate (Dartmoor has also been an island for a great period), we find elephant, lion, wolf, hyena, rhinoceros, beaver, and even—this is only about half a million years ago—evidence of humans. Juniper, pine, hazel, oak, elm, dwarf birch, and willow also cover the heathland.

As a primordial farming community develops, this heavy woodland cover starts to get cleared, usually by an extensive burn and then an intensive grazing of the uncovered land. It was this very combination that led to the evolution of peat, something that now covers vast tracks of the moors. The peat is more than fifty centimetres thick, in certain areas over seven metres.

Around the late Neolithic to early Bronze Age, a ritual sensibility starts to emerge within the scattered Dartmoor communities. The land is littered with stone circles and stone rows and often accompanied by ditches and raised banks. There are more of these rows on Dartmoor than any other place in Britain. The speculation about their use is vigorous but vague; we can say that they certainly seem designed to address the mysteries.

As it stands, on the day my walk begins, Dartmoor is a distant, bleary lump on the horizon; it will take another story for us to get to stomp its grasses. But for now I have to get to where this tale begins, and to do that I have to get nearer the coast.

My destination is a crow's view of the Dart estuary—the lanes are slurried pink with heavy rains causing rivulets of mud from the fields. It looks like a battlefield, a heavy reckoning.

Soon I am off the lane and heading downwards towards Sharpham Vineyard. But it's not wine tasting that I'm here for. Halfway down the track I lean against a fencepost and take in the scene below. The estuary is an undulating serpent, dramatically curved, with exposed marshes here and there. The tide is out, and the thousands of burrowed furrow shells, cockles, and ragworm provide swooping heaven for the local bird population. Across the way I see three ranges of hills, densely scored with the sharp lines of a farmer's ambitions. Beyond them, several television masts blink out over Torbay.

The air is fiercely sharp, intoxicating. The Dart—"river where oak trees dwell"—is a frequent shifter of shape, from an almost entirely freshwater system on its high moor to largely marine habitat at its maw.

It always begins with coins. I hurl my libation out for the delectation of the osprey, beech, and mud bank. I hurl silver to break the straight line of history. I pay compliment and service to the understory of this gurgling, salt-licked, wetling place.

The fields appear to have alopecia; in the distant green is unexplained pink, patchy, not regulated. The light is extraordinary, yellowish-gray skies then suddenly parting into blue. When it does, the lime-white beeches on the other bank flare up into a kind of eerie luminescence, burning bushes almost. This goes on for several minutes, the sullen light breaking these previously ghost trees into splendid, silvery array.

My eyes draw back again to the estuary. My memory had been confused—I had remembered this stretch of the Dart as a triumphant arrow of unbending waterway. It's nothing of the sort. It's true Celtic—a Merlined stretch of serpent curve and mud, a briny trail, not as eager with its secrets as I had remembered. In the upper reaches are yet more animal powers—the green sandpiper, the mute swan, and the sedge warbler. For those with patience, the whole area is bristle-thick with wildlife.

Today is a limited palette as regards colour: a bright silver overhead and mottled greens, browns, and thin hummings of orange lacing the banks of the sun-glinted waves. Everything feels sluiced through with moisture. The river is thick with worms and snails that prove good feasting for some of the shell-fish, otters, crabs, gray seals, and the occasionally spotted dolphin found on the banks or waters. The reed bed is housing the reed warblers and buntings, whilst the heron abides in the shallows, waiting for word of a Trojan stranger.

I've occasionally been ferried across this river over the years—for fish suppers and Guinness in Dartmouth, but today it's hard to imagine the water being deep enough; it's fast moving, but from up here in the crow's nest, not incredibly deep.

Directly underneath me is a worked field with a hollow tree in its centre. Around the field and above and beyond me are leafless oaks, their branches gnarly limbs. My head being so full of Brutus and his arrival, it feels like they are beckoning him on, these crooked fingers of the branch. I get caught up in the trees' slow excitement and stare hard into the thin glare of the January sun, waiting for the thrum of a hundred oars.

There is a noise: a Toyota Hilux carrying what appears to be a small group of teenagers. They dismount and start straggling up the field. Desiring privacy, I decide to leave the perch and follow the river. Amongst the steady minimalism of the colour range I can spot the occasional blue or manufactured pink just past the bend to my left. It can only be Totnes.

I wind across swampy grasses, juddered with moisture, till I get to the edge of the water. It's colder still down here, and the light catches the surface like a glint on the scales of a rusty dragon. But before I know it, my clothes are jumbled in a pile, half-tucked into my boots, and I'm wading out into the brown surge. Not having overthought the moment, I'm not in a wetsuit but just as God intended, taking the deep cold as the good-natured slap that it is. I bury my head and shoulders quickly into discreet but freezing laps of wave. I can feel mud sucking powerfully on my ankles and see a smeary green kingdom when I open my eyes. There is a pungent smell of river water against cold air when I wrestle my head up again, gasping. My brain is a jabbing blue slab of ice.

Quickly I'm on the other side of the river and starting to warm up. I take little dives down to belly-scrape the bottom of the waters, seeing little, just groping ahead in the murk with glowing white shapes that must be my hands. Having swum the Dart high on the moor, I've experienced the dangers of subterranean juts of granite out of sight.

This time, I reach out and recognise the confirming roundness of tree roots sloping in from the Dart's bank. For just a moment I float in the brown river, bobbing by the glistening wood. In the strangest way I feel as though I am remembering something. My hair drifts in clumps and I keep just my eyes above the line of liquid. Everything is deeply still.

Suddenly I am witnessing the arrival of Brutus. Right there, fifty feet down the waters, I can see the surety of his ship's passage, those salt-browned faces peering over the sides, the aura of conqueror that glides with them. And I, some dark wretch of the swamp, watch on from the wet roots of the shallows. It's there and then it is gone.

I shudder how the story of Brutus risks too much attention to the high world. Our founding story. I push out from the bank with broad strokes and keep my head under.

I sludge over the other bank to my very welcome pile, still just about warm, and, hopping from foot to foot, quickly layer on shirt, sweater, jacket, and scarf, with only sandy socks and sopping hair as evidence of my impulse for water.

I walk a little inland to keep warm and I notice that, despite its lack of forest and resolutely farmed appearance, the land surrounding the estuary seems relatively free of houses. Whilst for a moment I fall into a sentimental reverie about sympathetic local councils, Cara later reminds me that the empty spaces probably have more to do with prohibitive sums required for housing rather than with conservation.

As the Dart enters Totnes, it straightens and becomes more that hard line I remember. Dotting its sides now are small shipyards, housing developments, and various eateries and cafés. It's also starting to rain and getting even colder, so I have the riverside almost entirely to myself, apart from two women walking an inquisitive spaniel.

A small population of gray seals, said to number twenty, have been spotted as far up as here, so I can't help but scan the waters. Nope. It's less stirring now, but by no means unpleasant. Breaking from the waterline I walk up the high street—Fore Street—to the very place where (legend is insistent) Brutus first set foot. There it is, the Brutus Stone, a small granite boulder—a boulder

I have seen drunks enthusiastically piss on, hooded lads spit on, and most ignore as they strain up the steep hill to the emporiums of wheat-free bread and lentil bakes. It does not feel like a charged spot.

I can feel that I have transgressed from the myth line of Brutus's story, in the accumulative bustle, incense-thick air pouring out from local New Age bookshops, the accented cry of the insistent big-issue seller. It all feels ghastly after the wet, dense-feathered, nesting, silvering-waved estuary. But isn't all of this the very kind of mix that Brutus founded and that was even prophesied by the *being with the moon in her hair?*

Out of the nest

Surely it is the business of all youth to one day aim an arrow at a parent's heart. Even with the most benign childhood, usually the severance into life's next stage has to be pretty direct. Otherwise, how do all concerned get the message that they are not dealing with a child anymore? Stubble on a chin is not reasonable evidence.

Brutus grows up in a tense confluence—on one hand the son of a king, but already marked by a prophetic hand that he would bring the death of both his mother and father. We presume that this cheery state of proclamation has spilled out into the general community. His royal position requires etiquette from his dignitaries, but how much genuine affection is present? How old was he when he became aware of the ghoulish dynamic surrounding his ascendancy to the throne? We are confronted with a number of questions.

This is clearly a tale that begins with transition. It is the end of the old order and the beginning of a new. Whatever has been going on under the King's reign requires a shake-up, a renewal. However, the whole affair is heightened when it is the son of the king and not some far-off villain who causes his death. It is his own hand that sent the arrow. King killing is a traditional way to claim power, but we get no such conscious intention here.

There are many ways to start an adventure. Some wander for love, others for wealth, but almost all wanderings involve leaving the anesthetised, one-size-fits-all groove of the domestic and setting out into the wild spray of unpredictability. This first story, the story that lays the ground for the others, begins with an anguished pitch. Unseen forces push this young man on. Certain experiences are so charged they seem fated, that we have collided with the iron fist of prediction and can do little but follow the hard cards it presents.

This is a progression that was dictated before he was even born—felt in the salt wave, the stars overhead. Maybe he signed up for this.

"The Deal Beyond the Things of this World" is a phrase to describe the moment when we synch up with these fateful openings. These deals are bargaining for deeper life, and what the deal contains is rarely something that has financial or commercial viability attached. The currency usually comes with a little suffering.

Prophetic words droop over many of us. Maybe not so celestial, but spat down through the generations in the mindset and expectations of our own families. It is the business of every soul to, at some point, push against the death rattle of the predictive, the flat eye of the punch-drunk uncle saying we'll never rise higher than the factory floor. Whilst there are toxic prophecies that are simply hereditary bitterness, others are wrought tough in the very fabric of the cosmos. Brutus is tasting this latter brew, sharp and desperate. So it is when you are to found a kingdom. As we stretch out I will draw largely on the Mediterranean textures of its roots.

The altar in altermodern

It is clear that, just as in the story, culturally we are in a period of huge and speedy transitions. Old kings, old notions—traditional fixities are taking arrows to the heart on an almost hourly basis. The writer Nicolas Bourriaud (2009) claims that postmodernism is *over*, done. The corpse is stiff, waxy, and congealed. This new emerging he calls the altermodern.

The twentieth-century modern and postmodern attention to a primarily Western-fixated culture is at an end. There is no clear centre anymore, but an emerging polyglot. The exposure to endless varieties of society, opinion, and texture is cooking up an enormous creolisation at the expense of multiculturalism and regional identity. For the emerging generation, culture is resolutely globalised; slow ground is no ground.

Bourriaud sees this new universalism as being based on subtitling and generalised dubbing. How could it be any other way when the heavy chore of actually learning a new language or being immersed long term in another culture is a ridiculous labour compared to subtitled, uninformed, but absolutely instant montage of image appearing on the glowing laptop screen? We are receivers of a vast backdrop of information, but identical to the vastness is thinness of relationship.

Whilst the turning from a Western-fixated centre to wider culture should be celebrated, you can send back the clowns when we realise that the replacement is not rich diversity but globalisation. This is the very opposite of a myth line—something found slowly by diligence, place, reaching out into history, myth, and the slow thinking of a landscape. This is more like the smoke streams from an airplane, briefly visible but with long-term effects.

The *alter* in *altermodern* refers to multiplicity as well as notions of otherness. What happens to otherness when everything is subsumed into the blinding light of the new creole? Will otherness become the new constant? It would appear so.

Of course, some can see Hermes, Coyote, and Loki scampering around in this new, dislocated, un-Olympian, flattened-out barrage of instantaneous connections, but how long will it keep their interest? All three are in service to speed and a little chaos, but only when it serves more than the profane. No matter how grubby their appearance, Trickster is pushing us back into encountering divine forces. But this thinness of knowledge, this denial of the local, where does this place Saturn and his diligence to long-term goals? What of the steady logic of Apollo and Athena, or of home-loving Hestia? *Have we forgotten the altar in the alter?* I worry that we bore the gods.

Time is often perceived within a kind of straight-line history; but the altermodern is no straight line, it is a maze—a maze with no centre to locate, no flag to be embedded. Like (and I do stress *like*) Coyote, its life force is not really gathered in one place like a heart, certainly not in Old Europe, that being one of its positives. Realms are no longer stratified and boundaried, but gateway-riddled plateaus.

Here's the rub: We have information, but do we have meaning?

We would do well to remember: Coyote requires settled areas for his wider travels to take on real significance; he needs something to run up against. He enjoys some sovereign heft. If everyone travels, we encourage a form of his demise. Occasionally Trickster establishes as well as transgresses boundaries. But if the boundaries no longer exist at all, then where is Trickster?

The issue here is that the gods are a *complicato*; Hermes is at his best when relating to other forces: fierce Hera, Aphrodite, Zeus's kingly gaze. The rough and tumble of their shared intrigues creates culture; they are not to be separated. Globalisation is monotheism. Hermes within this format is not Hermes at all, but a mimic. Bernard Neville talks of "Hermes inflation" as a psychological, not mythological, alignment with Western hubris.

An attempt to reorient could be to recall the specific tone of Hermes's communication—to communicate the gods' messages by psychic means—from *soul to soul*. So if the soul does not open, then Hermes is not present. If there are no other gods to send messages back and forth to, then Hermes is not present. Remove the flowers and the bee is taskless.

So, we all are sailing out like Brutus, on protean waves, with no sense yet of what this will all bring.

We remember that Brutus is originally from Troy, not Italy. The Romans were not keen on seafaring, and when Brutus takes to the waves it is Trojans (Turks), not Romans, that he takes. The Romans had enjoyed many tactical successes without ever requiring great naval battles. They had a culture of shepherds and farmers, not great fleets heading out on the whale road. It wasn't in the blood. They had brought a terrible hand to the Volsci, Samnites, Latins, Aequi, and Sabines; their capacity for strategic violence was never doubted. However, even when they straddled much of the Mediterranean, they tried to avoid the sea. It wasn't that the Romans didn't have ships, but their relationship to them seemed oddly hesitant, especially when we regard the depth of ocean knowledge available from many of their subjugated foes.

Brutus, then, is heading to a place of some dread to the civilisation he is leaving behind. The sea holds a similar sense of unease to the forest in European folktales. Its untrammelled waves could very well lead us off the edge of the world. All deserts, woodlands, oceans, and mountainous regions hold titillation/terror for those of us nesting hearth-warm in the village. The mountain peak is closer to the gods; the ocean depths extend down into the Underworld. Best stay clear of both.

We are all horse thieves

Brutus is an immigrant, an "other" to these people he has uneasily existed within. As a travelling storyteller, I find that there is no character more lovingly regarded than the orphan, whether found cradled in the bulrushes or at the lonely crossroads outside a German village. We all have an instinct for growing up in a place that is not necessarily where we really come from; *surely this can't be our real family?* Despite the limited horizons, maybe there is some magical other family hidden way back; maybe we are really descended from Hungarian horse thieves or jovial Dublin poets that got James Joyce dancing every now and again.

These little shoots of grandiosity are not to be mocked, despite some wobbles in factual validity. They are a deeper kind of truth. They are a reaching beyond the brain-insulting grayness of much of modernity to an inheritance from the wind, the unfolding sash of a galloping bandit queen, the hard snort of the cornered badger backed in by hounds. It's our mythic inheritance we are sensing.

So, some of us sever. We cannot *but* aim the arrow at the heart of the old life, the old king. From the moment the mother dies we know the prophecy has legs, is going to play itself out, so to hell with caution and a neat shape for familial approval. When we know this was never our story anyway, our setup, our kingdom, the wandering immigrant within us will shake the cage and not count the cost.

When the nice boys or girls in our neighbourhood suddenly go wild, won't return calls, get into street brawls, have sex indiscriminately, shut down entirely, or sleep for twenty hours a day, they are pushing for a sea journey. The question is, do they have the Trojans to bring with them, or do they set out alone on a leaky raft with a bottle of brandy and a broken compass?

When the story refers to the ship, its general finery, the serving men, it tells us that this is not a mere boy. Something has been honed, worked out, stretched inside him. There is a focus. Within us is the supporting cast of warriors; they need to be activated, marshalled, or positively ordered into putting their muscles to the oar. No doctorate gets finished, no child raised, no language learnt without them. The story tells us something about strategy: that when the time is right to head out, it's best to have some skill developed, something that supports us, no matter what hard weather we encounter. The ship isn't butchered with leaks or drifting in circles. It's the kind of ship that Sylvia Plath sailed when she launched into a poem: firm, powerful, and unafraid of storms.

Addiction to disorder

A perverse twist to departure is when it becomes addictive; we all know those who become predisposed to turning over the apple cart of their life as a kind of nervous tic—if they cannot taste the brine, they become nervous, afraid of death amongst the dishes and school run. So roll up new lover, new town, new horizon—an addiction to the act of severance. But as the years roll into decades, we find no woman at the edge of the world, no healing in the deep, no kingdom to claim. We endlessly shake the cage without the deeper message getting through. It's about timing and a certain internal attention. The genius in these stories is the sensitivity to specific moments—*this* is the moment to act, not next week, not last year. But they also tell of seven years underground adding kindling to a small fire, accepting wood shavings as payment, working in the thrall of a forest lord. Images of patience. This all has to do with the business of discipline.

The word *discipline* derives from the Roman goddess Disciplina—a Latin noun that indicates training, faithfulness, self-control, and determination. Disciplina was especially adored by warriors, and many Roman legions outposted to remote stretches of the empire drew on her qualities of both loyalty and frugality to keep them heart-connected to their mission, adaptable to less-than-luxurious conditions. So to know the moment to set sail, to stay the course, to have warriors at your arm requires an offering in the temple of Disciplina. Each study with a scholar up late, bent over a difficult text could be said to be a temple to her.

Many caught in the addiction to upheaval define their character by their very readiness for movement. We all know the friend whose face is perennially contorted in bitterness, endlessly bringing the conversation around to *their* endured traumas and *their* seemingly endless and frankly self-induced changes of circumstances. This temperament can become a prideful scar. But the stories say that this slower pace, this gifting to Disciplina, leads to sovereignty, a claiming of queen- or kingship. If you are continually caught in disorder, then your aim is off and your boundaries trashed. The call to the ocean journey is not to be made cheap with continual furor. We cannot anchor a kingdom with that kind of hysteria around.

Disorder is a kind of cheap trick to mimic the psyche's desire for initiation. When it fails to be ritually provided, we try to compensate by creating the mayhem without the magic.

One who stays

A frequent complaint is that myths are always about big sexy moves and large personalities. What about the ones who have to show loyalty to the nappies and the dishes? An antidote to this bravura is to enter the presence of Hestia.

Hestia, goddess of the hearth, eldest daughter of Cronus and Rhea, is not known for adventures. But to be in her presence is to be warmed—they say she cannot be distinguished from the hearth fire itself. Troubled lovers came to her altar for resolution. Her hearth was a place of peacemaking and mercy. She had no time for war; she offered sanctuary and refused any sacrifice involving bloodshed. It was not a travelling temple, you had to come to her; she would not and could not leave her hearth. She was immune to the beguilements of Aphrodite, and even Eros's arrows fell lame at her feet. The lady was not for turning.

Ovid claims her as "nothing but a living flame," robustly elemental. It is Hestia who draws you not to a voyaging out there, but *in*, in to that delicious stilling that arises from time by the fire. No heroics, no grand claims, but a limited rather than limitless horizon—a horizon that encourages quiet awakenings. She's an eternal principle, a light that never goes out. Why would something like that need to travel?

Hestia is a refuge that some have found when enforced, by prison walls or a body that refuses to function in the way it used to. As hearth fire she is public, available to all, but her inducement is to settle. It was a kindled fire taken from her embers that would serve as talisman when Greek colonists wandered into the wilderness. When they reached or founded a new village, Hestia's embers forged the new fire. So, while she herself does not travel, she carries a boon for those who do.

In our lives, Hestia is a soul bridge—the turn inward. The delight of padding the house in early morning light as all busyness seems to be bustling along some place outside. The joy of closing the door—a constantly open door is an insult to many sacred things. She is a great settling, a room dappled by firelight not bulb, deep reflectiveness, a stationary constant in the squabbling hysterics of the gods.

And for those who cannot take the voyage, then maybe they gather by her hearth and dream alongside—intricate and boisterous dreams. Of course the hearth fire is the natural place for any mythteller. Sometimes there is a joy in staying back.

When we sail at the attuned moment we encounter prophetic insight—knowledge that not everyone is ready to hear, hence the warriors' being left on the beach. That which has shown stamina at the oar, strategy following the waves, now steps back. Dogged persistence will get us many miles, in fact to the very gates of a temple, but it is the sovereign who takes the final steps. At some point in Brutus's upbringing he has been steeped in ritual: the burning of the three fires, the sacrifice of the deer, the drink, the realisation that he needs to offer a prayer. We note also the sweet detail that his intention animates this etiquette, even with a broken altar.

There has been much speculation about the name of the deity Brutus encounters at the temple. Some insist Diana, others Artemis; some lazily make no distinction between the two or believe that Diana is a late, Roman photocopy of the Greek Artemis. Diana has an entirely independent origin in Italy, being worshipped on the Aventine Hill in Rome and specifically invoked as a protector of the harvest against storms. She was also a goddess of fertility, but somehow holding the virginal aspect that Artemis is so famed for. As the Greek influence grows ever more pervasive in Roman culture, a kind of fusion seems to start to take place. Both deities become connected to the moon and the wild things. Homer refers to Artemis as *Artemis Agrotera, Potnia Theron*—"Artemis of the Wildland, Mistress of Animals." But as well as the mistress of the animals she is also mistress of the hunt, taking life with as much swiftness as she puts into preserving it. She was supported by Pan, he gifting her seven bitches and six dogs, whilst she hunted down six golden-horned deer to pull her chariot.

Her sanctuary at Brauron was the haunt of adolescent girls who were put into religious service to the goddess for one year. During their rite of passage in the temple, they were known as *arktoi*, meaning little she-bears. The origination of this name was a rumoured story of a bear who had wandered into Brauron and been killed. Artemis was furious and insisted that from that moment on there would be an atonement for the bear's death. The young girls learnt and enacted several sacred dances whilst disguised as bears.

It is a potent image that, at the age when young girls are being roughly sexualised by much of modernity, these young women were taught to withdraw under the fur of a bear as their bodies began to bud. Rather than a time of erotic display, it was a period of aligning with a tremendous animal potency, to allow this flowering to have privacy and also a cosmology around it. By the time the girls left that temple to move into the intensities of courting, they had some sense of their value, what they were aligned to. Our daughters should be so lucky.

Within mythology, virginity can indicate a kind of truth teller, one not caught up in the lusty grunt of life's intoxications but sharp minded, fresh with a certain spiritual clarity. It is less about abhorrence of sex, more some part of us "set apart," invulnerable to the influence of the things of this world. Given their fierce associations to the lunar and to taking and protecting life, their ambivalence to men, their sometimes contrary nature, Brutus is lucky he showed some etiquette at the entry to the temple.

Rather than tear out too many hairs over the goddess's identity, it feels appropriate to acknowledge her otherworldliness and some generosity displayed to the young man. Much human sacrifice was committed in her name, so it is naive to assume this is a cuddly figure offering some mentoring over a latte.

This being will not be met in sexual ecstasy or in a commune feeling groovy, but in the quiet solitude of the temple in the forest. If you do not bring the appropriate gifts, she will not appear; if you have not encountered storms, she will not appear. If you are not comfortable with aloneness, she will not appear. The nature of this being is complex, many shaded. She is not the goddess of the dance floor; she does not instigate warm, relational, sexy feelings. You won't meet her at a five rhythms class or on Facebook. She is austere, strange, in service to things we cannot quite see, pristine—a being who could strike raw fear into even her followers in those days when her name echoed the hills.

They could not be sure what would be handed to them—the blade requiring sacrifice or the cheery face of a baby. To arrive inappropriately, as in the story of Actaeon, stumbling on her while she is bathing, is to be ripped apart by your own ravenous hounds, your own uncontrollable urges. If you're not suitably cooked, she will act decisively.

But the story tells us that when we go looking for vision, when we hold a subtle ear for holy unfoldings, she just may appear. She is not *comfortable*, and many of those who have received her visioning have not been the most benign of characters or led the easiest of lives.

A goddess of moonlight has a subtle, nuanced texture, no longer the bright, single-imaged, mono-infused TV commercial. She gives him the vision, sure, but does she tell him the way? That is for him to find. To follow moonlight is a commitment to waning, waxing, and fullness, to a path of silvery movement, to uncertain steps of utter faith when the only sound is the death hoot of the owl. Moonlight is reflected sunlight and so, far less visible then the indelicate strut of the sun blazing all before it. So, for Brutus, to find this kingdom is to take lunar steps: to stay active, certainly, but sensitive to more than just the brilliant aggression of youth.

This is the being who haunted Robert Graves so much. While he was living on the outskirts of Brixham in Devon, he felt compelled to write *The White Goddess* in churning bursts of script whilst witnessing abject horror from waiting publishers. Yeats was always convinced he was moon favoured rather than abiding in the crasser glare of the sun. This energy will hurl us on with descriptions of places so wonderful we have no choice but to pursue them. As goddess of the hunt she is releasing the "questing beast" in Brutus. An animal—part serpent, lion, and goat—that, once viewed (normally in the glades around Camelot), makes the hunter helpless to do anything but pursue its maddening trail.

Once we encounter this beast, we experience a flooding of the nervous system with the intangible but ferocious desire to follow its call. This being with the moon in her hair even suggests to Brutus that this is a place to which he is meant to offer stewardship. A home.

There is a pain in glimpsing the possibility that there is some far-off kingdom to inherit. Maybe some anguish in this deep, pushed-away knowledge, a truth that arises in myth again and again. That we have a vast inner kingdom:

> *Of boar and bee,*
> *towered flanks of oak,*
> *western tip surged with apples,*
> *the north blue with*
> *remote and lonely mountains.*

This is way too much for most of us. It reminds us of the "I Am" poems of the ancient Celts—poetry in which you made lofty associations between your temperament and the curlew, the nut-heavy branch, the purplish sky of a lightning storm. You take up a lot of space, an awful lot of space. No longer is the head bent in either piety or shame; it is bent back and roaring loud into the hurricane. You are the swift-footed wolf singer, the mud-smeared fish that learns to breathe, a mighty procession of snow-tipped mountains, a curly god with a harvest of lovers. Many would rather stay fetal, defended against an experience of their own beauty.

To ensure that we don't get into this kind of disorientation, we can try two other methods—one is never to get to the sea journey at all, and the other is to set off so unprepared we don't have the experience to get to the island. Society is very good at offering both possibilities—tranced-out domesticity or rootless abandon. Many potential leaders die out there on the waves, hexed fatally by drugs.

The encounter with the being with the moon in her hair is a root experience of awakening. William Blake and Frida Kahlo have followed her lead ruthlessly. And I mean ruthlessly; she is not about many different options or Albion as a holiday home; she is painting a picture so magnetic that total pursuit is the only option. Hand in your casual flirtations at the door; this is a marriage proposal.

Marriage

This proposal takes us to a new temple, the temple of Hera, wife of Zeus. She grapples marriage in a deathly firm hold. Hera is less about the ideal partner or romantic love as such, more about the constant, sometimes frantic desire just for coupling—to be part of a couple. Bearing in mind that Zeus is actually her brother, it is hard to imagine a more intimate, weirdly tangled familiarity than that offered by a Hera marriage. The absent husband will be met with wrath. Men and women that stare woefully into their coffee, desperate for a mate, any mate, are in the thrall of Hera. When the coupling occurs, magical gifts at her altar are the labour of making house together—picking colours, choosing curtains, cleaning drains, fitting washing machines. You are bound together in murderous proximity.

In the case of Blake and Kahlo, this is not a marriage to a human but to an art. As we age, the desire for meaningful work can descend on us almost as strongly as romantic love. The soul reveals the desire for significance, for heft, for some psychic resonance over and over, and will crash our lives against the rocks until we take notice.

Hera is not a mother figure but three faced: Hebe—a young girl, light loving, full of laughter. Then there is the Matron—the strident, powerful matriarch established and in the midst of life. Then finally Chera—the most mysterious of the three. Why? Not because she is old, but because she is *left*, alone, all to herself, a distant figure. A Queen of Swords, a Sigune in Parzival, the Grail story.

Within Hera's realm of marriage, these three do not play out in historical progression but in sporadic bursts, maybe all in one day. The part that is left, that floats lonely by the side of the dance floor, will always be in the mix, always add poignancy and distance to the wider binding that Hera insists on. It is a useful loneliness, and it would benefit us all to understand its part in our own marriages.

For those who experience the binding through art, it is the intimacy of the studio, the careful selecting of oil paints, the refusal of party invitations, that serve as Hera's altar gifts. Chera is encountered in the times you are distant from your work, suffering writers' block, can't find connection to the engine you are fixing, the house you are painting, the literature course you are completing. In truth, it is this dance of distance and intimacy that gives the relationship its longevity.

The seriousness of Hera locks resolution to innovation; it burrows down into investment, monthly payments, regularity, even boringness. Books can't get written without slog, albums recorded without repetition—Rome doesn't get built in a day. Hera extends loyalty to the vision, to the making of *house*, past immediate personal happiness. So there is some relationship between Artemis and Hera: Artemis opens our eyes to the possible, Hera grips us tight with the resilience required to see that possibility through. Relationship to Hera is a crucial move to a sense of place. Brutus has signed up.

Giants of regression

As I've said before, the departure of the giants evokes some grief in me. How many times do we view history from the plumped cushion of the hero, not the tired-eyed wisdoms of the defeated? How many thousands of years had those giants abided there? There is much to be learnt by shifting gaze within a story, so that the lens is not one always with the victors. We see a steady line of animals disappearing alongside the strange, large ones.

The insistence of the Being with the Moon in her Hair—her emphatic speech to Brutus that the time was right—is the only element that calms my disquiet.

So with that lead, I will take another tack, another way of apprehending the mythic giant. This is the giant less as an original people of the land, more as an interior energy.

We can see the Dart estuary as a birthing canal for Brutus, leading to the emergence of his new life, his inheritance. The predictions were absolutely accurate—rich soil, verdant forest, teeming animal life. All is just as it should be. There's just that one thing—the inhabitants. Vision brings trouble with it.

Giant energy is a brutal force when not aligned to a great cause. Giant energy is what pours through a community when they tie a woman to the stake and light the kindling. Giant energy has no eye for nuance or the diligently coaxed herb garden, the subtle array of grays and blues in a painting by Cezanne. It towers too high off the ground to catch the scent of the wild lilies; its irritable eye struggles to make out distinctions on the small canvas. Giant energy is distrustful of difference, of paradox, of ambiguity. Anything other than a yes or no enrages it.

Growing up in the eighties I would encounter it firsthand in the terrorising of our local pubs by right-wing skinheads. They had a rigid dress code and brutal fists, were utterly aligned around an intense but basic symbolic language, and, if you did not fit within that frame, would gleefully inflict as much damage as they could.

In the Greek world that stands behind much of this story, Zeus had to defeat the giants, or Titans, to instigate culture and civic order. Hesiod, the oral poet and shepherd (of somewhere between 750 and 650 B.C.E.), claims that the etymology of *titan* is "to strain." So the feeling of the Titans is one of stress. With stress as a major killer and disease instigator in the new century, we see it is creating a flesh harvest in Hades. If domination by giants indicates that gods are no longer present (i.e., no Zeus), then in losing our mythos, we allow a damaging flood of exhausting strain.

We all have giant energy. Harnessed elegantly it is a tremendous source of will. It is giants in service to saints who get some of the great cathedrals built in old Gaelic stories. It is a raw reserve of sheer grunt power; if we deny it or fail to educate it, then we exile a great deal of momentum and stamina. We are not to deny giant power but to refine it.

Brutus encountering the giants is like moments when we face up to powers within our own being that have grown hostile. Whatever we neglect or unduly abandon will end up waving a bloodied axe, greasy, mean eyed, and sadistic. To get to our own mythic ground we have the challenge of inviting closer what we would far rather ignore. But, in the process of any real growth, low and behold, out they trot—sharp yellow teeth and club swinging, God only knows how long they have been languishing.

We have a tendency to view these exiles with great suspicion. We may decide to be a free-thinking artist, loose and unconstrained. Immediately, anyone in a suit looks suspicious. Down into the cellar goes that part of ourselves that keeps a close eye on the contract, works to a deadline, balances the books—frankly, that's so uncool. But as the years pass and we end up selling our work for far less than it's worth, or get tied up in knots with the tax man, or are beset with rip-offs, we may have to pick up the key and wander down to the cellar, where we threw that part of ourselves so many years before. Do you think it will be pleased to see you?

For others, the lover could be down there—starved of dusk, the scent of sun on skin, the joy of erotic friendship—locked up by a life rigid and focused only on statistically viable results. No one down there, no exiled energy, is going to show you anything but the giant when they emerge. Whatever is down there is *pissed*, regressed, woefully hostile.

Some who had difficulty absorbing the fury of some feminism towards the masculine may benefit from studying this story. If you had been squeezed down, relegated, abandoned, what would your mood be when you finally got some space? It's no great mystery.

Blake regarded many of these cellared beings as more than personal—as "divine influxes"—and felt that rage and lust and grandeur drew us closer to a world soul. To repress them entirely is to numb routes out into the wider, listening world.

Being named after Mars, associated with war, has been an interesting dynamic in my own life. But I use the word *dynamic* deliberately. Few want associations of mass bloodshed, annihilated villages, and heads on poles as immediate connections to their name. But Mars, when allowed out from the cellar, has other things to do.

It may be tempting to view the accomplishment of Mars, and indeed all these giants, as apocalypse, nuclear war, the end of everything. But James Hillman (1989) reminds us that Mars asks us for engagement, not wipeout; even victory is not essential. Mars is about instigation, a god of beginnings. The ram god mobilises. No Mars, and we have paranoid fumblings, stationary vagueness. Apocalypse is not on his radar, because it is the ending of all things. When Mars (really a god of agriculture, not of the city) arises, we need to get closer to the message, not further away. *We need to differentiate his passions.* So to illuminate something that we dread involves knowledge of the deity behind it.

The Homeric *Hymn to Mars* (Ares) calls for a devotion that assists understanding, that grows ever more subtle: "Beam down from up there your gentle light on our lives and your martial power so that I can shake off cruel cowardice from my head, and diminish that receptive rush of my spirit, and restrain that shrill voice in my heart that provokes me to enter the chilling din of battle." So, real attention to Mars creates discernment; helps you choose your battles; calls on an expert's eye in the field of rousing activity; hones a point to angry, aimless spears. Throw all that away, and you invite mayhem.

Giants can tower over us, block out the sun with their girth. But, of course, Brutus and his men are not following the sun, they are following the trail of the moon sent by the goddess of the island. Moon thinking outwits.

But moon thinking also requires a sovereign—a queen or king—to carry it. Someone with gravitas to hold it together, a clear earthiness. Without that rootedness its nature overwhelms, all is mist, everything is mystical, revelation, no boundaries. Everything is speaking to us, all the time. Think of those using the tarot constantly or those who find it impossible to hit even the remote control without consulting a horoscope. The greatest magicians in this area always have good boundaries.

The sacred and the insights it offers can overwhelm if the mundane is not pacing doggedly alongside. It is not advisable to stay on the mountaintop after a four-day fast; it is what Lakota call "too much Great Spirit." Our fragile systems are deluged to the point where the sacred loses its usefulness. Mystery needs to be digested slowly, and that requires a patience, sometimes a distinct lack of excitement. When we try to skip the graft of being a good sea captain and jump straight to the epiphany, it is unlikely that we will ever truly "drink down the moon." Rather, we get caught in the fogs of paranoia and crash the hull. The moon's occult sensibilities are dangerous without a hand in a hundred yards of moist soil.

This denial of discipline, struggle, and sometimes flat-out boredom is why some modern art is so unconvincing; it lacks life resonance. The artist plucks the flower but has never planted the bulb, and somehow we sense that. Many wish for the encounter with the *being with the moon in her hair* but try to ascend over the difficult sea journey that leads to her. This is never going to work, for the same reason that we would trade one Patti Smith over a hundred florid young men playing harps.

Ochre art

Some years ago, my friend Cara and I visited the cliff faces of South Devon, still red ochred with Goemagog's blood. It was a blustery autumn day. After the usual trouble parking on Livermead seafront, we headed off. Rain clouds started to spit as we climbed down treacherous steps to the beach. The tide was coming in fast as we skittered over the last stretch of sand to the ancient cliff face. The lurching gray wall of cold foam spluttered towards us. With a small hammer we quickly chipped away enough particles from the cliff wall to grind into ochre, to make a deep-red paint. As we filled our battered old rucksack it felt as if we were in a *participation mystique* with the old story. We were gathering the blood of a giant to make some expression of beauty. Days later, Cara was in several local schools assisting children to use that very ochre to paint on animal hides—patterns, tusks, dreams.

This story has taken us through the burning ground of prophetic incantation, judgement, heartbreak, sea journeys, vision, conflict, and finally, sovereignty. It is intensely mythological, more so than some of the later tales, in which the human dynamic grows stronger. It has shown us that vision is a bag of trouble and that to get near our own will enrage the giant. It's rarely easy. The story cautions readiness for the great sea journey, etiquette when you face a deity, and a willingness to draw close the exiled.

CHAPTER THREE

Chaw Gully Raven

Snow. Wet flanks of it, half covering the crumbling stone walls of the high moor, making these field borders look like Aztec glyphs, concealing some great and burdened secret. The sky is iron, utterly.

Gazing out from the ice-slick tarmac that separates the north and south moors, my eye struggles to truly recognise the landscape. Certain curls of granite are simply missing or walkabouts. This new seeing is quite a development, especially considering I have deliberately neglected to bring a map.

The absence of map is not haste or a deliberate foolishness, but a desire to walk these stories in the old way, to hold in mind, rather than language or grid, the root to and from my destination. As the mythteller handles a story entirely through memory, I intend to do the same in the walking line. For some stories this is easy; for others, less so. When I had started up from the southern ridge of the moor, all was green—cold, but green. Up here, it's snow all the way.

I am picking my way slowly to Chaw Gully, with a charge to tell a story to a raven.

The cold slips defiantly and easily in through my layers, so I pick a brisk pace down a thin path. Ridged with clusters of drift, the trail of ruby-red soil seems outrageously vivid against the peppered white flanks on either side of me, like a tribal scar. The air is startlingly fresh.

Within minutes there is a pronounced dip, the first of many. What appears to be a flat, easily negotiable landscape from the road is nothing of the sort. It is layered, mystically sliced, and slashed with sudden descents and bogs. What has seemed a straightforward walk to the gorge and back is now a very different scene; with the winter covering I'm lost as to where to go.

❊ ❊ ❊

DEER

Almost as I am having that thought I notice fresh deer tracks on the crisp snow in front of me. Looks like a roe deer, possibly fallow. The cloven-hoofed print is delicate—the two sides of the hoof curve inwards like two sides of an arrowhead. Were they branching out, I could have continued a brief fantasy that it was wild boar returning to the high moor. There are rumours, but not today. There are pellet droppings—dry—and as I impulsively decide to follow the tracks I start to pass trees with frayed bark here and there, a sign the trees have been used by stags to rub the velvet off their growing antlers. It's a couple of months after rutting season, but still I glance quickly about.

The prints shove my thinking out from my numbed, icy skull. In reverie I see my old tent, wood burner blazing with dry ash, the floor three skins deep with red deer, goat, rabbit, and sheep. I remember years of living in a circle. It was following tracks like these that got me into all that trouble in the first place. I can hear hail on canvas like a hymn of God, and the inked darkness of dusk bristles with the scent of the roe just feet from my thick, felted door flap.

Or are these hooves another magic? When I travelled around America, I heard natives tell of a deer-woman—sometimes deer, sometimes maiden or brown-eyed crone, always hoofed. She belongs to that charged tribe of feminine animal powers—the Xana from Spain, the Lara from Brazil, la Llorona from Mexico, even the Naag Kanyas, the serpent women of India. She loves to dance and arrives at times of transformation but will not hesitate to kick with those hooves if you look a little stuck. Today she feels close, and I follow.

So now I'm clearly off map time. If I'm going to find this gully I'll find it with a mixture of instinct and animal trails. In this weather that gully must provide good shelter. The tender prints meander but slowly lead to a fast-flowing stream. Next to the stream are the remains of an old cottage and some rather more recent tangerine peel left on a wall. Tracks start to converge here, and it's clear the action was happening around dawn, just after the snowfall. There're plenty of wintered bracken and brambles to munch on, as well as a couple of seedling trees that must have seemed like high feasting in this iron-cold month.

Any confusion deepens when there's a quick divergence of tracks, some heading directly north from where I stand, some east. The east tracks seem to be aimed at a cluster of scrub-like trees and undergrowth about half a mile away. I am reluctant to follow, as I suspect the trees and undergrowth may contain the animal's home.

RAVEN

Raven sweeps overhead. Silent, ebony against the freezing gray. In a second I trade trails. The one I choose heads eastwards, over the other roe tracks and far beyond, just disappearing at a slight dip in the granite-tumped horizon line. Seeing Raven is a big lift. I am now stomping through thick, dead bracken with a crusting of snow and ice on top, facing a long incline. My breathing is shallower, but I feel a charge seeing those casual black wings marking tracks in the bone-cold air. The wind gets up. That low, elemental moan. My ears are red and my Levis soaked to the knee.

There is that mingle of slight panic mixed with excitement as I do nothing but follow the bird. My logic is berating me every step, assuring me that the gully is several miles to the west, that I even started the walk in the wrong place. I'm no longer tucked in by field walls but right out in the wide flank of the rise now, directly in the impact of the wind. I catch my breath and glance back. I can see roughly five miles in each direction. The thrill of seeing not one human being—no sudden red of waterproofs and the glint of a compass—is a deep one. I can see pines clustering on my far left like a dark army, and forged acres of pistol-hard ground to my right. There is the sudden sense that behind these hills are other hills and behind those are moor and mountain, all empty of human snare or ambition.

Raven takes me a long way. Farther than my body wants. I miss the delicacy of that roe track and the stream bank. My North Face jacket is stuck with sweat to my shirt and unzipped; I'm taking handfuls of snow and letting them melt in my mouth as I climb. Following this air trail is spinning me out.

PONY

I look down to gather, to ground. A third trail: hoofprints of the Dartmoor pony, fresh scat too. It seems that there is an almost tangible warmth to them, that snow has actually melted around the shape. They and Raven's trail are now aligned. I climb the last section of hill and turn again. I've come some distance.

There have been bones of these wild little ponies found up here dating back to around 3500 B.C.E.: immeasurably tough, kindhearted beasts. Small head; large, wide eyes; full mane; the foreleg rising to the shoulder. They have carried hard yards of tin across moorland, descended as pit ponies into water and darkness and scraped rib cage, escorted prisoners with guards to Dartmoor Prison. This is their place. No wonder the snow melts with tenderness when it sees their resolute hooves blessing the white.

I find a small gully; is that it? But no, the sides are far too brief. I don't even bother descending and, fighting some disappointment, continue along Challacombe Ridge a little farther. I sense, rather than see, a drop-off to my right and wade through a final section of sodden long grass. There it is.

Raven did its thing. I see a savage gash in the ridge, hidden until you are almost on top of it. The few photos I have seen tend to be of its entrance, but I have come at it from the side. The sky is threatening another flurry, and a few flakes drift down past my nose. I look around for a possible descent.

It may have been exhaustion, or exhilaration at suddenly finding the gully, but I find myself simply swinging onto a canopy of brambles and clusters of bracken that feather the drop and freefalling down the frozen foliage. I'm simply too tired to negotiate a more sensible way down.

Feeling like a slightly wayward sleigh ride, I hurtle down the brambled cape and enjoy the discreet padding of the snow till I land, crumpled and exuberant, at the bottom. I have entered another world.

I have rarely felt such a shift. I did not expect it. I feel like Gawain entering the valley of the Green Knight's chapel. The wind has utterly ceased. The death moan that has accompanied me the whole walk here is just memory. Even the quality of the air feels different. Utterly quiet. There are no conks and no aggressive squawking, no sense of malevolence, only the steep banks, the handsome granite outcrops, the icicles hanging in row after celestial row, the leisured silence, the firm bounce in the ground underneath the snow.

Having followed such a gut-low-instinctive path to get here, I feel as though I have walked through the back of the wardrobe. I start to pray, steam leaving trails in the air, and place offerings appropriate to a raven in the snow's crust.

After longer than I expect, I pick my way through the gully, feeling a sweetness of spirit I could not have predicted. I need goat hooves for the ankle-twisting breaks in surface under the snow's crust, but I love the experience. I feel light, like a kid.

About halfway down the gully, I come to a triangular opening near the ground, opening right into the maw of a side wall of granite. Suddenly all is vivid green—ferns and ivy literally crown the entrance, melting snow causing silvery droplets. There is no end to the opening; it twists and disappears, way beyond the reach of my arm. It feels gorgeously unhuman, lively, charged. I know I have seen it before, but I don't know how. Here it seems even more silent.

And it is here, in this freezing fullness, that I begin my speaking for the raven that is and always was.

❊ ❊ ❊

Raven is the cave priest.

Every strong word in every good book,
conks from the dark wishbone of his mouth.

Sleet pebbles his prehistoric feathers,
as the small black prophet

Preaches thistle speech
to his patient congregation
of stones and bog.

Raven loves hard weather. Raven carried Noah's ambition for dry land. But Noah should have known that Raven's fondness was for the vast wet. And if it ever found such turf it would have to be moss-drunk and fat with prey. And it might forget to come back to the ark. Our Raven is the Raven of Chaw Gully. It has always been there.

Raven brought light; it remembered to itself. Way back. In a box wrestled from the chief of the Otherworld. It took some smarts to do it. But people forget; there was no light in this world. There was no way that Raven could drop berries and fish down to the first people; it couldn't see a damn thing. So Raven became a leaf in a stream, was drunk by the chief's daughter, became a baby in her, got born, stole the box of light, got feathery and beaky and jumped through the pin-prick hole back into this world.

Raven became two and nestled on Odin's shoulders. All its genius, thoughts, and memory it whispered into his ears and almost improved his mood. Chaw Gully Raven has been busy. Now it watches.

The gully is a deep gash in the rock up near Challacombe Ridge. All moor people have a memory of coming not from sweet above but from the rusty below, where the god of tree roots is slow-silent below the hysterics of the everyday. But even that memory in our blood brains gets turned from longing to a clutching desire. Something is *down* there, we know that much. And down go we, brutalising, cranking the rock, all for mother tin, the glimmering ore. Our will becomes a muscle, unbending, as we place our lusty hand into the vast black slit, crazy for the glint.

In the pub, old men say the Romans did the work, found the seam. That we, as a culture, have just followed their straightness ever since. Sending us barking—us of the orchard and the spiral energy. But we are loyal dogs when beaten hard enough. So generation after generation of men clamber on slippery, gray rock to find the hoard below—the greasy dragon mountain, a shingle of jewels.

But what comes back with the men is more than good news. Men get drizzled by terror down there. They hear things. Yes, they bring tin to the surface, but they hear things. It's often in the dimpsy time, when they should have packed and crawled back to the pink light of dusk. They hear the Knockers.

There are other things down in the gully. There is the knock of chisels, picks, hammers—finding seams, but from the *other* side of the rock from the men. Miners have been known to piss with fear when the scraping begins. Or the sparks of light leading men from their companions farther in. Or the backward singing. Sometimes the miners claim they left offerings in the old way—hunks of beef, strong beer—and that they were led by the knocks to a new seam of ore.

But the old men know better. They know that the Knockers could get right inside a digging man. Could walk right through his spleen and lungs and squat in his mind, dropping wet horror into his dreaming. After a time the men would start to leave the gully alone. Even with the talk of Roman gold.

Oh, they speak of it.
By the hut fire,
stumpy fingers
point into darkness
out towards the gully.

All night the timbers shake,
with bellow-talk of foreign wealth,
and cider brags of risk and valour.

But come sour dawn, as they
shuffle to the shape that day requires,
cheese and beef is their only directive.

They shake the stories loose
from the blue cloak of night.

Raven watches. The hard-beaked sentry. Never sleeping, never turning the post to a younger, always the same one. It watched the centuries when dozens of men clambered their way down into the blackening; it watches when twenty years of hail is the only offender to its solitary reign.

It knows what the Knockers are. They have an accord; they always have. The Knockers were here when the giants boomed above them over gorse. They heard the victory cheer of bright Brutus on the hoe. No matter.

Raven watches. One day a boy comes from over the ridge, plump with cheese and ale and sporting a straight, unthinking look. That look, Raven remembers. It was that look the miners had when they broke up the holy stone avenue up on Challacombe Ridge. When they go home and look through their piggy eyes, the kitchen is still scrubbed, the china daintily arranged. No evil occurred, surely—my bed is still made.

The boy unravels rope and gear as Raven courses through his thinking. It's the same old stuff. He doesn't even glance round, catch the atmosphere. No up or down. No cosmos. No holy smoke lit, no empty belly as he waits for permission. The transgressions are endless. Just his lardy arse clinging to the rope as he lowers himself down. Around his head, his thinking has become guttural and nervous; Raven watches that brain become a waspish cone of ambition. Down he goes.

No, says Raven. A decision. Hands come from nowhere, a blade. One steadies the rope; one smoke-dark hand starts to cut. Oblivious, the boy descends until the fibers fray. His body will be taken and laid on the heather beside the entrance to the gully.

Do I look pretty?
says the boy.

Where is my mother?

It is autumn, and the
House of Falling Leaves
crafts his cairn.

❀ ❀ ❀

Well, it's not autumn as I finish the tale. My hands are raw and tingling with cold, my breath a dragonish steam. The gully takes the offering in one gulp; the offering barely hits the sides of the gully's immense stillness. This place is so untrammeled there is a reluctance to describe it much further or to leave too precise instructions for finding it. It's time to leave.

The pony trail leads me back to the roe track. I feel cleaned out somehow. Soaked, hot, and at peace, I climb the original incline from the beginning of the walk. From behind, right over my shoulder, sweeps Raven, then down into some low-slung bush. From the corner of my eye, I see two fly out and away.

By now glowering clouds are bucketing wet snowflakes onto spindly gray trees, and the mood is changing again, a swift eeriness laying its ancient gramarye on the land, reclaiming certain secrets. An odd gust of wind eddies around the frozen roots of an oak, pushing humans out—back to the hearth fire, thick buttered toast, and little kids' chuckles. I've lived this changeling atmosphere before and head on into the growing dusk, not looking back.

When I finally make it home I sleep for hours. My dreams bend into weather patterns and beaked old faces lurching from thin trees. When I wake, cosy in bed in the dark, I see an unending wave of flakes through a gap in the curtain.

Black mouth

To many of us, Raven carries fear as its herald, its mojo, and is not afraid to scatter the clingy substance here and there to get what it desires. It's preference for the flesh of the dead and its willingness to gobble scat make it an edgy presence. Its ink-black plumage, elongated Roman beak, and patterning of honks and ghostly croaks make it a bird with a rep.

Still, beloved of the Norsemen, the Haida, and the Greeks, Raven has startling associations with the sun rather than endless gloom and corpse-picking. There is the old native Trickster tale of Raven actually bringing light to the world in a small box stolen from a big man of the Otherworld so that humans could hunt fish and collect berries. Odin bent his great ear daily to the litany of genius gossip that Hugin and Mugin (his raven consorts) would report to him of the world's occurring.

We know that an alpha raven's mouth turns black on the inside when the raven takes a position of leadership (always by force), and that the followers' mouths tend to stay pink unless they are making a bid for dominance. There seems to be no way round this black-mouthed leadership, even in our most refined universities. Violence can be deeply subtle. Knowledge can quickly become a form of intimidation used to bruise your way to tenure. This way, physicality is no longer so crucial; even the solitary can think their way to stature rather than swing a fist or kick a football.

Initiation has always placed emphasis on colour. Black is always one with knowledge of the Underworld, of failure, of stuckness, or depression, fatality, listlessness. Whilst having endured all that, they have somehow slow crafted it into a crooked and beautiful song. The colour red is showier—having more to do with the young buck—than is the patient depth of black. This mouth colouring reveals much about relationship: that too much subservience around the leader cripples development for an individual.

Remember the painter Willem De Kooning's refusal to work in Arshile Gorky's studio? "Nothing grows around big trees," he said. Depends what kind of tree, I would suggest. For animals, pack living often greatly assists survival, and they know well that leadership will require constant display, strategy, barracking, and generally large behaviour. It's exhausting. But for initiated tribespeople, the West is a pink-mouthed society, a society that runs from much of what initiation offers in the raising of an adult—becoming kin to nature, facing the underworld, staying connected and indebted to a cosmos. When we stay distant, protected, coddled, ironic, our mouths stay resolutely pink.

The seemingly contemporary notion of a raven or snake or parrot as an inner figure within humans is not so modern. Recall the third-century Church Father Origen (1982, 115): "Understand that you have within you herds of cattle, flocks of sheep . . . and that the birds of the air are all within you. . . . You see that you have all those things that the world has." And maybe the world has all the things that *you* have, as we roam a wider psyche. Origen's awareness has been a poetic step from seeing cattle as a mere meal on legs or a resource only for labour and feast. We also realise that there is plenty of order, logic, and upstandingness in the animal world. All kinds of habits and cautions. Real animal nature is not just a byword for sweaty exuberance.

The trouble with this animal association is that too rigid an interiorising robs the animal of its independent vitality; we risk degradation in too many attempts to assimilate something that we recognise but that should in some ways remain usually "other." Raven is a *spiritus rector*, a guardian deity, not a mere symbol "representing" our mysterious side. That's a ghastly affront to many secret things.

Although enjoying a kind of solitary ambience, ravens are effective team players when hunting. Terry McEneaney, an ornithologist from Yellowstone Park (Heinrich 1999, 133), reports seeing a raven landing on the rim of an osprey nest and stealing a fish. Whilst the osprey was agitated, another raven working in tandem sneaked in and stole an egg. There are hundreds of such accounts.

This seems to indicate some kind of forward thinking on behalf of the ravens. Professor Dieter Wallenschlager (Heinrich 1999, 134) witnessed a raven feigning injury—dragging a wing—to incite a swan to attack, whilst again its mate rushed the nest and stole an egg. While opinion ranges on how much forethought is required to pull this off, what is clear is mutual dependence of both birds on the anticipated outcome.

The Tower of London still clips the wings of its ravens because of an old superstition that if the ravens leave, England will fall. It is a bird close to wolf-mind: it will deliberately lead wolves to prey and then guzzle the greasy leftovers. It was said they did the same thing for old Devonian hunters; they would be left the guts when the deer was killed.

They are mystifying, smart, aggressive, and strictly hierarchical; they don't sit round on beanbags in talking circles—they have black-mouthed leaders who intimidate to get themselves to the top of the pile until they themselves are toppled. Ravens are into power. Butch. The raven expert Bernd Heinrich (1999) tells the story of watching a particular dead beech tree for some time and noticing that a succession of dominant ravens in the group would all choose a specific perch when their time as top bird came. There were many other trees to choose from, equally plush, but somewhere in the wider mind of that group it became established that *that* was the power perch, and so that was it. After years of careful and sometimes painful observation, Heinrich also noted that leadership amongst ravens came with a cost. All leaders have large bodies, which require more feeding; all leaders have to constantly display their grandiosity, their example, which requires many battles, much blood on the snow. You can't relax; there is no one for you to follow. You lead, always.

Raven carries the nigredo black of the alchemist on its wings, beak, and body. It is like some charcoal stain on the optimist's blue horizon. Fifty thousand years of gobbling scat and flesh, a constant at the battlefield, make it a companion to putrefaction. Black is a potent tonic, even when it is denied that black is a colour at all. It is the robe of choice for any decent occultist. The black of night is the cover for illicit liaison; to be "in the dark" is to be wandering, confused, unsettled; it is a hint of what could await at the moment of death.

At the same time, archaeology tells us that black is the place to go. It's long been known in England that any place name with the word black in it—Black Meadow, Black Woods, Blackingstone Rocks—is a place worthy of digging. The reason? The darker-coloured soil will indicate an old settlement—generations of fire ash, food remains, and general use. To a crafty eye, black means to dig deeper. To a certain eye, it offers reward.

Raven carries this rattle bag of contrary wisdoms, invokes a cautionary wave or grimace as it sweeps over the jolly street party. You and I both know who would be first to pluck out an eye were we to trip one rainy night. And yet, some memory remains of this bird and a box of light and a tiny hole to the Otherworld. It flares up mixed emotions.

We wonder at the permanence of Raven. These birds can live decades, and we suspect this one has always been here—it is every raven. It feels like an elder, and a harsh one. It floods into the boy's thinking and, sensing nothing much going on, wipes him out. A rather raven thing to do.

Heinrich tells the story of introducing a single wild raven into the aviary of four semi-domesticated ravens—Goliath, Fuzz, Lefty, and Houdi. After some showboating from Goliath and aggressive intimidation by Houdi, the dominant male and female, the birds settled to ignoring her, getting truly aggressive only around meat. If she went near it, they would not hesitate to attack her. Before too long she was trying to dig up caches of food they had hidden in the snow. On the rare occasions when she was successful, she managed to get them so distracted that she would snatch up the original food deposits as they were guarding later caches. She had her small successes and they kept her alive.

When returning from a trip away, Heinrich was dismayed to find the young female dead in the snow and, even more surprising, signs that her eyes had been attacked. Ravens have boundaries around pecking out the eyes of a fellow raven. It was clear to Heinrich that, despite this transgression of usual etiquette, the four ravens had teamed up and beaten this one to death. She had died lying on her back in the snow, feet up in defense against her four adversaries.

What makes this story distinctive is that Heinrich regards the killing as punishment for a constant overstepping of the line within the psychological framework of the five birds. Ravens can be merciful—even starving ravens rarely kill a weaker one—but to Heinrich, who has had a lifetime of studying the birds, this was a clear consequence of infraction. Having worked with gangs and also sometimes in prisons, I find it hard to ignore the similarities in, literally, "pecking order."

Maybe the boy was in a similar situation of infraction. How many times have men relentlessly and profanely excavated that gully? Ravens remember. At Cornell University, Kevin McGowan, a researcher of crows—a job that requires climbing up to nests and banding the young—has been resolutely hounded by the birds across campus, crows almost queuing up to attack him.

In the story of Parzival we encounter a ferociously potent hag of the woods called Cundrie—all tusks, red coal eyes, plaited eyebrows, fetid breath. The twist is that she, rather than a troubadorian ideal, represents the grail itself; it is she who is in service to divine influxes. If she detects any kind of vacuous or irreverent behaviour in a young knight, she will, verbally, peck his eyes out. This kind of combat was called "dark speech" in bardic circles and certainly assisted the birth of that lethal weapon *satire*. Cundrian values—and I would suggest that Raven is a holder of such values—will turn rapidly on one who lacks efficacy.

Raven is another manifestation of the harsh directive we detect over and over in these moorland stories of humans engaging with the gods. It detects an odd memory of some kind of emergence from the earth and the way that emergence distorts into endless excavations and ultimate mineral exhaustion. What twists in the gut of humans will not be satisfied by fiscal wealth but by vertical nourishment. When this flattens into vacant greed, that gatekeeper starts laying out the dark side of its job description.

Raven's tower

Raven is ruffling my mind as I pass over Tower Bridge on the way to an evening's teaching in London's East End. Only a minute later I pass the slightly surreal scene of the tower—an archaic black lump of belligerent stone surrounded by state-of-the-art high-rise business centres. My friend Jonny Bloor and I have negotiated the entire labyrinth of London's west-to-east roads to get into town early. Due entirely to his planning, we get good parking only minutes from the venue and plenty of time to wander. It's refreshing to be out of Devon for a little while. Even around the derelict car park I can spot collections of crows and a few ravens, perched and honking, on the Dickensian features of several local buildings. I quickly wonder if I am looking at the stately gatekeepers of a more urban scene.

The area has long been associated with successions of immigration—Irish weavers, Ashkenazi Jews, Bangladeshis, Chinese, African—sometimes instigating fierce conflict, sometimes breathtaking innovation. It's a delight to catch so many different cooking scents on the air—from bakeries, curry houses, delis, and street vendors. For two hungry lads, we don't know where to turn. Each tantalizing scent carries a story of travel, struggle, acceptance, and finding space for your customs and beliefs within this wider melting pot. Somehow these mythologies rubbing up against one another tickles new flavours, new eruptions of image. Maybe not at first; there's been blood spilt on these streets. But slowly.

My storyteller's ear starts to detect the stories from underneath the concrete: of sailors arriving at dusk on the riverside in the time of the Tudors and making a new home; of fledgling Caribbean communities springing up in Canning Town, way back in the nineteenth century. I think of a time when there were over 150 synagogues built for the growing Jewish population. That must have been hard for the cockneys and for the new arrivals, as well. A world in rapid movement usually is. I think of the fifty-seven successive nights of hammering attack this resilient area took in the Blitz, when all of the communities, regardless of race, dug deep into the collective soul and endurance of the East End and survived it. Every corner of the district holds something that I haven't seen before or that I am beholding in a new way. Rather than hoodies, I see several incredibly elegant young black men in tweeds, cap, and waistcoat, dressed for all the world like upscale Devonian farmers. The artists Gilbert and George stroll past, also immaculate—it seems the area's history of tailoring is being upheld with a twist by the current East Enders. London can be quite magical; it was in Peckham Rye that William Blake beheld a vision of angels in a nearby tree—"bright angelic wings bespangling every bough like stars"—and, when Blake was eight, the prophet Ezekiel loitering under a bush.

The evening is packed. I have to get up three flights of stairs just to fetch a chair for my telling; all seating is long gone. It's an evening of poetry and stand-up—rapid jokes, skilled delivery, very urban.

As I peer out at the rammed house and listen to the other performers, I start to feel more than a pang of unease. Regarding the story as an independent entity and not scripting my performance means I have little idea where the mood and possible humour of the story may fall. Listening to the punch-line-heavy and extremely well-paced performers and the constant witty references to urbane culture, I feel strangely placed as the show closer.

The story begins. The libation is an exquisite single malt that causes strong fumes for the front row, but so focused am I on reporting the images I'm seeing, I don't look up. The pulse of the drum settles me; the chime of the ankle bells pulls in the animal powers—stag, hound, wolf. And there I am, an Englishman of Scottish ancestry, playing a Turkish frame drum whilst telling a Polish fairy tale to an audience of Caribbean, Irish, Cockney, and many more ethnicities I cannot make out under the stage lights. It's sort of nuts. Especially if you are looking for some kind of bardic purity. It's a kind of mongrel activity. Woof.

The ethnicity of the audience doesn't bother me for a second. It's a blessing. But a kind of cultural framing for what they were seeing as Londoners did give me pause. The jokes were not rapid fire; the story held a great deal of grief, it was long, and they needed strong ears to hold it from beginning to end. This loose, fiery, unscripted, invocational thing called mythtelling could just be a step too far.

When I felt the warmth of laughter from an older Jamaican man in the third row or the embrace of a Polish couple when I stepped off the stage, I realised that for these East Enders, I was modelling something they knew very well. That collision of influence, sincerely carried, that births something again. This whole district carries this wonderfully.

As I wrote earlier, certain stories will always have a geographically specific resonance. We can intuit them when they approach, recognising them as stories from the old country. I have called it their slow ground. But what we heard that night in the East End was nomadic recognition—the wandering story that stands behind cultural display and makes straight for the heart of the listener. As I finished the story, many got to their feet and cheered—the bar was shut by the time I managed to get past the waiting well-wishers. Again, story placed itself in the primacy of the arts. A brave risk by the organiser had paid off. That may have little to do with me as a storyteller and far more to do with a little help from the old East End itself—a place with a very expansive notion of Englishness. This is the other side of this book's emphasis on getting claimed by the ground you stand on—that the place will be filled with beguiling contradictions, bizarre influences, and quiet corners. Do I regard the cosmopolitan nature of the East End as a worthy deepening of the idea of Englishness? Of course I do. It's exciting to witness.

As Jonny and I crossed Tower Bridge just before midnight, we located an off-license. Keen to enjoy the Guinness I had missed by making new friends, I stepped into the cosy doorway and bought a couple of cans. As I was about to leave the district of the ravens' tower, I again heard three wild honks from above a derelict shop across the shadowed street. Wildness is everywhere. I thanked the gatekeepers, hoped they enjoyed their story, got into the car, and headed west.

CHAPTER FOUR

Liminal Culture (1)

A TRAINING IN THE LODGE OF WORDS

It's raining as we crawl up the track onto the moor. My battered Saab (door savagely booted the night before by a stray cow) picks her way gingerly over the loose shale and occasional boulder. This black pearl is loaded with my threadbare tent, wood-burning stove, a trivet, several Persian rugs, the rattling clank of dark beer bottles, local eggs, and a staggering assortment of smoked bacons and sausage from Ashburton's finest butcher, Rodney Cleave. Stuffed in the pockets of my leather jacket is enough chocolate to barter my way out of the underworld itself. About halfway up the track, we pull over onto the glistening, skidding grasses of Tony's field. Tony is a local farmer—whip thin, skin as brown as a hazelnut, utterly generous, with an almost aboriginal look in his eye. It's also his cow that booted the vehicle, which may explain today's jovial attempts to put us at our ease.

We gingerly lay the thinning black canvas over the Saab rather than directly on the sodden grass. For now the rain is more an atmosphere than a direct assault. As I study the patched-up canvas and run my hand gently over thread, my mind turns.

It had been some years now since I first entered the lodge of words. Those solitary years of speaking the fragile, half-glimpsed names of the copse had unfolded exponentially into what I rather optimistically thought of as a kind of bardic education. I knew the proper behaviour around deep experience was then simmering the juices: slow elucidation, fierce study, garlands of mistakes, and the stubbornness to continue when all available evidence pointed directly to your enormous incapacity for the task at hand.

Despite this, a day had come when I had started to teach something of what I knew, directly from my tent. Three good people had arrived and for a year took everything I could fling at them.

79

They listened as folks listen when they know that in a matter of months they too will be splayed against the side of a Welsh hill as Irish winds bat their favours in from the nearby ocean, as the people of the sod boom up their curiosity from the soil beneath their feet. You could practically hear their teeth grinding.

I was still a baby storyteller at this point. Still shuffling words around curiously on the indelicate runway of my tongue. My experience of seeing gripping storytellers was still almost none. I knew that, across the waves in America, a very few had taken this to a truly admirable art form, unafraid to explore story in a way that, rather than reducing it, amplified it to something extraordinary. These were not thinkers who used the old tales just as a garnish to furnish their next psychological makeover; this was the stuff of life and death. Still, the possibility that I would ever meet one of these characters or even get to Turtle Island was so remote it was laughable. Like a kid playing blues in a Norwich pub getting to hang out with Howlin' Wolf. Never gonna happen. As it was, I had enough to contend with. I was preparing our small group for an audience with a deity.

My reverie is broken by a yelp. My right-hand pirate, Jonny Bloor, is walking swiftly towards me with a mouthful of blood. Whilst he was erecting the trellis for the yurt and stretching what we call bungee ropes, one flew free and the iron-hooked end, with lightning speed, lodged itself in the bottom lip of our hero. The bungee is now removed but a distinct hole that is pissing blood remains. I think it looks rather stylish. Not one to miss a ritual opening, I suggest that Jonny let it drip down onto the soil of the moor. At least briefly. Then fill up the hole with chewing gum soaked in vinegar, or tobacco, or maybe even something vaguely sensible. So Jonny parades the borders of the field with his dripping mouth, ever brave, whilst I notice the rain is picking up.

With the help of another good man, David Stevenson, we soon get our creaky home erected. A bucket is produced for sporadic leaks—very occasional, I swear—and, praise Allah, the fire is lit, trivet set, and the smell of roasting coffee drifts out from the smoke. Heaven, really.

Later, our tent fills with people. Cars parked at the bottom of the track, they have wobbled up to us with heavy rucksacks and anxious eyes. Jonny has met them in the darkening rain with a lantern and ruptured bottom lip, claiming I lost my temper. Far from it, but they're not to know. All are here for story, for the wild rumpus, for the night sea journey.

So focused am I on telling the first night's story, so caught in its marauding sea of images, I only partially register that the temperature has dropped. In fact it's freezing, even with the fire crackling out its story for all its worth. I glance up. The roof of the yurt has, utterly without sound, flown off and down the hill. So completely caught in the story's unfolding, none of us have noticed its departure. A hundred thousand stars twinkle overhead, but at that specific moment they are scant consolation.

Busted-mouth Jonny is first out the door, scampering like Finn's hounds after the far distant sight of a crimson guy rope disappearing over the tump. This rather introverted group, with some bellowed encouragement from me, follows him out, grabbing all manner of hand tools and rough coils of ropes as they go, Dave sweeping them all on, holding up the rear with a large bill hook.

By now the temperature has dropped below freezing. Hands have become blue claws as we scamper after this knackered piece of cloth that had been holding our world together. Finally, we catch our whimsical shelter, just before it takes a subzero drenching in the bottom stream. The wind is now howling, so the long-favoured technique of throwing a kind of lasso over the top of the yurt and dragging the canvas across is almost impossible. The enraged winds are throwing their spit right towards us. Two brave souls are splayed like inebriated spiders halfway up either side of the trellis as a brick tied to a rope is hurled just over their heads to land, just for a second, on the other side. Like a herd we lurch through the crunchy heaps of dead bracken to heave our shelter back onto the top of the tent. Murky shapes hurl me boulders to support the guy ropes, and suddenly the wind drops entirely. All is utterly calm. The story picks up perfectly from where we left off.

Later, when our fellow travellers sleep a traumatised sleep (we will be submerged in a local stream at six), Dave, Jonny, and I stretch out on the rugs by the blaze and reflect on what a ferocious gatekeeper of its secrets Dartmoor is. It has laid out some ground rules for our work. Like the ornate carvings on the doorway to an Asian temple, its images offer caution to those who enter. *Be aware*, go respectfully or you may taste blood; *be aware*, go respectfully or you may lose the roof of your house.

Days pass in the black tent of story. Image after image roves through the blue smoke. Rocks are gathered and heated, old stones filled with tales from the chilling green swirl of the River Dart. Squatting on Dartmoor soil in the sweat house, in the glittered dark of prehistory we give water to the rocks and hear their hissing disclosures. Many hours later we lie, naked and a-steam in the long grasses, with the unremitting grandeur of the stars overhead—

shield-rivets of the sun. Soon, the rich scent of venison stew and fresh-baked bread would lace our nostrils, issuing from the candlelit door of the tent, and our fasting would be done for now. We would stagger, like steamy new pups, towards that bay of lights.

The stories that cauterised our souls, the lantern pilgrimages through the midnight of Hembury woods, the rigour of the sweat house, the laboured construction of ritual speech were preparatory and absolutely justifiable endeavours for procuring just the right amount of readiness for what was to follow.

Early the next morning we were atop the proper granite drop of a Devon cliff into fierce January waters, each laden with armfuls of flowers, great chunks of bitter chocolate, hefty slabs of steak, good beer, and as tentatively excellent verse as we could muster.

Below us, chomping his foaming teeth, swirling his gnash dance was the god of the waters. No Scandinavian or Anglo-Saxon behemoth, but the denizen of the people of the Celtic North Atlantic—Mannanan Mac Lir. To Mac Lir, always a poet, each wave is a wildflower. Always a host, Mac Lir invites you to feast on his gang of moon-tusked boars, who will leap unbidden from under the feasting table every morning, reborn again, jovial and deadly.

So, quaking in our nakedness, with only the flowerings of our simple gifts, we made offering before it became sacrifice. The boom-slosh of the slate waves would, for a moment, be laced with a bobbing adornment of flowers and parchment, dark beer, and a scattering of speech. The great maw would swirl and gnash and swallow our fragile giftings. Then, our small troupe would come to the very lip of the cliff, face the pagan imagination below, gaze the untrammelled depths, and, as one, *jump.*

And why? To behold something vaster than ourselves. Not to find ourselves but to lose ourselves for a moment, to give shape to some strange and restless memory that has been tapping quietly on our bones since the moment we could walk.

I would be scorched, woefully singed, twenty sheets to the wind, exhausted after these assaults against the ungenerous amnesia of our times. But, at some point days later, I would surface from under the skins, pour strong black coffee, poke the kindling, and redouble my study. Each word I pored over had travelled immense distance and paid properly to get to me. So I took them seriously. After my time in the bush, it was time to start to really study some great human thinkers. It was a significant help that every few weeks there would be a small group gathered for us to study these broodings. Form such a lodge yourself. I was beginning to feel useful, at least a little. It was a rather new sensation.

Some years later

It has been a difficult night and I've been woken by singing. And not just one voice, but a kind of eerie choir. I sit bolt upright, head fusty, push the sheep-skins to one side, and lean out the flap of my tent. In early light, base camp is looking tight: the plates are stacked and washed, the fire pit still twinkles with embers, and a robust pile of kindling and hardwoods are heaped under a tarpaulin just a few feet away. The soil glitters with dew, and there's a flirtation of blue sky above the oak canopy. But where are the choristers?

Camp is on the Venford curve of the Dart river, discreet. Scattered over a short distance are a group of men and women undertaking the wilder-ness vigil. This is the morning of the third day. Again the singing breaks my reverie. It's extraordinary: layered harmonies that then break off into polyphonic stutters, a rhythmic pulse underneath that picks up and urges the whole composition along.

I'm impressed. This is the first time a group of fasters have sneaked out of their spots, hooked up, and formed a choir. They must be just over the ridge, below the tent. I subdue a momentary irritation due to their wayward disregard for protocol, but the sheer joy of their music washes it away. This I have to see.

As I crawl up through the bracken to a prime view, I'm smiling to myself. They're busted. I can hear Tim's bass tones providing a steady ground for the lifting trills of Paula; Phil and Roz seem to be scatting over the top, a jubilant pattering of freeform sound. Wow. They are good. I peer over the edge and gaze down at the scene. There's no one there.

Not a sign. Nothing. Just acres of late-summer grasses, rotting trees, and a thin, winding path that passes their spots. It's not them; they're not the choir. I'm perplexed, because the singing is in full voice, it's everywhere. Then, finally, I see where it's coming from. It's the river.

This is not just the roar of water over rock; these are the sonorous pitches of the water's many voices. Deft, with intricate deviations and ruminations, it feels like the sound of something divinely pleased with itself.

I've never heard anything like it, and I've walked the river's banks dozens of times—at all times of day and night, soaked in its muses. But this is quite something else. Dark booms and high ecstasies surge the celebrant air. The entire valley seems to be shimmering, animate with the sound.

What can I do but sing along? My croaky, just-woken warble finds its bashful way into the mighty tide. Hours pass. Two days later, I see the wobbly figures of the fasters slowly emerging from the undergrowth, crawling out from hollow trees and weaving through bracken. Sometime later, with tea warming their bones, clutching fruit, they start to share stories. But there seems to be one big one. The singing. Soon there are raw smiles and waving hands: "It was you!" "No, you!" "I heard your croon every morning, Tim, and it was a great tonic." In the end, I have to fess up and tell them about the fluid originator of the big sound. We all go quiet for moment, as we realise we've had four days of getting threaded into the specific disclosures of that curve in the river. Even a mile away, its melodic curvature would be something entirely different.

THE MNEMONIC IMPERATIVE: BUFFALO SPEECH AND THE MYTHTELLER

Orality

Despite the miraculous possibilities of literacy, the ground of most of these Dartmoor stories is to be found in oral culture, in a time when human speech was clearly a sound in a far wider music, the roots of these tales carrying the twigged musings of the magpie tucked tight in their thinking. The teller was placed within, rather than on top of, the textured web of sound the living world creates. This baseline consciousness creates a negotiation with the temperament of sea foam and black bear. Everything is intelligent, animate, filled with vitality.

Let's dig in a little: I want to explore some characteristics of oral culture and then move towards the Welsh and Irish bardic schools as a bridge between orality and literacy, and then enter the English liminal stream with the medieval dream poem. These chapters (there are three) are to follow a kind of thought that is in keeping with these small stories, liminal as a culture that is open to the unruly and prophetic, to transmissions from dream, lapwing, and snowflake.

An authority on orality, Walter J. Ong (1982) reminds us that the Hebrew term *dabar* means both "word" and "event." In oral culture, a word is an event. It carries weight and mighty influence. Ong goes on to give us the illustration of a buffalo hunter being able to smell, taste, or touch a buffalo even if it is quite dead, but if he *hears* a buffalo, then he'd better get out of the way quick! The sound is direct, active, informing.

When we realise that, in such a time, the sum total of our knowledge was what we could recall—no internet, no shelves of books—then we start to understand why a word would be considered an event. Recall is not endless, so a certain sense of selection would be necessary. To allow a word into the granary of your thinking would be something thoughtfully negotiated, not a scribbled note in a journal to be picked over. This association of action with a word helps us understand the relationship between language and spell casting. To assemble words into your memory is to increase verbal breadth into this wider web of sound; it is a form of power. And because it is power, the impulse is to remember things of true significance; the mind becomes the fetching tip of an arrow rather than fluffy with media-driven detritus.

Conversation between villagers, the seasonally related telling of stories, and land-specific rituals all would assist as mnemonic triggers—that is, helping the memory establish information to be retained. This mnemonic imperative would influence community syntax. Information would be stored in collectively registered patterns of communication—nothing resolutely abstract, otherwise its very use would falter, requiring the refreshment of shared conversation.

Just as with any formal contract, deals and alliances had to be made, but without pen and paper the details would have had to be memorised by both parties in a mutually agreeable format. This increases the sense of ritual—the retained phrasing brings both parties back, by the use of incantation, to the origins of their arrangement. Early poetry is partly an attempt to store cultural knowledge in a retained format, an oral framing that carries history down the generations. As this gets more ornate, specialists are brought in to do the labour of retention—the storytellers, poets, magicians, and priestesses. There is a very real element of conservation in the task—too much free-wheeling in the language and it starts to lose collectively approved inflections. The task would be preservative as well as creative, the job of the tradition bearer.

Tradition is surprisingly agile; it can be ground down to nothing within a generation or, if allowing enough innovation to ride alongside, be sustained for thousands of years. This kind of volatility is what usually claims a tradition as a living one. In this context it can't be compared to the abrupt changes in modern music, for example—Frank Sinatra to Jimi Hendrix in a matter of years. Proximity to a community was much more acute, and there was less slaughter of the previous generations' traditions because all were in such close contact. You still had to negotiate the same mountains, the same traps, the same frozen lakes. You didn't sharpen the word-sword for no reason. It is indicative of the trade for comfort over shelter when you can so liberally destroy your elder's art.

Oral culture in those times was about the business of revival through new breath, not slavish imitation that would have little life-giving in it. When you told the stories you did ancestor work, not just to twenty generations back, but to the immediate uncles, sisters, grandmothers whose mouths had shaped those tales before you did. They would step out from the back of the cave. To tell stories is to attend directly to the dead.

As a storyteller I have long suspected that the motifs we find in tales—three daughters or sons, an animal ally, a wedding—are remnants of this oral learning, this need for repetitive scenes to lock down the story in the memory. It is a wonderful discipline for an apprentice storyteller to learn stories by ear only, to activate this sophisticated application of memory.

This is not to equate imaginative flatness with retention—certain descriptions will go alongside the characters. As Ong describes it, the participants would prefer *brave* soldier to soldier, *sturdy* oak to oak, and so on. Whilst the image is fleshed out in nothing like as much detail as a modern novel, these brief inflections create just enough rooting for the story to reach its tendrils into the listener's imagination, for the listener to actually *invest* in the retaining of the story.

The creation of a living mythology requires a tremendous amount of work—simply in the human retention of its complexities (not even getting into its occult dimensions). It is an aggregate business, to be absorbed as a whole, not picked over and dissembled by earnest literary analysts. As many anthropologists have discovered, when you open the sacred bundle of a tribe or gingerly enter the shrine room, you may find nothing visually there but rather a referral to invisible realities that are partially tuned in to relatable experience by the story—if you dislocate them, then it may cease to function. These mythologies are a highly prized result of lifetimes of mental and psychic labour. So the stories told and worked through with the muscle of retention and epiphany are to be transmitted in a specific manner so the mythos can continue to flourish in the listener's mind. The epiphany is crucial, the continual opening up to the earth through fasts, ritual, and wilderness time. That assures an evolution in the stories (even if incremental) and keeps the prophetic aligned to the pastoral.

I have sometimes worked alongside tribal people, generally North American—Chippewa, Lakota, Seneca—who have an ingrained relationship to orality. In some (but not all) I have noticed how their spoken tempo would often pick up considerably when directing prayer or ritual speech. There would be few gaps for breath, a heightened sense of occasion, a rapidity of image that would pour beautifully off the tongue, but quite unlike their regular speech.

The reasons for this are varied—personal style, casting of atmosphere—but again, I began to wonder if there was not a remnant of old orality in this style of speech, rather like the repeated motifs in story. Oral culture is in love with *copia*—the abundant and ready supply of inventive language. Like the variations in the movement of sea waves or the trilling delights of a jungle foliage, if voice retains its inherent relationship to the wider panorama of sound, is it not natural to enjoy a similar breadth of description? Descriptions that, when on a page, seem a little overbaked but when roared or whispered, can have an invigorating resonance.

When I asked about it, I was informed that they had learnt that style from nonreading elders who had retained large tracts of knowledge in much the way I am describing. To them, silence within a ritual prayer could disable the flow of sound that they were drawing from both memory and spirit; if a gap emerged they would rather repeat a phrase than allow too much space into the grand procession of sound. Without the resources of an alphabet, too much silence was a danger to retention of certain holy phrases. The value of repetition within speech is also a throwback to a time when groups may have struggled acoustically to hear the speaker or the imperative was to ground the words in the oral memory of the listener. In a culture that is oral, knowledge not repeated soon evaporates.

This evaporation is useful for forgetting specific tribal traumas (although they often linger for some generations), as there are no written texts reminding the group of a great abuse or loss, thereby weakening their wider mythos. If the group changes location and the geographic anchor to genealogy and story changes, then before too long the storyteller stops repeating the story and it drifts into a great forgetting. Of course, there are variants of this: far distant memories of homelands have been sustained in certain cultures—for example, the Gypsies—for many hundreds of years. But as a loose rule, there has to be a collective decision to "keep remembering" for the old patterned genealogies to stay clear in the group mind.

Oral storytellers, although flat out insisting they don't deviate from the narrative, almost never give a verbatim recital. Being placed in front of folks frequently—even faced with those you have known all your life—alerts the teller to the collective mood. There is also the way the story itself wishes to be told that night. As an independent agency linked to both memory retention and supernatural agency, the story has its own peccadillos. It's a contrary beast.

If, gathered under threadbare canvas or by the hearth fire of a Cumbrian farmhouse, the old stories are told, then there is an undeniable sense of *communitas*, a reaffirming, a brushing up against mighty images that remind the group of their history, place, and values. The characters who elegantly waltz into the room are ancient companions. All laugh at the three gossiping ravens or hold their breath as the young woman wanders forest paths at midnight, despite knowing the outcome. The characters in these stories have to be remarkable or they simply *would not be remembered* within an oral climate.

The boundless chaos of living speech

It was literary tradition that actually brought the idea of oral culture into public consciousness; to the medieval mind there were not yet clear distinctions made between the written and the spoken. Aristotle's *De Interpretatione* presented the idea of the written word as an image of the spoken word, which in turn was an expression of mental experience. Thought to speech to writing—the clear stream. Aristotle's progression was enough for most Dark Age thinkers—simply a change of medium. It would be a later era, the eighteenth century, that started to take into account the issues of gesture and intonation (so crucial in orality) and the near impossibility of expressing them on the page.

Samuel Johnson's *Dictionary* (1754) includes a preface where he complains that attempting to duplicate "the boundless chaos of living speech" only reflects regional dialects of a brief moment and that this should not be encouraged, as it could never be set as a standard. With his obvious preference for the literary, he was one of several to start making distinctions between the spoken and the written. Johnson was squaring up to the old Aristotelian idea of writing as just an image of speech and was claiming that writing raised, refined, and improved speech. Johnson wanted to do away with impromptu orality and go with erecting dry stone walls of considered and permanently reflective bedrock writing. No more ugly, collapsing, reconfiguring, mischievous, animate, obscure speech tangles, and more smooth, shiny lines of lettered laws.

The elocutionist Thomas Sheridan (Fox and Wolf 2002, 246) also emphasises difference between speech and writing: "When we come to see them in relation to others, we see clearly their utter independence of each other." Professor Nicholas Hudson (Fox and Wolf 2002, 246) sees these emerging distinctions, both for and against, as the fact that "European scholars were beginning to acknowledge the inherent limitations of what could be achieved by visual language." Sheridan goes on to claim: "Some of our greatest men have been trying to do with the pen which can only be performed by the tongue; to produce effects by the dead letter which can never be produced by that but by the living voice, with its accompaniments" (Fox and Wolf 2002, 247).

As a society grows more conscious of its literacy, then so too does the notion of orality appear and, with Hugh Blair, Rosseau, and Sheridan, a reassessment of the beauties of dynamic word power. Robert Wood's *An Essay on the Original Genius and Writings of Homer* (1767) goes all out by claiming that it is *because of* Homer's lack of letters that his verse has its power. He avoids "cold and languid circumlocution" of modern (for his era) writing through a kind of direct experience rather than the reflected glories of yet more book knowledge. There is speculation that there may be no single Homer at all, rather a kind of bardic tradition that composed epic poetry under that name. And it is to the bardic tradition that I now wish to turn.

The great plough and the circle of Gwydion

So let's go back, past the eighteenth century and these debates, back to a discipline that was a fusion of the two forms of communication.

The great bardic schools of Ireland were a bridge between orality and literature. For starters, they were run by laypeople, not clerics, although they flourished for a time alongside monastic institutions. Their roots went deeper, already being regarded as bewilderingly ancient by the time of St. Patrick.

The business of the schools was mainly history, law, language, and literature. The history would have been that of their own country, as were the law, language, and literature. Running quite opposed to the rest of Europe and its anxious clinging to Roman law—by now a rotting corpse in a foreign land— they encouraged and repeatedly polished the diction of their own tongue till it was truly an art form. Speculation remains on the sympathetic teaching of Greek and Latin too—possibly with the arrival of Gallic scholars in Ireland in the fifth century, in flight from the barbarian invasions.

Night and darkness was an ally. Students would be given a subject at the burning edge of their abilities—perhaps something on concord, quartans, termination, syllables, and union—each subject with its own abstruse set of instructions. The student would take to his bed, turning the conundrum around and around in his head. The next day, too, the student stayed in darkness until, at a specific point, lights were brought in and then, and only then, the story was committed to writing. It had to take root in the brain and be retained orally before the hand skidded ink across the parchment. The student then gave a kind of presentation to the master poet, who chided, advised, or approved before the student finally got to shuffle off and eat something.

In this fertile darkness, surely we see a remnant of some druidic practice: a turning within, a reliance on the old oral stability of mental mnemonic to hold the images in place, a shutting down of any distraction into the totality of knowledge that sometimes lurks in holy darkness. The bardic secret. A grappling of poetry's hazels in the ebony cloak of privacy. It is easy to imagine the young student drifting in and out of dreaming, allowing the task to become luminous, far past book smarts. This was an entrenched practice, a constant discipline. In an institution that gradually becomes far more domestic and court orientated (poetry for the approval of nobles), I would suggest these nocturnal journeys kept intact an older, earthier route back to the experiential origins of bardic practice. Night was a gateway.

The school was not so much about a geography or a grand house (often a hut or home) but focused around the charisma and knowledge of the *ollamh*, the big man, chief poet. The ollamh's influence radiated out in all four directions, and when he circuited Ireland amongst kings and nobles, the school, for all intents and purposes, went too. The ollamhs were intellectually fierce, opinionated, and full of the pomp their status conferred. On visiting a dignitary, it was not unheard of for an ollamh to remind his host of his own standing, much like that of king or bishop (Corkery, as quoted in Matthews 1998, 32). The word *bard* was actually used for a lower rank of untrained poet; a student aspired to be a *fili*. A bard in Ireland was more raggle-taggle: a wandering jongleur; a teller of tales; maybe, heaven forbid, a singer of songs. There were heavy fines incurred when trained students tarted their gifts in such a way. This naughty underbelly of performing rogues became known as "bad fellows" when they wandered England, or *filous* in France.

However, payment for the noble strand could prove difficult too, even with the amount of praise they rained down on their employee's head. If the poets arrived en masse, they brought with them an enormous cauldron called the Pot of Avarice. With this they grandly emphasised the need for payment in gold and silver or, at the very least, food. This cauldron was made of pure silver and supported on the points of nine spears. There they would stand at the entrance to the compound. We can see them now, dusk settling, chill in the air, the great cauldron glowing silver in the gloom, the line of poets standing in the mist. They would pass a poem down the line, man by man, stanza by stanza, to demonstrate their recall and honed poetic tongue. A brisk encouragement for praise, a bed, or payment.

Much later in Wales, and preserved or rediscovered or made up by Iolo Morgannwg (or Edward Williams, Welsh antiquarian, 1747–1826), we hear of a bardic astronomy: constellations of stars with names like these:

- The Circle of Gwydion
- The Grove of Blodeuwedd
- The Hen Eagle's Nest
- The White Fork
- The Woodland Boar
- The Conjunction of a Hundred Circles

This is thrilling, especially when aligned with Morgannwg's revealing of the bardic dividing of the seasons, ancient chronologies, and descriptions of poetic trials.

It is less thrilling when we realise that *The Barddas* (1862) from where this language arises, is certainly a forgery, a fake, either by Morgannwg or texts he studied that were themselves bogus. It is less thrilling when we realise that he was actually doing jail time in a Welsh prison when he started to gather the fragments from which his heady imaginings created the above.

But this is far from just a calculated attempt to deceive. Indeed, he and another forger, James Macpherson (the "Ossian" poems) did more to preserve a notion of the bards than anyone since the Middle Ages. Who on earth knows what was going on in their heads when they wrote this down—certainly much creativity and imagination. The trouble comes when artists try to place their effervescent results into a space and time that is not authentic. No matter how much we hunger for union in these old fragments, a devised "whole" such as Iolo attempts to provide tends to a fictitious atmosphere—for obvious reasons: it's a fabrication.

Many of the controversies in Robert Graves's *The White Goddess* (1948) come from his taking Morgannwg's utterings as inherited knowledge. A lively poetic sensibility works at a tempo different from the kind of absolutely proper, snail-paced scholarship required if you are to produce major statements about goddesses within European poetic tradition. In a peculiar way *The White Goddess* has continued a tradition of historically wobbly but conceptually vigorous ideas that could, at a push, include this brief "holding of the flame" by Morgannwg and Macpherson.

Geoffrey of Monmouth, when composing his *History of the Kings of Britain* (1136), claimed to have come into the keeping (or loan from the Archbishop of Oxford) of a book in "the British language" (probably Welsh) that gave extensive details of major figures from Brutus to Cadwallader. It is from this document that he supposedly mined all kinds of facts and detail—although again, there is a great speculation that the book never existed and was a device for Monmouth's florid imagination to run riot. We begin to detect a pattern, though I think there was an older thread behind Monmouth that he was consciously tugging on.

These days both men—Macpherson and Morgannwg—would probably have happy careers as writers of fantasy, or even be regarded as "channellers" and make a living that way. When something beautiful has been lost but a fragment of memory remains, hungry to the last, we will accept even a mimic of that beauty. What makes the work of Iolo really complicated is that he did copy some authentic documents that are now lost, which means, as with any great lie, there are hidden spools of the real within it.

So much of the New Age follows similar lines and understandably offers irritation to the scholar. At the same moment, some of these fabrications have intelligence and yearning at their core; what they lack is something rooted in deep personal experience. What they lack is a certain kind of truth. Not a factual truth exactly, but a loyalty to the imagination, not the fantastical. In my sense of the word, the *imaginal* has more cooking in it than just our intelligence—it's a bigger thing. The fantastical seems rootless somehow, untouched by the wider realms.

I suspect that what many of us long for in the figure of the bard is not the courtly reciter of the post-Norman world but the older, more loosely mystical, land-connected lover of the primordial earth, a road that by its very nature is, as the storyteller Robin Williamson states, made of the "quality of mist and starlight": something profoundly druidic, magical, but also hard to access in modern times. This old figure was already being promoted rather clumsily by fourteenth- and fifteenth-century bards in an attempt to stop a steady decline in interest in the form. Some academics insist that their earnest speculation is the root of what we now regard as "fact" about this earlier stage.

Returning to the regional

For anyone interested in wildness in the vehicles of orality and literature, the later bardic world is problematic. First, for its frozen flavour—wildness and creativity grow steadily more absent after their chief concern becomes the history of court and nobles. We get far less of an ecstatic nature stream pouring through the compositions (this is why we get so excited about Taliesin, although he is another figure under fierce debate) and more stodgy praise of dignitaries, accompanied by the shaking of the money tin for another round of beers. Poetry is rarely vital when tenured.

Second, the diminishing of local dialect in favour of a unified tongue is absolutely at loggerheads with the bioregional flavour of this book. We need more burrs and rasps in language, not fewer. It may have been necessary at the time to create a clear Gaelic art form that was internationally recognised, but that time is not this time.

The *regional* voice reveals trails back to the soil. We could go down to the specific—to dirt, twigs, streams, family roots, geographic understanding, the spontaneous and natural—more than up and general, honouring wealth, status, stilted poetry, the status quo. We need to take our praise back to the natural world, *not offer it to the "land" owner.*

Whilst we waywardly salute the stories of reciting by memory sixty thousand lines of verse, and the practice of darkness as a strong leap towards luminous awakening, and its use as dark speech—a form of verbal combat—it would be fitting to return to an original source of the bardic inspiration: the land.

When we get swept up in the recreation of flowing robes, badly played harps, and forged histories, it all starts to feel like a clumsy theatre, and surely we are missing the point. But the word *bard* still has protein in it, a little mystique, and so could respond to a re-visioning with the move back to *forest* consciousness, *moor* consciousness, *ocean* consciousness at its centre.

The intimacy of reading

With the medieval era, reading became elevated to an art form—an energy all its own—not just accompanying a primary orality. In the monastic tradition, text was originally read out loud to increase meditative intimacy to the words. From a pragmatic basis, reading out loud also proved essential for comprehension: there were no gaps between written words. These early monastic communities sought engagement, not manipulation, of the text. It glowed to their eyes. When read out loud, the syntax bore itself into memory, thereby increasing the text's moral potency to the earnest scholar. However, even as far back as the second century, there had been concern that reliance on the skill of recall compromised lively and associative thought in the moment. This memory resource was the birth of rhetoric, of planning in advance what you are going to say.

Plato speaks of the esoteric skill of creative recall and the exoteric skill of learning a written text by heart. These practices create argumental structure and planned stressed metaphors. Ivan Illich beautifully tracks this progression in his book on Hugh of St. Victor (1096–1141), *In the Vineyard of the Text* (1993). To Illich the book contains sounding pages: the line is scooped up into the mouth and given voice, and understanding deepens through literature taking occupancy of the breath. Hugh worked out of a monastic community where reading was paramount to the absorption of wisdom and wisdom was a being—Christ. So to seek wisdom was to seek Christ. What Hugh sought to amplify was not just memory but his own consciousness.

Most medieval documents were untitled; you cited the first and last line— the *incipit* and its *explicit*. Whatever constituted the first line became the title in the way we would understand it.

However, fifty years after Hugh, the move from the auditory to silence had begun, and with it an increased level of authorship. Hugh enabled for us an oral record, but from then on in, writing becomes the launching point for the development of the writer's thoughts. As Illich reminds us, Hugh spoke to his students; a hundred years later Thomas Aquinas lectured to them. Hugh's students read his utterances; Aquinas's read his compositions.

By the fourteenth century this level of exegesis was creating such complexity from lecturers that we see visual aids being created to assist in their apprehension of the teaching. Copyists would write out the lecture's outline; soon it was commonly understood that to understand the argument you needed the text in front of you. Can you sense the dislocation approaching?

This is an enormous move: writing, no longer to assist sounding patterns but elevated to a symbolic tapestry for imaginative development. A cathedral of language can now be carefully erected, constructed, and deconstructed, no longer just the musings of orality documented. There is a whole construction crew moving out of the ink, onto the page. Again, the nomad of the mouth goes down under the hooves of the farmer of the pen.

It is also worth remembering that there was no break between written words—hence a necessity of reading out loud. When paragraphs appear, and space around the words, there seemed less imperative to read the words out loud. The words were no longer a herd, but easier to isolate, to corral. The tongue could move through the minute gaps between beasts, discern differences in species, temperament, scent, intensity. In this way, orality offered surprising disclosures to the reader. You experienced the text with a wider holism, a wider sensual range. But by now, your ears and my ears were not tuning to a shared thought; it was the individual eye that was now the primary receiver.

Kindly recylining

Medieval man was not generally an ecstatic or dreamer but an organiser. Not a wanderer but a codifier—a builder of systems. People loved to separate out, to arrange, to tidy almost to the point of cosmological claustrophobia. Drinking deeply of the era's love of systems and general bookishness, they created a single complex and harmonious model of the universe. This cosmos was a great and finely ordered multiplicity, C. S. Lewis claiming it as a classical rather than gothic sublimity. As a model it was not totally abandoned till the end of the seventeenth century. Lewis declares the model to be vertiginous:

> Looking out at the night sky with modern eyes is looking out over a sea that fades away into mist—or looking about one in a trackless forest—trees forever and no horizon. To look up at the towering medieval universe is much more like looking at a great building. The "space" of modern astronomy may arouse terror or bewilderment or vague reverie; the spheres of the old present us with an object in which the mind can rest overwhelming in its greatness but satisfying in its harmony. That is the sense in which our universe is romantic and theirs was classical (Lewis 1964, 99).

This explains why all sense of the pathless/the baffling and the utterly alien is so markedly different from medieval poetry when it leads us—so often—into the sky.

And it was into the sky that the people viewed their impulse systems writ large. The spheres transmitted what were called *influences*—the planets affected our psychology, our plants, our minerals. With their night literacy the people saw and were confirmed by what they beheld above them. They were contained and in relation.

Even theologians claimed that the influence of the spheres was unquestioned, though they rallied against (1) lucrative astrology; (2) astrological determinism—something that excludes free will: "The wise man can overrule the stars"; and (3) anything that encouraged worship of the planets. We locate a kind of Christian nod to animism at work—and not for the first time. The mythological commingled with the celestial in the divine naming of the spheres: Saturn, Pluto, and the whole, roaming horde.

Whereas now we stare, incontinent with awe, at the unimaginable miles above us, Lewis insists that in the medieval model you would have felt that you were looking *inward*, your inner fates scattered above you.

Once this interior-above was so deeply shaken by the Copernican revolution, we started to query what we once beheld with awe. Our eyes narrowed, and we claimed all sorts of wisdoms: where once I mistakenly beheld, now I *see*.

Even the ordered cosmos needed areas of ambiguity to complement the whole, otherwise we were bolted down too tight. The medieval worldview has legitimate claim for claustrophobia.

So loping along discreetly from the pagan world came the faerie, the long-livers, the gentry, the Benji, to keep a door—albeit a small one—to an Otherworld that was not just heavenly. This small nod to porosity blessedly allowed many stories to crawl through. And few places are as porous as a dream.

What is emerging is that, rather than favouring an oral primacy over a laboured literacy, we were seeking in both a relating to the wild—both startling and ordinary. Orality is not necessarily a guarantee of finding that; tribal groups and remote villages can be just as closed off, misguided, and mythologically frozen as anyone else.

We have seen how anchored the bardic schools were in darkness and dreams as a natural companion to the outward cloak of their learning. *There is privacy before revealing.* As Europe grew more distanced from the older druidic practices, the dark retreat became an access point to the inner world that could be undergone in any situation.

Is night not a kind of underworld? Blind Homer, at the epicentre of the classics, revisions a heroic past through his descriptions brought from his luminous beholding to the outer world. Morda, a blind man, adds kindling to the fire of Ceridwen's cauldron, vast and enlightened in his hidden terrain and pivotal to the creation of the potion drunk by the great Taliesin, the most famous bard of all.

The medieval dream poem is an honouring of visionary information. These poems were afforded tremendous popularity in their day, and many are still held up as genius works in literature—Langland's *Piers Plowman*, Chaucer's *The Parliament of Fowls*, and the Gawain Poet's *Pearl* are but three plums from an indecent orchard of riches. What distinguishes the dream poem is its adherence to soulful revelation.

The Christian tradition has blown hot and cold with visionary material, but the significance of dreams as a conduit of sacred information is made clear by Elihu in the book of Job: "By a dream in a vision by night, when deep sleep falleth upon men, and they are sleeping in their beds: Then he openeth the ears of men, and teaching instructeth them in what they are to learn" (33:15–16).

From the third-century's *Apocalypse of St. Paul* onwards, we note a surge of visionary work, material that would have certainly been firmly in the minds of Dante and Chaucer. So, clear word from the good book must have, as A. C. Spearing (1976, 12) says, "provided a major justification for a literature of dreams and visions." We recall in the book of Numbers, God speaking to Aaron and Miriam:

> If there be among you a prophet of the Lord, I will appear to him in a vision, or I will speak to him in a dream. But it is not so with my servant Moses who is most faithful in all my house. For I speak to him mouth to mouth, and plainly: and not by riddles and figures doth he see the lord. (12:6–8)

What a fascinating statement, of two very different communications between a deity and a human, and also of the place of intrigue—"riddles and figures"—in celestial communication.

Whilst we can make connections between the bardic and the older oral relationship to darkness and dreams, it is clear that the Christians are no slouches in this regard either. Just as the bardic schools continued in Ireland, Wales, and Scotland, almost side by side with them, monastic orders would have studied these biblical images very carefully.

Chaucer's *The Parliament of Fowls* is a glorious straddle of both persuasions: in it the dreamer is led to an extraordinary garden—a kind of eternal

Eden—where every tree that ever was flourishes next to a river and verdant meadow, teeming with animal life. Rather than Adam and Eve, we find Cupid; as a supporting cast of characters such as Pleasure, Youth, Foolhardiness, Flattery, and Desire pass by the young dreamer, we realise that the garden is a kind of allegory of the love affair.

It turns out to be St. Valentine's Day, and when Cupid beholds Dame Nature, the Great Mother herself, she is surrounded by birds—birds given glorious attributes: the meek-eyed dove, the thieving crow, the wise raven, the gluttonous cormorant, the noble falcon. They are all there to choose mates.

A formel, a spectacular female eagle, is being pursued by three male eagles, and they all burst forth with eloquent bird speech, protesting that they and they alone will treat her more as a sovereign than a mate (shades of the troubadours). After more bustling debate on the notions of love, fidelity, and even a suggested battle to sort it out, Dame Nature wisely claims that only the formel can choose, who equally wisely requests another year to decide. Signing off, the birds sing loudly, which wakes the dreamer. Dissatisfied with these cloudy images, Cupid returns to the safer climes of his books, hoping to get more "sense" from them. The end.

In this poem we detect a still-lively relationship between the nature of animals, of gods, and of the unconscious. When we are unconscious, that is, dreaming, we fall into these underworld patternings. When loosened from the literary (and dream poetry is very bookish—lots of in-house references to earlier authors) we fall again into a den where we can apprehend the animal powers, where they are cackling revealers of our own human predicaments. This is wonderfully and outrageously shamanistic, a throwback to the immense stretch of human existence when we willfully entertained lonely disciplines to enter bird consciousness or elk consciousness, to barter dreamily for the hunt, to join our voice to their feathered cant.

Chaucer is more anthropocentric but still intriguing. We see characteristics that both species share writ large in the birds' personalities: slyness, nobility, fierceness—something also enjoyed in tribal stories all over the world.

The Parliament [based on a root word "to talk"] *of Fowls* draws on both the mystical awakening of the dream and the bird council but also draws in comedy and the business of romance. It's a poem that looks both ways—to the everyday tussles of life but also to the mythological energies that stand behind those tussles. It even breaks into a kind of throwback to orality, a bird-chatter language, with cries of "kokkow" and "quek, quek" in the poem.

The role of the lettered, rather unworldly poet not versed in love is a medieval staple; the hierarchy of the birds displayed in gradients of nobility (a mirror of the society) was another literary trope. Even a squabble that breaks out between birds is a sly dig at the warring aristocracy and the Commons of Parliament. Even so, in this agile literary work we see the dream elevated to the position of revelation—even if the dreamer is not up to the depth of its insights. Chaucer points to the value of the experiential (are your dreams not a kind of myth system?) rather than the secondary sources the dreamer anxiously turns to for interpretation. It is a most ribald blessing that we cannot manipulate them, and in that, dreams do indeed offer wildness at the heart of the domestic, every single night. Even the most humble of nuns crafts a treasury when she dreams, and there's little she can do about the extravagance—colourful, lusty, inventive, shameless. This reveals to us much of how soul covets image. Wild horses over the hill.

Narcissus and word power

So this briefest of sketches highlights just a couple of moments in the European relationship between orality and literature. As we close, let's turn to a deep rumination on such a dialogue. Let's go to the work of David Abram.

To Abram, the move to the vivacity of alphabet is not something dismissed or even quite disapproved of. It's held in appropriate awe. But awe can highlight danger, and his work choreographs the losses and the gains involved. Both *The Spell of the Sensuous* (1997) and *Becoming Animal* (2010) are landmark texts.

Rather than banishing the written word, Abram amplifies its potency: the work gets us conscious of its *power*. The human animal has woven its steady way to a truly bespoke form of animism, but a kind of aliveness that reflects only *our* nature. Like Narcissus transfixed by his own reflection, we find in written words a swift insight into ourselves—what some call a mirror—but at the same time can be trapped in a wider picture.

We see only ourselves. Oral culture—when speech volleys up and into the wider canopy of bird song and hedge rustle—catches glimpses of a shared conversation wider than just the grind of our own mental kingdom. Speech gets tenderised and inflected and challenged in a manner most unlike that when we are squatted over the glowing screen of a laptop.

But let's own up. Isn't it glorious to do just that? In a world seemingly growing so abstract, a universe so unutterably vast, the split-second reward of a finely crafted sentence can feel like something tangible, robust, something to shelter under. And hours later, when we are glutted by language, doesn't the wider world sometimes seem a little grayer, a little farther away in comparison? That's the word power of the alphabet.

It enables, for me, a wonderfully false sense of security.

Do you remember, a few pages back, talk of the medieval universe? Remember the moves of Copernicus to seemingly reveal the wizard behind the curtain, *that we revolve around the sun, rather than the other way round?* That kind of thing rattles a sensual being. As Abram writes, it replaces *qualities* with *quantities* (Abram 2010, 155–56). Our own emerging, scenting, intuiting way of being in the world is, in a moment, absolutely secondary to the mechanisms of an exterior universe, quantifiable but staggeringly huge. Who are we to presume our little stories of the oak with the moss on the north flank or of the night the River Exe became an adder are anything but whimsy? But stories are like cobwebs; they collect a hundred secrets in their net. Impacted, intentional secrets between wolves and pines, trouts and river people. Well, that storied world and its implicit relatedness have mostly fallen around our feet. A few hundred years of this and it's not surprising we are nervous wrecks.

And where does that vast, aboriginal interior go? Entirely into the confines of a human body, a frame woefully too small for its majesty. But we have to get a sense of an interior, of being *held*, from *somewhere*, and so we finally draw it reluctantly into the bone house of our own body.

And it's there that we enter the temple of Narcissus. There that we build our little house of words to cope with a cosmos wrenched asunder. It makes us feel better, at least for awhile. But down the line, are we not busy devising a kind of hallucination? In Devon there is old folklore that insists it is fatal to catch your reflection in still water. Dartmoor, with its preponderance for fast-moving streams and rivers, is more like the oral tradition—words fly by you—but the still pool of literacy is more like the magician's circle, a greater compression to the conjuring. And, as with all magic, there is a cost.

When I go to the trees and the long pale beaches of our south coast and the rutted little streams of Dartmoor, they don't provide me with easy mirrors. They do away with my feeling in control or on top of something. I don't necessarily feel powerful. So, let's be pragmatic a second: What does that look like?

It looks like me walking a stretch of ground, telling a story and bearing witness to how the earth reacts. The long, fettered silences, the moment when a buzzard lurches from a tree, the bubbled sigh of foam on sand enable for me (to use literary terms for a moment) an entirely different sense of punctuation, full stops, and adjectives. They get to work on my imagination; they seep into the spoken words and rearrange some of the rhythms. I don't see myself mirrored back to me; I see myself flooding into something far bigger. The mirror has cracked from side to side, and I slip through the eye of the needle.

I lean over the side with my fishermen's net and get pulled into the big sea.

So, much of anything worth admiring in my own work I can't take much credit for—other than being a faithful witness. In the living world the stories don't immediately bounce back to me; they don't reflect necessarily what happened with me at my kindergarten when I was five. They take me on walkabout.

Hours later, soaked, sobered, or a little high, depending on the journey, I may arrive at my little hut and scrawl a few lines. But when I glance up, there may not be that tin roof any more but a hundred million stars whispering in their high, cold language, and no solid timber underneath my boots but a fragrant rug of pine needles.

Nature will show more than ourselves, back to ourselves. That's one of the inestimable privileges of a life. A core of aboriginal thought. No one, least of all Abram, is calling for book burning or unthinking hysteria. But I think he calls for a proper appreciation of *power* and how, somehow, written words could actually enable ways to rehydrate the terms of our narcissistic relationship to the alphabet. We need breathing holes for the seals in our syntax, lush passages of word grass for Scottish cattle to bend their hairy, gingered skulls to.

This is not just a flight of fancy; this can be practice. Localised, maintained practice. When I tell a story to a group of people, I've *already* been soaked in the responses of the natural world to that story. Wit has arisen, tensions have been defined, and unexpected flights of imagination negotiated by the sturdy presence of the Dart River. So a kind of braiding to the living world can take place *before* a wider human sharing. There's already the fragile print of a starling's claw in its mud, the perfume of apple blossom some way back in the odor of the telling. Your conscious mind may not catch it, but some way back, your animal body shifts in the bracken and says *yes*.

Another move from Abram. At some point in this kind of conversing, a good soul will often stand up and berate the speaker for attaching any kind of human characteristics whatsoever to the living world, insisting that it's all still anthropocentric to claim a cloud as grumpy or the wiggle of a bush as ebullient. They have a point.

If our emotional education has stretched no further than our fiercely protected inner self, they have a point: that it's nothing but a land grab to start prodding plants and passing rooks and describe their moods. Cheap. But that's not what Abram says we did. For thousands and thousands of years, that's not what we did. When you wander freely in a wider psyche, then a ruby-dark sky filled with juddered thunder is inexorably bound to the sharp thump of feet in your gut. It's not an affectation, not a metaphor even, but immediate, beautifully devastating relatedness. That very thunder is the initial educational image for a young girl on the plains, a-swarm with anger for her sister. It is from Earth that she draws self-knowledge.

> If we listen, first, to the sounds of an oral language—to the rhythms, tones, and inflections that play through the speech of an oral culture— we will likely find that these elements are attuned, in multiple and subtle ways, to the contour and scale of the local landscape, to the depth of its valleys or the open stretch of its distances, to the visual rhythms of the local topography. (Abram 1996, 140)

This is wise thinking, properly spell-breaking syntax. The use of alphabet to actually *wake* us up from its often entrancing capacity. We witness here an enormous clue as to how to rebraid ourselves to the living world. To take ourselves out into, I suggest, a fairly small stretch of earth and reconsecrate our speech to its contours and grit.

Again, I say, this isn't whimsy; this is something that can be learnt. This is a tangible skill. Reread the section about telling stories as a way of their being shaped by the earth and start there, maybe. Move back into the sensing range of your own body. Commit to a decent stretch of time. Not an afternoon, not a workshop, but real damn slow. Like a rock is slow.

Abram's work is so arresting because it's not just startling poetics, not just philosophy—it instigates something in us honestly deep. It does chthonic work, something rare. It instigates, dare I say it—remembering. A remembering that is hard when beset by the twenty thousand things you have to do before lunch, but it's there. Now that's magic.

In the caribou dust of your bones, it's there. In the prehistory of the flames that lick your hearth, it's there. We're old, y'know. Whatever they like to tell you on the television. When we bend our heads and sob without reason on entering an old oak grove, that's not sentimentality, it's animal memory.

CHAPTER FIVE

Grey Wethers and the God of the Sun

I'm squatting in the jaws of a Dartmoor beast, taking refuge from the wind. My face, pallid after months of autumn, is tingling, slap red, prematurely sunburnt. This isn't meant to be happening; it's winter, for God's sake. The beast? Sheep. The jaw? The Grey Wether stones. As I ease my shoulders back on a granite tooth jutting from a bustle of thick grass, I roll some local folklore round my body, that at least once a year these stones return to their original assignment as four-legged, curl-flanked grass munchers. Those unofficial chompers of the British landscape.

My eyes are suspicious slits peering the big blue sky; my beard hangs as a peppered stalactite in shrill cold, a weird contrast to my scalded face. And gloves? Why do I never bring any? I really should know better by now. Ah, but I have coffee, and lumps of local beef, and just a little of that Christmas blue cheese, perfect on a sourdough crust. I offer some black drops of liquid to the grasses and a crumble of cheese and hurl a good chunk of beef. I'm feasting up here, in the silent presence of some ancestors. I'm knackered, actually. My Levi's shirt is still hot-stuck to my shoulders from the stomp through the forest, and an ankle is twisted from the last half mile, but I've come to tell a story, and that's what I must do. Any minute. I'll just get my breath.

But I'll never get used to the sharp velocity of Dartmoor air and its insistence on sleep. I'm under. Blessed rest. A brief but energising nod. It seems to last just a moment, until the stone my head rests on seems to almost jolt me awake, as if by poking me. How can a stone do that?

Weird. Okay. I stand and walk to the centre of the circle—there are two— and I'm aware of little tweaks of pain from that ankle, as well as a distinct twinge from the knee to go along with what appears to be a frozen shoulder. I am maybe not in my fullness today. This winter I seem to have gotten old very quickly.

If the stones could become sheep again at any moment, I would do best to proceed whilst I have their undivided attention. This gray parliament of stones, nobly strewn with lichen, peer up at the travelling man. I'm nervous, more so than when in a room full of human folks. Rocks seem to listen in an entirely different way. Especially when it's their story you are telling.

I've spent several decades, now, looking at and talking to stones. They are a varied and often cryptic bunch. Tell them a joke and it could take weeks to get a response. They don't tend to give it away too easily. They are rocks, for God's sake. But I've felt them change under my own hands, from a deep blue agelessness to a shard of flint that hummed hot like an Arizona tin roof. I've wept over glowing river stones in the sweat house, heard them gurgle and crackle their tales in the fire pit. I've held them at dawn and dusk whilst folks sat on the hill: the stones bearing witness to the fasters' condition, each stone taken from its place up there, then returned. They are message carriers. I've spent hours in rolling Welsh thunderstorms at the feet of secret cave boulders and witnessed entire worlds unfold on their surface. Unwritten histories of a time before ours have paraded themselves majestically on a thin slab of limestone near Gloucester on a Tuesday afternoon. And this isn't even rocks being particularly mystical. This is just us growing mute to the many ways they have of being their nature.

But the members of this ensemble—these circles, this council—have a particular sturdiness to them. Next to their squat, regal countenance, this storyteller and his transitory bones feel like a moment's distraction to their day. But I have something with me that isn't. I have a currency they value. I have a story.

GREY WETHERS AND THE GOD OF THE SUN

Spade hit peat. Muscle to the turf, the rough sweat of real labour. Peat to be gathered and sold to Dartmoor farmers as fuel for the winters. Families scuttled up close under woven blankets as blue smoke rose and the kettle wheezed into life on the trivet. Peat is a life giver, a grimy champion, as bleak spirits of ice and rain roam the remote settlements of the West Country.

It was late summer. Three peasants toiled on the bog-heavy uplands next to Sittaford Tor, carving the peat into blocks and letting them dry out in the sun. For weeks they had done nothing but hack into the ancient ground. Hack till the turf shuddered like a trembling bell. Shirts were salt-stuck to their burnt backs, minds woozy with the slosh of beer going man to man. Come the end of day, they would load the dried peat onto the skinny backs of their ponies.

The sun finally began to sink from view and the three men wearily gathered their gear: budding irons, slicers, and turving irons. Home was humble but solid, granite boulders with a thatched, mossy roof, long laced with lichens and moss. The hut was owned by a man called Rogne, who stayed there when working, along with his companion Varnes and Lynhur, a stranger to the moor but there for the digging. Lynhur was from some far distant place—the east of the country—but did his best with the subtle language and roguish turns of phrase.

Work makes men wolves: starving, gulping down cold pork, bread, and cheese, booze on tongue. It was getting dark; a steady rain lashed the entrance to the hut. Soon a storm; thunder hurled dark sound through the valley and the wind was a hundred voices, none with good news. The aching men dragged their weary bones even nearer the fire and pulled warm blankets round their shoulders.

> *Rain loafs from hill to hill,*
> *up from old Torbay—that*
> *apple-bite of coast,*
> *receiving its portion*
> *of the trouble.*
> *The stones of the hut*
> *settle back for a story,*
> *warding off*
> *groaning black air.*
>
> *Granite speaks:*
> *Men of the turf, give us tale:*
> *barter with weather, make account*
> *of your shape, hurl language*
> *to the four quarters.*

Rogne roused himself from the fire gazing, scratched his chin, and began the ritual. "Thank God for this hut on a night like this," he muttered.

"Ay," said Varnes, "but I would rather take to the hills naked in this storm than visit Grey Wethers on a Midsummer Eve."

What were the Grey Wethers? The Grey Wethers were two broken stone circles comprised of thirty blocks of granite on the southeastern slopes of

Sittaford Tor. Wethers is an old name for sheep; from a distance they look like a flock of grazing sheep.

Lynhur, as a stranger, knew little of the Wethers and asked Varnes why he was so afraid. Varnes settled back and started to tell.

"There was once a Dartmoor man called Zorac, one of a tribe who still worshipped Belus, the god of the sun. In his early days, Zorac was so devoted to Belus and conducted so much ritual, threw so much hard graft to the blazing god, that he was favoured and became rich. But, surrounded by wealth, he grew lazy in his ceremonies and slack in his language.

"The Midsummer festival was the time when relationship to Belus was at its keenest. All the other folk toiled endlessly in their ceremonies. Offerings were abundant that year. Early one morning, Zorac wandered down over the dew to choose one of his sheep for the God. Scratching his full belly, he yawned and decided he couldn't be parted with one of his sheep—it simply wasn't worth it. So he picked out a young lamb from a neighbour and slaughtered it. No sweet words, no effort, a clumsy killing on the green slopes of Sittaford. From his golden seat Belus watched on, saw the whole scene, gave license to his fury. Something must be done.

"That evening Zorac returned to his flock. Where they had dotted the grasses only hours before, plump and healthy, he now found two circles of granite stones erect in their place. Belus had acted. Zorac grew distressed, distracted, his wealth fell away, and he grew sick and died. He is buried in the cairn up on Cosdon Hill.

"Every Midsummer Eve, at midnight, the stones take their original shape as Zorac's sheep. There they graze till morning. The storytellers say that should you succeed in shearing one of the sheep before sunrise, if you sprinkle the fleece with water from the ancient rock basin on top of Kestor, it will turn to gold. But this is part of a wider ritual, a righting of Zorac's greed. It won't work if done for nothing but gain.

"And just to make your head swim—none of this will unfold without using Zorac's original shears, which are buried with him up on Cosdon Hill. Not only that, the shears will then have to be bathed in the River Teign at exactly midnight. You need to wrestle the shears from the bones of the dead and then bathe them in the flowing water."

At this Rogne leaned in, and with a little flourish, recited an incantation on the very subject, whilst Lynhur listened on, boggle-eyed.

At midnight by the Tolman, upon the River Teign,
The shears within its water, shall carve thy weal or bane.
Strike on thy left, then on thy right, red blood the flood
shall stain.

Beware lest trembling fingers, withdraw the blade again,
But hold it firmly neath the stream, till tress of hair appears,
Which seize and keep to bind the sheep, then use the magic shears.

The weight of the words left heavy silence in the hut. The three men gazed into the embers, minds adrift with ambition. Keenest of all was the stranger, Lynhur, who repeated the incantation over and over silently as he curled up in his itchy blanket, the rain thrashing the roof, the small fire spluttering its cautions.

He returned east, to fen country. All through the deadly winter Lynhur brooded. As he fished in the shallow ford he brooded; as he trailed the scat of a long-distant stag, stirred a feeble stew, stroked his gaunt belly, repaired his weapons, he brooded. Come summer he knew he would return to the moor. He would live out the old prophecy. His dreams were of blood, gold, a woman's tresses. Riding a stolen horse he would cross many miles to return to Dartmoor, to take up the challenge.

Ah the horse thief.
Kept his secret
from smithy and sheepherder,
tinker, weaver, net-mender.

Just grinned into his
cup of beer, gestured for a refill,
in those taverns of the far west.

Nothing like a secret to keep you warm.

But the opportunist's ear
does not catch the nuance
of the deal, and stolen hooves
will crumble under the hard melt
of the Midsummer God.

Seven days before Midsummer's Eve, Lynhur swaggered up to Cosdon Hill. His feet ached; his brow was a river of sweat. After circling it several times, he found the entrance to the cairn. With some rough tools he set to work, humming low, imagining his fortune. After half a day's work he prised open a stone coffin. The old ones were right. In amongst the skeleton, amber beads, and a smattering of bronze and tin, there they were. The shears.

Then on to the ancient pool at the top of Kestor, to fill a goblet with water. finally, he made his way to the Tolman Stone on the River Teign. It was late, just before midnight by now. He sung out the incantation with full tongue, his voice hoarse with the exhaustion of the day.

> *At midnight by the Tolman, upon the River Teign,*
> *The shears within its water, shall carve thy weal or bane.*
> *Strike on thy left, then on thy right.*

He plunged in the shears. The water writhed around the blades like a dozen fish in ecstasies. He glanced up and he swore the moon was red. Then it seemed the water spoke, in some braying froth of word:

> *Strike! Strike! Crimson blood shall stain the flood*
> *and whet the glistening blade. Strike! Strike!*

In shock he withdrew the shears and at that moment realised the water was bloodied; from what, he didn't know. In courage, he placed the shears back in the occult flood. Again the gurgled incant:

> *Strike! Strike! In the stream*
> *To bind the sheep, fair tresses gleam.*
> *Strike! Strike!*

From the water rose the long, strong tresses of a woman's hair, like gold, like sun, like treasure. He was so entranced they almost floated past, till he frantically reached out and grasped part of the tresses. Just part.

The ritual enacted, the archaic words spoken, and Lynhur fully committed, the moor grew quiet. Almost benign. Were it not for the sodden, golden, ropy strands in his arms, Lynhur could have thought it all a dream.

The next day he took up his place by the fire in Rogne's hut, was warmly greeted, and took up his place cutting peat. He told no one of his midnight ambitions.

On Midsummer's Eve, he made excuses and hurried to the Grey Wethers. As he waited he grew drowsy. Some hours later he started awake, and to his joy he saw many sheep grazing in the moonlight before him. The old story was true! Still, he had wasted time by slumbering, and he had only a short rope made from the few tresses he had managed to catch.

It was farcical as he tried to catch sheep after sheep in the mooning light. Time after time he fell, goofy, to the turf. Finally, he caught just one and hacked away with rusty blades. Blunt blades. A little wool started to fall in brutish chunks, and his fantasies of wealth grew vivid. So overwhelming were those imaginings, he failed to notice the first pinks on the eastern horizon. But he noticed when the tresses on his far-too-short rope loosened and the sheep made a getaway. Sweat and exhaustion stung his eyes as it wobbled off.

Despair took him. Why had he pulled the shears from the river too early? Why had he hesitated to grab the tresses? All would have been well with sharp shears and long tresses for rope. He was bent with regret for even following this wretched prophecy. We all know that feeling.

In a flash he remembered that he needed to sprinkle the Kestor water from his goblet onto the fleece. As he reached for the cup, the air around him grew dead cold. The sheep hard flanked him, surrounded him, herded him, and kept moving between shapes—animal and stone—they seeming vast, he tiny. As they closed in, he heard the gurgling shrill again:

> *Thou that seek to gain the treasure of the dead,*
> *Shall in the fatal gift the grave does give instead.*

The following day, Lynhur, the stranger from the east, was found dead, pinned hard to the ground by one of the stones that had toppled onto him. Some called it an accident, but the old folk, gathered by those peat fires in the long winters, knew different. Vast currents of power curl tight under the soil and lurch up into celestial heavens. If you are to walk with such energies, then follow them to the letter.

> *Our man of bad listening*
> *the great jug of his ear*

scything away the
wise grasses
of caution.

Even as the hut rain-rattles,
even as the fire cautions,
he gazes up at the golden roof
of opportunity.

and there go we
and there go we
and there go we

We are all horse thieves,
sailing a mile from shore
with the neighbour's gold.

Embezzling their mares,
for just one stroke
of the wine-maid's thigh.

❋ ❋ ❋

I'd headed for the stones early. I scrawl the destination on a note and leave it on the large wooden table. The car is an ice shell, a dragon of frosting. We tilt northwards, with cries of huzzah! and a firm whip hand, up towards the blue sky and glazed, frozen brown hills beneath. My breath steams onto the window as Ken Bruce witters quietly on the radio. Gears feel thrashed; great muddied spurts of earth cake the doors; every piece of plastic on the car is hanging daintily from its righteous position. Good. I'm just starting to get comfortable with this car.

It's third-time lucky for walking this particular story. First time, I got within sight of the remote rings but got called back due to a sudden darkening of the sky—night fell quick with a forest to negotiate. Second time, I got turned around by jagged weather. So this bright, freezing day, I am grimly determined.

Hawk

Without a map I descend into the spillage of muddied lanes between the Postbridge Road and the descent into Chagford. There is hay bound in black lining like huge sticks of licorice on the fields' sluiced edges. Somewhere en route I am looking for signs for Fernworthy Reservoir and the pine woods that surround it. It is through them that I will get to the open moor and the circles. Today, all signs seem to suddenly vanish and I am almost on the descent into Chagford before I realise that something must be up. This can't be right.

I'm hot and irritated. Why is it so hot? I have been up and down this steep road more than once, assuming I would get spoon-fed by signs for the route to the forest. As this sits angrily with me, a large hawk bursts from the low cover to my left and sweeps across my path, only several feet ahead, initially at shoulder height. Epic wingspan, mottled with dashes of exposed white, fierce mouth—that's about all I can take in. I could have reached out and touched it. And lost a finger.

There is a great thrumming blast of feather and clarity, cutting utterly through my pouty mood. The bird's wingspan clears five feet, easily. It's not a buzzard—I know the colourings of the common and rarely seen rough-legged buzzard and even have a fair idea of the more obscure honey buzzard. This is something else again. (The buzzards have grown more visible on the moors since a lessening of game-keeping aggression, large "wakes" of them being reported.)

Hawk hefts itself upwards, catches a current, and forces my head far right. In the distance I can suddenly behold the formal shape and "cut out" pattern of a conifer forest past more lanes, dips, and old-growth copses. Thank you.

Hawk, friend to Hera, Isis, and Circe, clawed instructor of patience but companion to lovers—king-lover Gawain's name derives from Gwalchmei, "Hawk of May." Its vigour makes me done with whines.

I lurch into some purposeful strolling to cut down the time spent on tarmac. All Devon lanes are crooked and seem to lead you round on yourself before you get anywhere near your destination. Rather like a Devon conversation. When I finally enter the forest at its sweetest spot, I see that the dry stone walling at its entrance is almost entirely covered—the old stones like mossy loaves of bread or the curls of a green sea. There is a briny scent, up from the coast, that leaves only when I move farther into the shadowed forest, and the unmistakable aroma of pine drifts fragrantly around me. At the centre of the dirt track is a wide ice ridge, although most of the ground is without snow. I can't help but enjoy jumping from puddle to puddle, breaking the blue, icy skin. There seems to be no one about.

Tracking the ridge I slip, scamper, and steady myself on this white track leading, some miles ahead, to the Grey Wethers stones. Was Lynhur so enthused on his traverse to the stones—was it a glory swagger he carried with him? Had his winter starvations burnt all caution from his whip-thin frame? Today my companions—the peat diggers, the solar worshippers, the transgressors of the sacred—are invisible, but they stomp alongside. I am many.

These pine trees, planted out of necessity for wood in the First World War, *carry* war-paint—dashes of white horizontal against the steep trunks and endless shades of black. They seem poised for the chainsaw, to suffer without complaint. Occasionally, in the soldiering lines of timber, a strong gold light warms small areas of earth. It is strange to think that these non-native forests were planted out of a sense of anxiety. Maybe it can be sensed; I see no animal tracks but the occasional horse and sheep scat as I get nearer the moor.

These trees are voracious wanderers. Read the statistics: from the Canary Islands to the far east of Russia they are found, from Africa to Scotland, from New Zealand to Chile. They have become a tree of empire, of building; they have a knack of wiping out the local. Like most invaders they are tall. Tall and long living—some going for as long as a thousand years. A god stands behind them, the immortal Prometheus, the stealer of fire from Zeus. Well, like their inspirational deity, they too have spread like a wildfire. A pine found in California was a true ancient and, aged at almost five thousand years, was named after that god whose liver is eaten daily by an eagle and regenerated every night. The woods feel efficient but lonely. They absolutely do not hold the panache of an old-growth stretch of oak and ash.

I come to an earlier stone circle. Twenty-seven small stones, roughly twenty metres or thirty strides in diameter, probably four thousand years old. When these stones were first discovered, their inside faces were black with charcoal—from ritual: funeral or feasting. Hair, teeth, flickering flame, lurching figures, raised incantation, tears, offering. As I make my way towards them I can see sunlight glittering, taking my attention to something placed next to one of the stones. There is a bundle—letter, photograph, map—curled now by weather, but clearly a message to a lost and young friend. The photo is taken at a rock festival; a group of young men with handsome, wide-open faces lean together, broad and fearless in their camaraderie. It's clear one hasn't made it.

There are waterlogged and ice-stiffened pieces of cloth, purple and red, dotted about. And then more—witching gear, *fifth fath*. A bound, rough figure in lightning-struck wood, placed on the top of a stone. I leave the wood, the letters, the map, all of it, well alone. The very publicness of the offerings seems a little clumsy. This ancient circle is clearly still in use. Maybe it doesn't have the elegance and precision of original design, but there is something here that drags the bereft, the mystically ambitious, the straight-out curious to its breast.

The track rises, passes a crossroads, more air, more blue sky. As on all these walks, I relish the sheer aloneness. I can see for miles and there really isn't anyone around. Some part of me uncurls into that space as I start thinking about my life. About age, illness, regret, sorrow. As those unwieldy thoughts crash about, I refocus my attention to the present; I gaze around.

Piled up, probably a dozen on either side of me, maybe fifteen feet high, are stacks of bones. Bone hills. I blink and look again. It's not bone, but erratically assembled piles of bleached wood. They look like Mongolian shrines; I await the yip of the swift-ponied Asian rider. Where is the dark Altai cry? Each skulled hump looks like it deserves flowering orchids, bowls of frothing beer, silks tied to branch, rough slabs of jungled chocolate, quiet attention, goat meat for the circling hawk. Each one looks like a little death, some small ending that has occurred during this strange unfolding I call my life. All the grieved and ungrieved moments I have dragged my still-limping frame through. It's a kind of review. Really, it's a very strange moment.

And oddly, for now at least, it's okay. In this pop-up graveyard I can map my own travels, places I have lived, erratic betrayals, crooked loves, emphatic healings, street brawls, lonely Sundays counting the hard cards of grief. In the smaller piles, I see many little routes I have *not* taken: friendships cut short, choked at the hilt, strangled, mashed, and bruised with billhook flails. There are piles of hubris and simple stubbornness. We can't follow every trail. We are not meant to hear every voice that speaks to us. So it is. Things pass back into the composting earth. I feel a strange pleasure that there is something to show for these few decades. There is a story. The brightness makes it all visible, concealment no kind of option.

I have preferred moonlit shadows on the piles before now. The wind is up and freezing; I keep going. Apart from that insistent wind, it is deeply quiet.

I linger awhile on the edge of the forest and note a reluctance to come out from its shades into open moor. This appointment in the palace of the sun god is making me nervous. I've avoided it many, many times.

I finally cut out from the forest and head across open moorland, keeping in the tree line's shade, because although it's cold the sun is fiercely beating, too hot for my wintered face. The grasses are stumpy bolts blown into extreme clusters, meaning a constant meandering across broken-down walls and more moorland, over small frozen streams until finally the stones.

They are two circles. I count twenty stones in the northern circle; the southern has twenty-nine. This second circle seems far more substantial, with large, strangely shaped chunks of rock. Someone has placed a black stone, glittering with crystal, in a worn spot where a stone must have once been. Somewhere in Birmingham, an occultist feels a sense of self-satisfaction. Between the two courts of stone is a gap, a grassy runway, heading off into open moor. The sky is crisscrossed with airplane fumes. Again, my attention is drawn to the unusual late-winter heat. Then it hits me. Belus! This is his place. No wonder the rocks bake on a February day in a subzero wind.

And how did I get here? Not by Ordinance Survey map, not by compass or grinning local, but by the sweeping grandeur of a hawk. A hawk messenger of the sun gods. Friend to bright Apollo, head of Ra, feathered loyalty to Armenti, the Great Mother. Friend to Belus. The Celts said truly that a hawk's feathers carry sunlight with them. The hawk is more than a familiar of choice for Merlin, but actually the shape he would skin-crawl into. Dear hawk, bold path maker where there is no clear path, what the Seannachai fiercely declare the oldest animal of the Celts. Fly above me, fly above me, always.

Here, as in the other circle, are signs of ritual use. This is rather more charged. There are the remains of a flesh offering: a thin crimson crust of flesh and bloodied icicles hanging off a particularly distinguished stone.

These gray teeth were stoutly resident during the battle of Hastings, the witch hunts, the Tudors, the Great War. They squatted steady through the reformation, Cromwell, 9/11. Businesses go bust, empires go haywire, and proud people make love, have families, dream, fight, and die; endless thousands of dramas are played out. If the stones do occasionally tumble, strong hands reassemble them. And still the circle, the wind, the great empty hold their eternal council. It is a constant scene. There is no stagnation here, only permanence. I've never been in such a place that seemed so entirely to itself, its own ecosystem, its own thinking.

These stones are vast and elemental, but the current ceremonial detritus is scratchy and without consequence. It is like arriving at a theatre set without a description of the play and the actors gone for lunch, but having a fierce longing to see the full production. It is as if older eyes watch from the tree line, seeing us puzzle over the jigsaw. It is not strange that we bring our brokenness here, our fragmented imaginations; we have to have something to lean on.

Today I am confronted not with the drama of the Lynhur tale but with something of my own: the times I have shied from light, averse to clarity; my own skepticism of bright things, of success; the bone piles I carry with me; the understanding that it can be a fine and holy thing to sometimes follow a hawk's grand flight rather than a badger's earthy snuffle. I recall the blessings I have squandered into a slow-drip poison.

Alone in the vast and wintering moor, I pray to the one I hold dear, the Friend, and try to make good. When, hours later, I emerge from where I began this walk, my face is salty, scorched by the sun.

How a stranger hears

This is a story that begins in poverty. A saga not of kings and queens but of the deep-down exhaustion that comes from breadline living and the kind of labour that beats all subtleties out of the body. Many cultures whose people have lived poor hold in high popularity stories of buried treasure, often at a crossroads or someplace slightly outside the everyday jostle of the village. The story recounted by the men is even more magical: that shape-shifting is required for the old prophecy to play itself out. But an inherent warning is there from the very beginning, of the greed and eventual laziness of Zorac, that the sun-favoured one goes to the grave because of arrogance and ceremonial slackness. So for Lynhur, the stranger listening, his end is almost predicted in the beginning. When the devotional is absent, the divinities grow tetchy.

Lynhur is from some other place, a stranger to Dartmoor, and so hears the story with ears askance to the local. The locals have been utterly bent and weathered by the handing down of the tale by tradition bearers—the old women and men crouched by the fire. A god of the sun is not some abstract fancy for the teller of the story, and the story he tells transmits a holy message for those with the ears to hear it. But Lynhur does not have those ears, he does not detect its nuance; his lugs are bent only to the mention of opportunity.

Isn't he us? Western commerce could be said to have a major hearing defect when it comes to what the land is trying to communicate. We are listening through a static of our own making. Some would argue that we are all strangers to the myth world these days. As with Lynhur, maybe our own preoccupations dominate our listenings and we have lost the taste for its troubling commentaries. We are so caught in general sweeps of interpretation, we cannot detect the very particular advice of a particular valley or story. Rather than allow the obliqueness of the tale to unfold, we would rather turn it always to our own needs and ambitions. Hence the story goes from one of caution, reverence, and possible redemption to a shortcut to robbery and wealth. That's a swift and common move. We could extend this metaphor and say that this inability to "hear the story" is the very essence of our involvement with climate change.

This is a quite legitimate concern in the passage of stories from one culture to another—it gets messy. It's unlikely that a sixty-year-old electrician from Budleigh Salterton will ever quite draw the resonance out of a Miwok story that a native Californian will. At the same time, if the story is not just a product of diffusion but has its own desire for travel, could it be that maybe it has its own message for our middle-aged electrician? And that there are other models for receiving the story than just the greed of Lynhur? As it stands, I have witnessed startling insights on Hebridean stories from a West London Caribbean community, so this "hearing" can go both ways: ignorance or new insight.

In some tellings of the story Lynhur is called a nomad, a wanderer. This gives us some space to consider the notion of the nomad within the local as an ancient proposition. In the writing of this book, I've come to view the nomad as releasing some crucial flexibility between the faraway and the local. Otherwise we live in the fantasy that never the twain shall meet. The further we delve, the more we'll see that this has never been the case.

The nomad in the local

When we grope back far enough, we hear the clinking bells and animal croon of a vast migratory journey—way back, through the blue smoke. Press your ear to the mud and you will hear them.

From Africa, the Caucasus, the steppes, we hear the creak of the great wagons, the lively yip of reindeer song, the crackle of the fire. Movement has been one key display of our temperament. And not always on the run, not always adrift in ghosts, bloodshed, and oppression, but frequently styled with tremendous, hip-sashaying elegance.

Only a few miles from the Buckfastleigh caves, in the remote burial cairns of high Dartmoor, beads originating from the Baltics have been found, a sign of great veneration. They have been determined to be four thousand years old and adorned the burial site of an adolescent girl. I've picked my way through treacherous, boot-sucking mire to offer libation there myself. But it was the degree of migration in those red beads that really caught me. I thought I had given myself entirely to the local!

Many nomads travel for pasture (the word comes from the Greek *nomas*—meaning "the search for pasture"), beautifully rooted in the wealth of the word *herd*—the fed bellies of the animals in turn dictate happiness to the wanderers. The sustenance of the four-legged ones is a homing device for the tribe, a humbling incentive.

These ones-beyond-the-city-walls still amount to some forty million, some traveling to gather wild herbs, whilst others—like the Lobar blacksmiths of India—are craftworkers and travel to trade. It was nomads—the Mongols—who gave birth to the largest land empire we have ever seen. Under the unification of Genghis Khan, the land of these nomadic tribes stretched the great flank of Asia. It was nomads who carried the banner of Islam across North Africa, Spain, and Iran in the early seventh century. In early books of the Bible they are claimed as God's children; it is the city folk who are outcasts. Nomads have made a substantial hoof print on what we perceive history to be. Pragmatism, intricate social networks, and an often dazzling degree of weaponry ride alongside.

It's too loose a connection to claim them as hunter-gatherers: they are not. They have consciously entered the business of management, of proximity *to* and cultivation *of* herd. They clack with their staffs, directing the migrations, not just aimlessly following the chomping amble of the animals. There is an easy back-and-forth between the desires of both. Venkatesh Rao (Dark Mountain 2011, 32-41) claims just part of their bounty as the invention of the wheel, falconry, leather craft, rope making, even sewing (from the construction of hide tents with needles of bone and gut strings). If mobility is the pressing issue, it's likely a nomad designed it.

We could ask, what does *local* mean to a nomad? Proximity to a fireside or dwelling under a ragged canopy of stars, cradled in the soft fur of the desert grasses? Nomads seem to represent a modern aspiration—the wider earth itself as home. But still they resolutely maintain their specific song lines; their passage is still deliberate, often worn into an ancestral groove under their hooves, paws, and feet.

Soil

When nomads claim the rich soil of farmers, we usually locate a change in their thinking, what George Monbiot calls "a belief in progress." Transformation and salvation become an unstoppable highway cutting through the previous hard-wrought perception of the cyclic, seasonal world—loss and gain, abundance and scarcity. So where once was the spiral, now exists the gleaming road of future security. The crops are dry-stored, and nature's rough grip is to be overcome. We get to dictate some terms. The greater purchase we have over nature's whimsy, the better.

Professor Greg Retallack (Monbiot 2005) claims that differing soils dictate the religious emphasis of the people who work them. Whilst collecting samples from ancient Greek temples, he noticed that thinner soil existed where nomadic herders worshipped Artemis and Apollo, but as the soil becomes capable of supporting a robust farming life, the gods in the mix are Demeter and Dionysus, deities of harvest and the vine. The emphasis becomes less on hunting more on planting. The gods do not just exist in lofty Olympus but wander the fields in the evening light. The deities reflect the intricate concerns of the local; maybe they guide them.

The nineteenth-century writer Thorstein Veblen (1899) (Dark Mountain 2011, 36) makes a resounding distinction between two different kinds of pastoral nomad: lower and higher barbarian stages ("barbarian" is high praise in Veblen's eyes). The lower stick pretty much to the lifestyle I've described, whilst the high gradually become civilisations whilst maintaining an eyeball in the direction of their roots—an example being large herds of animals maintained for sport rather than sustenance. They in turn get deeply settled, forgetful, and comfortable, till nomads from the edges charge in, kick over the applecart, and claim dominion. Then over time they make exactly the same moves towards surety as did their predecessors.

Venkatesh claims that one on one, the nomad displays more innovation, street smarts, and flat-out aggression than any civilised person, but en masse, the porridge-thick, comfort-sucking horde will almost always win the battle. The mono trumps the feudal.

Traditional nomads rarely worshipped much local in the way we understand it; rather they hurled their praise up at the vast tent of the sky. The sky enclosed all. The Mongols loyally offered libation to vast Tengri, god of the air. Everything under its great sway was related. But, as we see, this old view is affected by the knowledge of life's inherent fragility, the seasonal patterning of what is stripped away, and the green buds of spring's recovery.

We have in large part inherited "the belief in progress" and now stand in the debris of its consequence. Maybe we are on the verge of becoming a post-progress society. There's enormous relief in that.

The amble of the last few paragraphs has been a pen sketch of how a book like this might approach the word *nomad*. I meet many people for whom the word produces a visible glow; they wear it as a kind of sash round their waist or a rose in their hair. It's become a phrase or get-out clause to describe the kind of floating busyness and continent hopping that makes up what many of us associate with a successful Western life. But let's slow the wagons a little.

I think very, very few of us are nomads in this ancient sense, and to insist on the word for our cross-continental scurries is a slander, to my way of thinking. I would call this the condition not of the nomad but of the scatterling:

scatterling: *One who has no fixed habitation or residence.*

We hold the keys to the kingdom and the kingdom is everywhere and nowhere. But hey, we travel, we make connections, we trade; why can't we claim the title *nomad*? What is the pasture we seek? Why is it different? I think we might begin with the word *bonded*.

Nomads do not travel *over* the land; they travel *with* the land. Their travel is not an abstraction, but an earthy pilgrimage deep with understanding of relationship to herd/place/person. These migrations root their hips and feet in the ordinary grandeur of ancestral walking. So—to use a recent phrase—they are bonded.

Many of us travel without that sense. We travel searching for something other than the trail itself. I think we are actually *looking* for bonding. So, bonded is the aboriginal ground, and if a nomad already possesses it, then for us to claim we *are* it while we seek it is rash and, as I say, a little slanderous. It's like a kiddie walking around with a fedora and sporting a wolf-tooth earring. Charming, but not to be taken that seriously.

Malidoma Somé (1995) tells the story of a child being born with the Dagara tribe of Burkina Faso. Gathered up outside the thin wall of the hut where the birth is taking place are all the local kids waiting for the first cry of the baby. The moment they hear it they wail out in response—to ensure that the newly arriving soul knows straight up that it is witnessed. Then the mother and child remain in the cozy dark of the hut for some days. The baby dictates its curious and woozy awakening—an Otherworld for this little being of the amniotic realm.

The circle of the tribe enables this slow-emerging sense of bonding. This bonding becomes an eye from which to apprehend the living world. Did you get that? I know I didn't. So I lick my lips and spend forty years trying to get a need met that should have been catered for within twenty seconds of my leaving my mother's womb.

Hut poetics

> *O Light im schlafenden Haus!*
> *O Light in the sleeping House!*
> RICHARD VON SCHAUKAL

It is worth taking a moment to examine the place where Lynhur hears the story. He is not *at home* but in a new landscape, something unfamiliar. He is already lifted out of his regular frame of reference; there will be sharp edges for his imagination to push against. It is this sense of openness that has an initiatory tone, of one's being deliberately exposed to something beyond the pressured traditions of the immediate social memory. From one way of looking at it, Lynhur is a young aboriginal, sitting in the magic hut with advisors, hearing of what lies out in the (as yet) untrodden bush: the murky spirit dangers.

Years ago, living in a black tent on a succession of English hills, I would enjoy tufts of grass sticking out from between the faded canvas and the trellis. Robins would fly round the tent-roof ribs then out again. There were always drafts; no feather could ever fall straight. In summer months, you could sleep with the tent ajar to the night's dreaming, the roebuck trail nearby, the badger discovering last night's dishes in the grass, old seasonal spirits shuffling about. Winter required endurance, pragmatism, muscle: canvas frozen on the inside, endless scouring for kindling, sleeping under a leathered mass of skin and blanket, throat creaky with temperature drop, only face visible from the dark pile, gasping wintered air.

The tent was a conjunction, a polyphonic murmuring, a den of natured languages. It was psychoactive. All this made visitors, sometimes even other yurt dwellers, uneasy. "Why not do away with that tent entirely and have done with it?" muttered one. But I needed the tent. The tent was the ritual marking out, the frontier inn that invited all the chattering denizens in for a drink and a gossip.

Gaston Bachelard (1958) knew well that all of us have such a den; that a house, flat, or apartment contains a kind of Russian doll set of other containments. The further down we go into ourselves, the closer we finally get to our own hut. All it takes is a lit candle, or a snowflake at the window, or rain on the roof and the hermit wakes, with its immense "in"-ness, from behind our daily face.

Bachelard reminds us that the hut is no bustling monastery; it offers solitude. He also poses the challenge of interiorisation, that spaciousness of the imagination rather than a literal change of location is key. We all know what it is like when you end up on a foreign beach and, to your horror, realise that you have brought yourself with you.

So, you can put this book down, light a candle, curl under a sheepskin, and find the hut anytime you want. The Dartmoor hut is an image of poetic reverie, utterly alive—the spluttering peat fire, the coming storms, the story as grounding in volatile weather. Bachelard loves the image of the lamp in the window of the hermit's hut as a symbol of the late-night mystic: a sign that someone is studying hard, a friend to the night, while we sleep on. Our image is even shaggier; it is the gasp of relief when a stranded walker sees a distant light in the mist and knows the walker's life is saved. The madness of the fog increases tenfold the warmth of the fire.

Rilke (1934, 15) describes the experience of seeing a lit hut at night from a distance with three friends as so powerful it could not but separate the experience for the friends, as their interior worlds all leapt up and went "See, see!" The inner life, so long enraptured in the embers of such a scene, could not share it around like a common item.

The favoured get lazy

What does it mean to worship the sun? Svarog (Slavic), Helios (Greek), Shamash (Mesopotamian), Ra (Egypt), Awondo (Africa), Tonatiuh (Aztec), and Amaterasu (Japan) are just a fraction of the many sun deities across the world, some male in character, some female. Belus himself drags Babylonian, Greek, Egyptian, and Roman cultures with him—all having slight variants on his name.

The sun, with many mythologies, can broadly indicate will, success, radiance, strength, and the fullness of midday. It is the sun deity's temple, more than any other, that brings in the worshippers, because it appears to hold what we all want—wealth, warmth, strength, clarity of vision. We flood the church and direct our lives to its attributes.

Some say that those who work in the great banks and Wall Streets of this world are sun worshippers, addicted to its golden rays, its vastness, its beaming and favoured heat. With none of the moon's murky ambiguities, the sun is good news for the hard worker, the ambitious young buck, the power-shouldered businesswoman.

But the story tells us that lusting alone does not cut it with the sun—that these great banks, these lazy vats of hoarded gains, actually irritate the Yellow One as it gazes down on Manhattan and the fat cats toasting with champagne the common people from high balconies. As the Occupy movements indicated, a cavalier attitude towards other people's money will bring consequences. Eventually.

Consequences because the Sun is not a profane altar, a refuge for the greasy handed. The sun brings warmth to the sick and skinny boned, a sophisticated hand to the turning of the seasons and to every animal, plant, and ocean that responds to it. Without its bountiful distribution of light, we have no Shakespeare, no Dickinson, no Goya. It is a gift almost above all others for us air-gulping wanderers. Old Belus and his other dimensions were not about making Zorac or the bankers or us fat cats.

Belus is a death bringer and life provider, delicately balanced, and aggravated when his favours are exploited. When the mythological layer of life collapses, when the ceremonies become toxic (end-of-year bonuses at the taxpayers' expense), then does something inside the lost worshippers not turn to stone? When we see the flat gaze of the corporate staring at us on the evening news, it is probable that something inside them—their sheep, their animal natures—has turned hard and without feeling.

Retuning: From field to herd

As we are seeing in this story, what one community holds efficacious can be as nothing to another. However, talk of gold tends to cross all boundaries.

Frederik Barth (Anthony 2007) describes such a story of retuning positions between the Pashtun and Baluch people from around the Khandahur Plateau in eastern Afghanistan. The Pashtun were field people, agricultural people, who toughed out issues in local councils where each landowner was seen as of equal standing. In the nearby mountains were the Baluch, pastoral herders and holders of a hierarchical power system. The Pashtun had more wealth and more status. That was about to change.

Pashtun status was tied up completely with land ownership, meaning that if your land was lost in dispute you would scrape out a life on the margins, bent crooked to menial servitude. Baluch power was tied up with the herds—something that could move—as well as to political alliances, not to stationary tracts of land. Amongst the Baluch, there was no shame in being in service to a chief, who in turn was in service to the khan of Kalat. Although on the surface the communal shindigs looked more favourrable to the tribesman, if you were excluded from those meetings you were in trouble. The Baluch said not all men were created equal, but there was far more opportunity for digging yourself out of holes if you became a "client" of the chief. All sorts of improvements were possible.

When warfare started between them, the two sides found that moving herds were far easier to preserve than were immobile fields. Before long, many agricultural refugees swapped sides, ensuring a preservation of language and culture for the pastoral Baluch. Ears got retuned, values reoriented, and the whole affair ambled on. But it would have taken some time.

By removing himself for the winter, Lynhur gets the initial message but not the deeper inflections of the story—the warnings. He doesn't dig in.

Within modern farming communities, we find the ear is also usually no longer bent to old language. The heady rattle-bag of ancient farming terms would baffle most Devon folk, texting with one hand as they drive their 4x4s up and down the cramped lanes. What of *ploughing abreast, pommel tree*, and *taking up the brew*? The post-tractor economies of Devon have seen language—rich, pungent speech—disappear back into its red soil. There is a vigorous poetry in many old farming words.

John Clare's poem "The Mole-Catcher" (Evans 1970) supposes old knowledge to be available at the listener's fingertips, that the listener will know that the trap is made of horsehair and a simple frame. The catcher uses a small spade—called a spud—to dig out the hole and install the wider trap, utilising a willow rod, a toggle of wood, and the tightening of the horsehair. Even when shiny steel mole traps could be bought at local village shops, many country people kept to the old method Clare describes. His words become a kind of history-magic, an invoking of both robust imagination and practical detail.

When melted snow leaves bare the black-green rings,
And grass begins in freshening hues to shoot,
When thawing dirt to shoes of ploughman clings,
And silk-haired moles get liberty to root,
An ancient man goes plodding round the fields
Which solitude seems claiming as her own,
Wrapped in greatcoats that from a tempest shields,
Patched thick with every colour but its own.

With spud and traps and horsehair string supplied,
He potters out to seek each fresh made hill;
Pricking the greensward where they love to hide,
He sets his treacherous snares, resolved to kill;
And on the willow stick bent to the grass,
That such a touched up jerk in bouncing springs,
Soon as the little hermit tries to pass,
His little carcass on the gibbet swings.

The black dog of winter

Lynhur does not act straightaway. He lingers in the threads of the story. God knows how it twists and contorts over that hard winter—the warnings subdued with every missed meal; the image of the gold fleece more radiant with every fruitless hunt, every shiver of iron-hard midwinter, the subtle body-aches of frosty autumn. Of course, at a time like that, the sun and its legacy seem more fable than reality. Without the jubilance of midsummer sun, maybe it is quite natural to get greedy; in its absence one starts to feel that the story is more invitation than warning.

We recall moments when we have enough distance from an experience to consider repeating it—no matter the warnings. The affair creaks back into life yet again; the crippled husband insists on another mountaineering expedition. We know our victim was sold from the start, with his memorising of the incanted verse. But what is life without a little risk, a little piracy? These moments of rashness are what stories contain—there are very few about a mundane existence. If the characters are not remarkable, or at least a little crazy, then they are not significant enough for the oral mythteller to retain in memory.

In many stories we encounter "ritual dis-information," in which a character is emphatically instructed not to do something because such instruction will serve as a trigger for that character to certainly do it and, in so doing, learn a deep truth. It's a contrary method of understanding the psyche.

That is not the emphasis here; the lesson is too harsh: it appears (as other stories do here, as well) a bleaker image of a gradual falling out of relationship with cosmos.

It is unrealistic to presume that rapacious survival issues were not partially at the heart of an ancient ritual life; of course they were. The mystery of death, the bartering for favourable weather, the lamb taken from the flock up to the bloodied rock—all were partially to broker attempts at stabilization in a savage and often brief few years, to erect frontiers against the gray winds of disorder.

But I do say partially. There would have been intense creativity, affection, even a sense of personal relationship—love—displayed to many of the old ones. Even by the time of these three characters, ancient to us, much of that has changed. The old *longing* for favour of a deity has been replaced by the steady chant of *want*. Favour be damned; the thing to do is to enact the ritual illicitly, grab the loot, and run.

The story does not forbid the ritual taking of the shears, the tresses, the water, but the action has to be efficacious, and it has to be perfect. Lynhur's greed and straight-up lack of reflection suggest it would be wise to avoid this situation rather than enter with a view to getting rich quick.

And of course, perfectly, he arrives on a stolen horse. Sometimes this can indicate a little piratical charm—some risk taking—but in this case the surrounding evidence is rather stacked up against him. We all ride a stolen horse at some point or another. We're easy to spot by the ungainly, probably wobbly horsemanship as we try to ride the energy of something entirely settled into its own rhythm. We lift another's ideas and pretend they are our own; we mimic a style of dress, even odd little mannerisms. But we must not be too hard on ourselves. It's through all this loafing affectation that we begin to find out what we love, who we want to be, what our tastes are. It's animal behaviour. But there is something nervy in Lynhur, as if this is his innate response to everything: nick it. In this he mimics Zorac's downfall.

It is highly unlikely Lynhur would have been able to afford a horse. And if he stole it, the peasant would likely be unable to replace it. To the village it is a vast transgression, enough to make him outlaw, *wolf's-head*.

Horse is totemic—to the tribe mind of the Paleolithic, to a present-day Exeter horse show, to the Gypsies, to the Celts, to anyone who has ploughed a field or had to get somewhere else. It turns both ways—the cherished friend *and* the wild thing, out on the edge.

Amongst the horse people of both England and Scotland, this makes the animal magical in any number of ways. And to negotiate that, you have to become something of a horse magician yourself. Two of the tools in the equine magus's kitbag would be the little-known milt and the frog's bone.

The milt appears on the tongue of a colt when it is in the mare's womb. Milt actually derives its name from the spleen, which it resembles. For hundreds of years, the horseman would carefully remove the milt after the foal was born; if he didn't do so, the foal would most likely swallow it. There is speculation about its purpose: some say none, others that it prevents the tongue from folding back during birth and suffocating the foal, others that it is there for the foal to learn to suckle on in anticipation of the mare's teats. In the horse-magic tradition of England, this has become a fetish, a heavy ally.

Suffolk horseman would "rap it up in a pice of thin white papper jest as it comes from the foal; then put a brown piece of papper over that." You would then bake it and "beat it up into a verey fine powder. . . . After it is baked out it in to a musseline bag and sweat it under your right arm. Let him or her [the horse] get the scent of it, and if he be ever so savage you can take him under your charge and do aney thing with him: only be kind and gentle to him or her" (Evans 1966, 214).

Some added oat flower, lunis powder, and olive oil, making it almost like a hard, thin biscuit. This combination of womb memory and scent of the beloved horseman seemed to calm the most crazed of horses. It's certainly a very old piece of information, George Ewart Evans claiming: "It is indubitably the hippomanes of antiquity. . . . Both Pliny and Juvenal mention its use in love potions."

For humans, as well as horses, hoods or caulds at birth are always auspicious, either devilish or divine: we have the *membrane adnelette* (French), *knabenhelm* (German), *sigurkufl* (Icelandic), *camicia della Madonna* (Italian), and *silly hood* (English). They are another frontier, a gifting from some other place we sense but can't quite recall. They tend to indicate psychics and poets. But for the horseman, it is the *milt* that could calm a savage horse or be smeared on a stable wall to call in line a horse that refused to step out to the yoke and the plough.

Second only to the milt was the frog's bone. You had to go out and kill a toad, then let it dry for twenty-four hours on a whitethorn bush. It had to be a "walking toad," one with a ring around the neck. Then the toad was buried in an anthill for a month, till the full moon. By then it was just a skeleton, a skeleton that you took down to a fast-moving stream. This is when the horseman had to draw all concentration in his body and soul together. He would place the skeleton in the stream. A bone, a crotch bone, would disentangle and start floating uphill *against the current*. When this happened, it was typical for a wind to pick up through the trees, crows to caw, all kinds of unearthly noises to sound—all very distracting. But the crucial bit of magic was to keep your focus on that etheric little bone defying the course of the waters. Some ground the bone into a powder but most wrapped it in linen and kept it concealed on their person. To jade (entrance) a horse, they would touch it in the pit of the shoulder with the frog's bone; to release the horse they touched it on the rump. They had their witching stick. The whole process of the toad gathering, drying, anthill waiting, stream dipping, concentration holding was called *the water of the moon* and was taken with utter seriousness by the horseman. With a wry grin the whole process would implode, become impudent, and provoke bad luck.

This level of efficacy is what is required from the stranger in our story—but he's looking for shortcuts.

Wrestling the dead

First test for Lynhur: To steal from the dead; to grapple the bones and take the jewel back to the upper world. In a story, as soon as you are in the business of disturbing graves, you are entering the Underworld. All instincts scream to leave the grave be, but Lynhur willfully breaks this taboo.

Some wrestling can be healthy; many artists tackle, successfully or otherwise, previous centuries of work. The wild genius of Picasso, alongside vice-like discipline, meant he clambered into many graves and brought home the jewels. His great legacy is that he refined that process into the highest realms of alchemy—what he stole did not gather dust but was wrenched into new expressions. His thievery of old masters' motifs was a form of honouring the very legacy he drew from. Such were his intensity and ritual sensitivity that he lived a long life and never wiped the tomb dust from his hands. The sun smiled on him. He made sacred transgressions at just the right moments. Great art is hot with these kinds of eruptions.

Picasso's *Les Demoiselles d'Avignon* is a mighty collision of influence: archaic Greek sculpture, the symmetry of Egypt, African statuettes, and even a lift from the geometric planes of Cezanne. We could say that his ear was primed for the message within this story—of audacious thievery, but also of a kind of cosmological efficacy: rather than hoarding, Picasso's wrestling with the dead creates new gifts for the ones yet to be born.

A hallmark of many initiations is the need for theft, the idea that a final piece in the development of an adult is some cunning. Not as a constant deceit or common rogue, but as mythological craftiness. In a Hebridean story, a young man gets to ride his father's horse only when he steals the whistle that rouses it from under his father's pillow. As the story progresses, he makes three steals: one, the whistle; two, embers from a crone's fire; three, a king's boat. Although the reasoning is not clear at the time, ultimately this audacious progression of "lifts" saves the entire kingdom.

We keep coming back to the word *efficacy*. The thefts within initiation are to reveal a psyche not immobilised by external pressure (they break taboo) and liberating some hoarded energy for the good of the cosmos. The Hebridean boy's father had long passed the point when he should have revealed the whistle to his son, and his failure to do so created a house with an extraordinary backlog of tension within it. Picasso opens a door to an underworld history of art, and all the holy dead pour through.

Lynhur is not in this category. There is no knightly "higher cause" to his stealth, just the grind of poverty. This scene has associations to a series of riots in many of the major English towns some years back; for the best part of a week, nightly lootings occurred, shops were trashed, and epidemic vandalism took place. This wasn't about civil rights and was widely condemned for its mindless rampage. The outrage many felt is very easy to understand. Within an initiation, a theft would not be of trainers and wide-screen televisions but of intricately carved bowls left in the women's hut, designed for ceremonial feasting. It would involve stealth, a leaving of tribute, and a crafty intelligence revealed to the elders that, in hard times, these youths would be able to figure out unusual and inventive ways to feed and clothe their families. It would reveal mercurial substance. Pizazz.

And yet this apparent pointlessness to the English riots creates the misconception that the climate these rioters exist in every day is sane and fair, that their very underclass existence—flattened out by absolutely no job or life prospects—is somehow bearable. It isn't. In comparison, a riot would seem an exciting place to be. Adrenalin, chaos, a brief flush of power before the deadening nothingness of your life returns. These scenes of youth gone feral are an echo of the old initiatory desire to wrestle death. And who really gets damaged? The local community, not the banking fat cats. The exhausted Indian shopkeeper, the mother on her way home from a twelve-hour shift at the supermarket.

Theft is a constant in the world of the gods. Look, there is the blue baby Krishna, wandering around stealing butter, locals actually preparing the most succulent butter so as to have a visit from the thieving, toddling deity. The great giant Thrym steals away Thor's hammer—source of creation as well as destruction—claiming the hand of the goddess Freya in exchange. This leads to some tricksterish crossdressing on the part of Thor, which leads a trail to the hammer's return. There is cattle theft all across Greek and Irish mythology; Coyote steals fire, and Ivan steals two goblets from under the nose of Baba Yaga. Any momentary ignorance has a greater insight hovering round the longhouse door; it is all bound within a wider brilliance.

It's a complex set of instructions: wrestle the shears from the grave of a dead man; collect golden-haired tresses from a river at midnight; sprinkle sacred water on the fleece for the golden transformation. When Lynhur's nerve starts to go, we suspect this may not end well for him.

Lynhur having already engaged with the dead, the golden tresses from the river now accelerate the situation into vivid supernature. In northern European mythology, golden hair has associations with golden wheat, with the harvest, with abundance. It is no surprise that this instruction has been dictated by a sun god, as the hair carries solar radiance and potential fortune with it. It is with the tresses that Lynhur will bind the sheep and make his fortune. If we connect the sheep with earthly wealth, it seems to indicate that to be aligned sweetly with the gods requires that our daily gain needs to be wrapped in tendrils of the immortal for true right living. So simple, so easy to forget.

Of course, the gathering of holy water is an old druidic remnant—the Druids preferred high spots for gathering snow or rainwater, as they were considered purest and nearest the sky and star deities. The water was charged, animate. Even today, Dartmoor is full of place names like *Druid's Well*, *Druid's Chair*, *Druid's Altar*, *Druid's Stone*, *Druid's Mine*, so it is not too much of a jump to associate the moor with those leafy thinkers.

The disappointment of the gods

On Midsummer's Night, Lynhur falls asleep, lets the sheep get away, forgets to sprinkle the holy water, and barely notices when dawn emerges. If the price for all of this weren't so high, it would be a comedy sketch. During the whole story there are few redeeming moments. Lynhur simply lacks charm; there is no befriended animal ally, no moment of generosity to a dwarf at the village gates. This has no faerie tale hooks—it seems an earlier story, harsher.

In Russian fairy tales, we hear tell of a "goddess that doesn't love us anymore." This isn't quite true, but it's a useful thing to fret about. There is a deity that rowed her boat to our very shore whilst we slept, adrift in trance from a sleeping pin. After a time she leaves and will not come back.

In our era, when we believe we can be anything and have anything we want, all the time, it is disarming to hear that we cannot snap our fingers to the gods and expect them to work slavishly in our favour; that in fact it is *we* who need to cross nine lands and oceans, to craftily get round Baba Yaga and her sisters, to emerge at just the right moment and display enough "awakeness" that love floods back into the equation.

It is as if the dignity of labour, a practice that is the very centre of bush soul—the slow scrape of antler bone on hide, the diligent picking of a path through a swamp to pay libation to a distant shrine—has become diminished. This labour is how to pay the ferryman; when we try to renege on the terms we muddy our relationship to death. It respects patience. The quickest route is by no means the most efficacious.

There is a tangible disappointment, in these Dartmoor stories, over a lack of manners on behalf of humans. Amnesia of courtship. Belus and the others gather at the edge of the fire to see if they are remembered. Feminine energies like the Great Vasilisa peer from their coracles to note whether any divine commingling can still exist across the worlds. Despite the hard ending of this story, some hope exists that we can still undertake the adventure, hear the story correctly, wrestle the dead, and make art that helps the waterhole stay wet and fish-thick, and that we can appeal to the disappointment of the gods with as much agile beauty as we possess.

CHAPTER SIX

Bear Standing Upright Under the Moon

EFFICACY, FRONTIERS, MIGRATIONS

It's rough weather up on Haldon Hill. As one of the main routes through Devon and into Cornwall, its exhausted motorway is straining to the very limit as truck after truck groans and grinds its load up and over this ancient tump. The road is a churning menagerie of sound: the thick flap of the wheels, high whines from frustrated engines, and the steady put-put-put of the exhaust pipes. In the darkening light of late afternoon, a curling snake of headlights stretches all the way down towards the city of Exeter.

Up here, Haldon has its own weather. There can reside here an arctic frigidity quite unlike the cold in the hidden villages and hamlets below. As the rain hurls its ravenous fangs down on the shining cars, only half a mile away I'm tucked into a thin scattering of wood, deep into ceremony.

I'm as dapper as I'm ever going to get, regardless of freezing downpour: grandfather's cufflinks, sash, tailored knee-length tweed, silver rings on fingers, waistcoat and bespoken old-time boots. An elaborate horse strap from the Hindu Kush is firmly woven into a large leather bag, which weighs heftily from my right shoulder, filled with gifts. Doesn't stop that rain, though, sleeting sideways though the gloomy verticality of the pines. For a second I gingerly remove my trilby and slosh out the gathered moat of rainwater under its upturned brim. Then back to it; the weather begets efficiency.

The story hut is looking almost ready for business. In the midst of the pines there is the rotted base of a very old oak, still rooted in crumbly black soil. A small bed of bracken has been diligently assembled, and on top reside a stash of dry kindling, a hip flask of Irish whisky, three strands from a blanket, money, and a slow-whittled antler-tipped staff, ornate at its handle with the carved appearance of a local denizen.

Above that is a simple woven roof of grasses and branches. And most important, it's near flowing water; otherwise I fear there's no possibility the guests will arrive. Fretting like a concierge at some fancy hotel, I pace the soil and glance through the dripping tree line for just a hint of their arrival. Just a few rustles in the glittering bushes. This story knows how to make an entrance.

I should tell you, this tale brings a very old arrangement with it. Though I've encountered it told as a local story, and through a local mouth, I intuit immediately that it's taken a migration across the Irish sea to get here. I can just smell it. It's a wanderer amongst the steadies. There's a subtly different magic to it that, I admit, settles wonderfully amongst the tussocks and green lanes of Devon. It works. I don't know if it arrived on a fishing trawler or on the back of an eagle or squeezed itself out into the confines of Newton Abbot library, but it's here. And it works. Some know it as "The Storyteller at Fault," one of its many names.

Stories have always done this. Some of them do like a wander. This touches on one of the most salient nerve endings in this book. There can sometimes be a ruction between those who insist on locality as prime for folklore and those who perceive the land as a fluid backdrop, fluid enough for the story to hop from country to country with nary a scratch.

The truth is, of course, that there are examples that will readily reinforce both positions. But for as long as people have loaded the wagons or set out across the ice flow, stories have been traded, migrated, and weighted. Weighted for their purchase, for their wisdoms, for their disclosures. True wealth.

But we already know enough of this Commons of Imagination; it's a note struck frequently down in the orchestra pit of modern story, the idea that all myths are talking about the same things at the same time. It's simply not true. I'm sick of it. As if the pitted cliff face of East Prawl is chanting the emerald song of Sherwood Forest. Different lands provoke different stories. Everything I've learnt from stripping down the black tent and moving tells me this.

When we herald only binding agents, we lift the human experience artificially above the earthy psyche in which it resides. We hang, loosened entirely from the tendrils of place, remote and universal, and wonder why we feel so discombobulated. The clinic of the existential.

When faced with personal transition—with trouble—in a culture worthy of the name, you would extend your attention outward to seek the worthy council of the wider psyche, the broader body that you were part of. We are not designed to wade through crisis without it. Doing so makes us crazy; it makes us appear deeply alone. Elms, blackthorn, and the crescent moon always had the power to keep busting open our cloistered thoughts, interweaving with our wider body.

So I focus on the local. The specific. But then this happens. Just as it always did. The nomad is back. A story rolls in, spits once on the ground, and beds in, claims some turf. Like some charismatic loafer crashing the party, by the end of the evening, stories have everyone dancing on the tables and a new blush to Aunty Ruth's cheeks. They get claimed. Naughty as they are, they get recognised as saying something new about the old place. I can't let this kind of messiness pass; it's too real. It's like life. But I suspect the story has not been deeply welcomed. There's an old way of doing these things, you know.

So, my task is twofold: to visit the land and barter some relationship to the story, to visit the story and barter some relationship to the land. What happens after is not my business, but I can't be slack in my duties. That's why I'm up Haldon Hill with my bundle.

We've established that storytellers have always had a hinge vocation between worlds, cultures, spirits. But, as I write elsewhere, there has usually been a gradient of protocol attached, a sensitivity, a way of doing things. It's not appropriate to grab some far-off tale and expect it to show up ready for business in a climate not suited. However, if the story *itself* has something of the migrational about it, then a courtship begins. A testing of the ground.

And that courtship requires a few standards: no Erin tale will settle unless it's near fast-moving water, if it doesn't have dry wood for the fire, or if there's no dram for the lip, no emerald bed, no staff to support its heft when the feet are weary and the road is long.

You have to be loving, generous, and attentive when a story arrives. You have to make a home for it. Give it shelter.

The three strands of blanket were part of a late-night gift from a storyteller representing some of the Tulalip people of the Pacific Northwest. A blanket that held one of their sacred paddles and was now freely given in exchange for a wild old Celtic story that he recognised and claimed as useful. It's always been done. It's a kind of magical practice. But the *way* in which it is done is paramount. You don't just grab a prize pony from a neighbour's paddock. That's how you get scalped.

Too many assume that oral stories are all up for grabs: as long as the story is repeated, then all is well. All is not well. When a story lands beautifully, we witness not just the spirit of the tale but the long apprenticeship the teller has served to it.

The turns in language, the lifting phrase, the moments of rapid improvisation are defining marks of service in the temple of the tale. To mimic such a diligent practice without the involved, cautious, and daily maintenance of a big story is theft. It's not "continuing the oral tradition"; it's theft. You simply didn't earn it, and as a friend of mine says, "You are still on the take." Stay in that groove and you may leave the West, but the West will never leave you. The fox-woman stays exiled.

These are words for those in the trade of speech to consider, those who claim a little prestige or maybe coin for their tellings. Now, for those on the front line of telling stories in the raising of kids, helping the sick and the poor of heart, supporting returning veterans, assisting the spell breaking of addiction, whispering tales into seal holes and across gray waters to a heron, well that is something else again. Long may you ride. But a similar education is required in the power gradient of the stories you tell. They are medicine, so understand the dosage. This is a call to do things right. Your heart has a true north, a sense of efficacy: use it.

The rain has hushed and a second wind has joined the first, a different tone entirely, this time coming in from the east. The air is so fresh it feels like it's soaking, like you could squeeze it out like a rag. The rocks and pine needles are an almost hallucinatory green. I reach into my bundle and pull out a couple of horse brasses—heavy amulets used for display and protection of the Devonshire heavy horse of the last century. I start my shake. The low clack of brass on leather, and a third wind enters the small glade. As all myth-tellers must, I beat down clock time with the clatter-pulse of my amulets until little pinpricks of somewhere-else-entirely show up. We are now at a proper crossroads.

So I bring language. Hard-wrought speech gathered from caves and clouds, kestrels and the hoof print of a roebuck. Gathered from sitting at the feet of women and men in service to language. Curated from all the ordinary heart-breaks and woeful betrayals we will surely face. And it'll still never be enough. But I bend my head and I try. I try to barter conversation between the tale and the land, conversation that the story and its beings recognise—if not a home, a place where they could occasionally shack up when over this way, where they can get a fire going, have a dram, get a sweet bracken bed like the old times.

This particular ceremony is quite a protracted affair and requires complete sincerity as well as little touches of fine, fluttering speech that the stories find charming. But the heart must be tenderised too—not with aimless flattery.

What happens between the land and the story afterwards is something only they can negotiate, but right now, in this spirit mediation, I am accountable. This matters; it's not free-form.

At a certain point, my knee drops to the grasses and I realise it's time to give voice to the story itself. They've turned up, one at time, over the last few minutes, and, although at a discreet distance, they're ready. I can see the glint of copper on their chariots, the hounds' breath-steam in the dusking. It's getting dark; crows caw from across the copse, and a car passes in the far distance, lights twinkling.

❊ ❊ ❊

The wandering storyteller

There was a time when a story was as precious as meat.

And in a time like that, down in this land of the west, lived a chief. A chief of what we now called Exeter. Now, the chief was sensible enough to treat his chief storyteller well, to place linen on his back, lamb on his plate, a roof overhead.

Yes, the word man and his strong wife were coveted. Valued. Every night the teller would take his place by the chief's fire and coax tales from the Otherworld. Small ones, funny ones, vast galloping epics, and then, when it got late, tales so magical, so straight-up eerie, that hanging off their edges were keen-eyed spirits who would surge into shadows and under the benches of the drinking hall. He could invoke such things. Because of this, he was venerated and, more than that, loved: a prize bull for the western chief.

One morning, up on Haldon Hill, the storyteller opened one baleful eye. He always did this to check which stories had rolled up for that evening's telling. None. He closed his eyes, sighed, and repeated the process. Nothing.

With this he panicked. Shot bolt upright, his nightshirt stuck queasily to his back. This had never transpired before. There was usually a den of stories competing for the job. Today nothing. To clear his head, he put on his boots and wandered out into the grasses around his encampment. Let the land speak to him, as it so often did up there. Some called the place Hawk Hill, because of the Goshawks that roosted there—supreme hunters, rarely glimpsed unless they chose. But nothing today; no distant roebuck, no robin on the branch. As he gazed the long gaze, he took in the distant south coastal ridge of Dumnonia to his right, and the still-waking settlement below. *Argh,* maybe the stories would show up later, he told himself, letting out a long breath. If they didn't, he'd lose everything.

It was then that he noticed the shape.

By the old oak and the small stream, there was a brooding lump. Like some vast crow that had crashed drunk through the branches and forgot his way home. It was a melancholy mountain that, on closer appearance, seemed mostly comprised of a tattered cloak and a battered black hat. Peering up from its shadowy depths was an ancient man, and as the teller got closer he realised the archaic geezer was doing something. On a thin slab of slate, he was throwing bones, gambling.

"Ah, my handsome," scratched the old bird. "Company. What good is a game without you?" "Well," sighed the storyteller, "I haven't had much luck this last hour. Maybe a quick bit of fun with you will rouse the spirits." At this, an odd laugh escaped the stranger; he gestured at the younger man to sit, and they started gambling.

It took only an hour for the storyteller to lose his money, his chariot, horses, hounds, hawks, and entire camp to the raggle-taggle scarecrow man. "I've nothing left to gamble with," he moaned. "I've lost everything."

At this his wife appeared, she of the sashaying hips, dark river hair, and roaming intelligence. She squatted down beside her man and took in the scene. "Not quite everything, beloved. Throw the bones for *me*, gamble me, and we could get our gear back. Do it." He'd heard this kind of certainty from her before and had learned to trust it. The stranger hurled the bones. They twisted this way and that and, yet again, they landed in his favour. With an odd look, the teller's wife crossed the grass and sat behind the old man, alongside the glittering hoard of bridles, saddles, jewels, and grazing horses. With every gain the ancient's shape had seemed to grow a little more pronounced, a little more robust, a little less feeble. When the storyteller even gambled himself against the hoard and lost, it was then that the dark man leapt up, quite revived.

He produced a leash and a wand. "What kind of animal would you wish to be? Hawk, hound, or hare?" On impulse, the storyteller chose hare. As the wand lightly touched his shoulder, as he surged into the new shape, he bolted for escape with all the strength a hare has. It was his own wife that caught him, even walloped hard blows in her handling. Even in the strange confines of the hare's body, he recognised the betrayal.

Having the man exactly where he wanted, the crow lord seemed to change mood.

"Having you here, all small and hairy, sleek backed and bright eyed, brings out a rare tenderness in me. For a little while you shall travel with me and see how I earn a crust. It may be that it gives you some little breadcrumbs of inspiration for your own sorry state." And with that, the two of them melted away into the dark grasses.

They reappeared some miles across country, at the entrance to the encampment of the chief of what we now call Monkton's. It was dusk, the dimpsy time, the time between dog and wolf. Cold too, breath piling out in white clouds from between the old man's teeth. Peering up at his master, the hare-man observed the mystic's new shape. He now resembled a fool. His ears poked from his hat, his cloak was threadbare, his boots sloshed with hedge rain, and he held the thin stem of a holly branch in his white hand. He had a sword without a sheath, and a small leather bag hung over his skinny shoulder.

When the fool claimed that he had an evening of tricks for the chief, the guards let the freak and his hopping companion in. In the torch-lit hall, the stranger began his show.

He pulled a simple lad from the crowd and had him place three straws on the man's hand. With lyrical breath the fool blew the middle straw away whilst the others stayed dormant on the white acres of his palm. Each trick procured more silver from the chief; each trick grew more audacious, more majestic, until finally the fool looked directly into the eyes of the chief.

"Great bear, wise power, and council of these western lands, for this next trick I will require more than silver. Will you give me ten pieces of gold if I show you something you've never seen before or will again?" The people turned their longing eyes on their slouching leader. They needed a treat. With a tiny nod, he assented.

At this, the fool reached into his bag and pulled out a ball of silk. He flung it slantwise up into the smoky rafters of the hall, and suddenly there was no roof at all but a dazzling array of cold blue stars. The line of silk took hooves and started to gallop up into the night, heading without delay to the yellow breast of the moon.

As it leapt, it wove itself into a handsome ladder. Without delay, the fool reached into his bag and brought out a hare that leapt onto the ladder and started for the moon, and then he procured a red-eared hound that bounded after the hare in swift pursuit.

"Now, would anyone take to the rungs and see if they can catch the hound that is trying to catch the hare that is trying to catch the moon?" A lad of the chief's, in his cups, bellowed assent and started his lardy rump up the silken ladder. Fool yelped after: "If you let my hare be gobbled, it's your head I'll have!"

All went silent for a time. Finally, the fool started to wind down his thread, and down came the boy, curled up a-snore, the red-eared hound with just a few tufts of hare fur around his greasy chops.

Fool did not wait for conversation but produced his blade and, with two lively strokes, severed the heads of both the boy and the hound; they rolled obediently to the fireplace to see what would happen next. The chief was on his feet, distressed. "A boy and hound headless in my hall! I've been trying to put a stop to this kind of thing!" The fool raised one long finger. "For five more coins, I would restore both lad and dog to their fullness. Do you agree?" Afraid now, the chief agreed.

With muttered magics, the heads rolled back onto the shoulders of the two, the hare popped out of the hound's mouth, and both mutt and leaper scuttled back into the bag. The boy ran to the fleshy kingdom of his mother's ample breast and slept fitfully for a week or two, but had taken on no lasting damage.

With gold now handed over, the fool and his hare melted into the shadows of the stunned compound and were of a sudden back on Halden Hill, with the teller's wife looking on.

"Ah, enough of the games," said the Crow Lord. "I've hurled the bones enough for one day. You can have it all back: the money, chariot, hawk, horse, hound, house, even your mighty wife."

"Not sure I want her," said the teller, now restored to his original shape and remembering her blows.

"She was just keeping you in the game, lad; had you strayed, you would not have received the teaching of a beggarly old crow."

The teller was visibly confused, and so the ancient placed lime-white hands on his shoulders and continued. "Storyteller: I'm not just a scarecrow. Not just a bone thrower. Not just a witch. Search your memory. You know me. I am a sweet god of the far west, of the Otherworld across the waters, and many times you have feasted me in the mead hall of your jaw. Many times you have toasted my name with the agility of your tongue. When you do this I break from my chains and the oceans are filled with flowers again, the barley floods with life. So when I heard that you had suffered desertion by your stories I had to make my appearance—*to give you a story fit for a chief.*

"Later today, take the tracks down this hill, cross the gateway into the chief's enclosure, and tell him everything that has transpired. This is my gift." And with that, he turned back into the tree line and was gone. Vanished.

That night and every night after, the storyteller told the chief the story. He never wanted another story. His shoulders would shake, his eyes tear up, his belly roar with laughter; his hand would knock the table for more wine. The tale never lost its freshness and in some way was told for the first time every time.

They say if you go at dimpsy time to Haldon Hill and place your ear to the soil, you will hear the sound of this story being told, a story fit for a chief. In the deep belly of the hill, torches are being lit, wine is being poured, and hounds lie content at the feet of listening heroes.

❋ ❋ ❋

By the time I've finished, it's dark. The story has had its way with me: the response of the thin and thrumming branch, the ripple of wind over mushy bracken, the gurgles of the brown stream, all have influenced the telling, set all layers tingling in this story man.

They're beginning their imprint: their local mythologising. Tendrils are bringing the words to their mouths, tenderly trying them out for succulence. They are supreme participants in the telling of this story. It seems to have arrived as an invitation, not an imposition; a melding, not a boot print. Encouraged, I do indeed place my ear to the soil and listen. Distant drums, friends, distant drums.

The hut is prepared for its occupants. Only time will tell if it gains generational roots in Devon soil, but at least it knows it has a little *pied-a-terre*, a "foot on the ground," up on Haldon Hill.

Sometimes I get letters about things like this. The madness of squatting near a busy road at dusk, attempting to broker relationship between story and a wintering cluster of trees. As if such a thing needed to happen. As if it mattered. As a recent note claimed, "We have words for people like you: the most polite of them is *nuts*. When you give up all this smoke and mirrors nonsense, give me a call."

As it goes, I don't think it's nuts at all. Just the right thing to do. Take such an image to the animal in your chest and see how it reacts; you may be surprised. The origin of all true ritual is fidelity to the senses.

Stories travel a mighty long way to get to our mouths. They've been flavoured by ancestors, and spirits, and the curvature of the land. They are big medicine. When you really feel a story claim you, it's not necessarily comforting; it can leave you rattled for weeks. And why not? It's a surgery of the Underworld at work. Every story that really works me reassembles me a little, straightens the shoulders, pumps a little more blood round the heart. People would pay many thousands to get that from a therapist or a healer, so why does a story not require maintenance on arrival? Why is this thing called storytelling so important? Here's a little story about why.

Cultural layers

Archeologists can drink. I mean really. The table is gleaming with pint glasses settled with chewy, warm, resolutely flat beer. A pile of paper plates, foil tins, and the remains of a curry slump on the far end, still issuing their come-hither scent of spice, salt, and grease. We're in a small coastal town in the north of Dorset. Globs of late October rain boom-patter the window.

Glancing up, the oldest man, a ceramics expert, finally says what the other men certainly appear to be thinking: "So why have they stuck a storyteller into a dig with archeologists? We want the facts and you just want the story!" There's a boozy grump of approval. Two days' digging in the rain for a priory that may or may not be there has not exactly sweetened the mood.

I'd seen this discomfort coming in the runes, I tell you. So, awkwardly, I stand up and deliver my little speech: "Well, point taken. But a mythologist is more like you lot than you may think. First of all, I know you'll often walk the mud ridges of an old field looking for, just on the off chance, something worth excavating. Well, that's what we do; we just happen to be looking in anthologies or listening to other tellers to find something to get us digging. So let's say you find something. You wave your machines about and stick in your spade. You find objects, you detect changes in soil, you begin to get a sense of the time span and the cultural history of the objects—if you're very lucky, maybe an Anglo-Saxon brooch or a Pictish ring. Well, for us the stories give all sorts of little clues to the time and attitudes of the storyteller who archived the story, or to the tradition the storyteller was trying to maintain.

"So you guys bring the objects up from the slow time of their resting place. Eventually they will be painfully examined, brushed down, and confined to a cabinet. They will certainly assist research, and the gathered facts will support scholarship. I admire this a great deal. But here's what storytellers do: when they get to the depths of the dig, they tenderly bring up the story, gather themselves, and start to speak it. Animation. They are in the business of revival, of bone-gathering, of bringing back to life something many thought was lost; they give us a *living* myth, a living excavation." Bless 'em, the ruddy-faced team took it with a few groans, the throw of a mucky towel, and another exhausted shuffle to get the tankards filled.

So, living excavations require certain tools long cherished: a flint-napped trowel and no iron in sight, rather than the impatient chug of the digger. The gradient of cultural history imbedded in the layers is not to be ignored: the hedgerow knowledge, the telling details of a particular element to village life, the mutable concerns of a community and how those can change. These are all more than worthy of study; they are part of the riches of the gift. But the heart of the story? Where the salty tang of life resides? That's in the *telling of the tale*.

Later in the night, a mother lode of weather descends on the moor. As I peer from the breath-steamed window, elms are crashing down onto shiny tarmac lanes and firm houses are caught in the swagger of the wind and looking for guy ropes. I place another couple of ash logs onto the fire and decide to do some bone throwing of my own. I reach down into that ever-present bundle and start a little divining—to peer into the afternoon's work on the hill and check that the many trembling layers of story and land got served. Otherwise it will be an early start back up in the morning. It appears the work is in place.

You will have read or heard many times now my brooding on the myth-teller as a negotiator between realms and dimensions. As I crouch by the fire I contemplate the myriad ways this plays out. For example, that the woman who carries stories in her bag is a kind of frontierswoman. I like that word; I like the flavour of some wild-turkey-feather-in-her-hat kind of presence that immediately arrives, scanning the cabinet for a good shiraz. I need to think about this notion of frontiers and the storyteller a little more. So I stretch out a deerskin, roll up some goat hides as pillows, gaze into the wintering flames, and ponder.

The writer David Anthony (2007, 102) is good to remind us of the difference between the notion of border and that of frontier. A *border* lacks the excitement of a *frontier*; it is nothing special, just a thin, officious mark between two areas of geography—usually halting a flow of movement. But a frontier, that feels edgier, richer, dynamic—more of the crossroads' tavern, less of the bored official flicking through your passport.

In the centuries before large states, frontiers were generally ephemeral; there was usually an ebb and flow of bodies in and out. Titles like Teuton, Pict, or Celt were often transitory terms for smaller ethnic groups that would have found this larger identity untenable. For reasons of negotiation, it may have been politically expedient for local tribes to team up whilst in negotiation over territory with outside agents, but it generally took a matter that pressing to enforce it. Once that matter was settled, individual concerns and identity took precedence.

A frontier also did away with the sharp edges of one language crashing uncomfortably into another. There was usually a gradient of language—connecting tissue—between dialects. You could bluff your way through. It is only with the creation of the nation-state that aggressive ethno-linguistic borders start to appear—in Europe it really increases with the late eighteenth-century arrival of the French Revolution. Borders with the least human traffic have the most pronounced linguistic difference.

Frontiers are also biologically mutable, not normally a defining indication of gene pool—people transgress all kinds of lines when it comes to mating. Frontier is more crucial as a statement than a constant geography—we have only to think of the Celt/Anglo-Saxon frontier dance across Britain in the years 400–700 C.E.

Despite this, Anthony evokes what he calls "robust frontiers." Welsh to English, for example, has remained strong for over a thousand years. And the Celtic Bretons are sitting on fifteen hundred years of difference from the wider French—clear in diet, art, music, and philosophy. There comes a moment when identity becomes tied up with *not* being like those others over the hill, and the intriguing give and take of a frontier sharpens up into the spear-bristled wall of the boundary.

So it is clear to see how diffusion could and did occur in the movement of stories from one place to another. Even in the "robust borders" of Wales and England, stories, like undercover lovers, sneak through and take root in another language, imagination, and yes, culture. There will be no immediate switch to entirely new ways of thinking but a kind of residual hinterland, a testing period, whilst the story goes "smoke's way"—snakily—through the fireside tellings and storyteller gossip, into the hearts and psyches of a new group. The firmer the move from tribal ground into civilised states, the harder this becomes. Could we not aspire to some frontier consciousness again? And as we track the changing patterns of frontiers we do well to ask: What of the emerging migrations of animals?

The migrations of animals and stories

We know that snow geese are wintering up to two hundred miles farther north these days, purple finches trouncing even that with a four-hundred-mile trek from their normal nesting areas. The ruby-throated hummingbird is moving from southeast to central Alaska in this resolute move northward. An Audubon Society study, recently released, reveals that an astonishing half of 305 bird species in North America—a lively assortment of owls, robins, chickadees, and more—are all wintering thirty-five miles farther north than they did forty years ago.

Urban development and deforestation both have a part to play, but the sheer variety and scale of these new migrations are bringing many to the inevitable conclusion of climate change. Milder winters mean less shivering for the birds, fewer hard nights to get through, fewer calories to have to gather. But there is confusion—cranes wintering in Germany rather than making their long-established southerly flights to Spain or Portugal. This is a risky strategy—to remain in a climate that could suddenly turn freezing, by which point the migration is equally hazardous.

Some birds, like the pied flycatcher, are altering the timing of their migrations in an effort to keep up with the changes. The problem is that the animals and plants that are waiting at the other end of the long flight are in a different state from the old familiar patterning—a state not conducive for the hungry beaks of their nestlings. The Siberian crane is facing a 70 percent decline of its tundra habitat. These wetland migratory birds are down to just three thousand in number, the last of a grand, ancient tribe. Their attempted migrations between the Arctic and the Yangtze river are facing a myriad of befuddlements.

The world is a-slither, a-crawling, ascending to higher latitudes as it gets hotter. The moths on Borneo's Mount Kinabalu have gone from a steady rise of forty-three-feet per decade to a staggering 475. After a hiatus of almost seventy-five years, mosquito-borne dengue fever has made a reappearance in the United States. Fish once seen as southern and exotic, such as the red mullet and the anchovy, have been caught on the coast of England's North Sea.

So the animals' myth lines are in a wild state of flux, reinvention, and flat-out disaster. No one knows how this is going to pan out. What we do have are exotic creatures arriving in new and sometimes hostile destinations; ancient fly patterns trashed in desperate mimics of new weather fronts that cannot be predicted; and nests of chicks born in a land that still sleeps, briar unbudded, soil frozen. Sounds a little like us.

These are all events that would have had an impact on the mythteller's life.

Frontiers extended out from the storyteller towards a communion of speech: an embodiment that drew in the hummingbird and the slowness of a volcano's thinking. The storyteller could grasp the body language between animals and allies—what bubbled up in rapid nods and trills, or the twelve-tine antler thrust in jaunty defiance. Verbal greetings were often secondary to the twitch of a shoulder or the rapid change in a bird's wing speed. To communicate a story deftly, this all had to be brought into the sound hut of the teller's body.

Frontiers also burst into spirit communication, the invisible world. Hair-raising vigils in the depths of a Welsh mountain brought back prophetic information to the tribal stories—of numinous, magical bartering—that utilised all the rapid-fire eloquence one had, ensuring that mythtelling was more than just a market-square theatre.

These changes in weather and animal migrations would have found their way quickly into the heart of the wider stories around the campfire.

Just as faerie tales and myth are moving into a new Commons of the Imagination, so too are the animal powers splashing, hovering, padding, and winging their way into previously uncharted areas of the earth, wrenched from their home ground. Even as I write this, out there in the dark and the wild stretches, these migrations are occurring constantly, in the thousands. As we sit in front of our flat screens, read our newspapers, and sip our cappuccinos, these changes may be just some kind of background noise at the edge of our thinking. For now.

What are the new stories that these migrations and desperations will engender to the animals? Who has the furry receptivity to absorb those emerging myths in the wider frame of stories that humans have carried like precious cargo? Unless these aspects of story come together, things will fragment with ever greater speed.

What these chaotic times are inducing is a rapid move back to frontier consciousness; the indigo bunting will pay no regard to passport control. But land it must, and negotiate new policies, bartering, and opportunity and familiarise itself to new stories. All these migratory animals are having a vast education in *emerging* mythologies; their own constants, their Olympians, are but drizzle over the vastness of the dark gray oceans they fly over. Tundra is becoming forest; jungle is becoming prairie. All is new.

It may be that stories are being forced to move from their old geographical habitations because they have something important to say about this wider crisis. As the crane settles in a new and unfamiliar German forest as snow falls, so a Seneca shaman story is told in the tentative surroundings of a Plymouth pub. I believe the two emerging migrations are connected. They are speaking over the frontier divides—crow to myth, to waterfall, to folktale.

What they have to say will arrive not as statistical data but as images that tug on the psyche of the listener, that are sufficiently weighty and straight-up startling to shed new light on many coming storms—a light that is suffused with the eternal, that "time before time," rather than just the strained, stressed-out strip light of the now.

This is the other side of the slow ground: the simple fact that any mythos of now has to include migration. But Hermes, the god of the storytellers, god of the crossroads, speaks from both sides of his mouth. The mythteller looks both ways.

Tracking moon on water

It's early morning now, and I've not had enough sleep. I've dreamt of a bear standing upright, under the moon, on Haldon Hill. That sort of thing wakes you up, gets you thoughtful. I open one baleful eye and glance round the room for any stories ready to be told. Seems they fancy a lie in. They're not the only ones. I pad down the stairs to make some coffee and prepare my daughter's breakfast. Soon there'll be the school run: shuffling precariously through the rabbit warren of early morning Ashburton, the car full of the anarchic gossip of nine-year-olds, with tall tales, short tales, and whatever they can glimpse out the windows. They are not yet immune to wonder, and witnessing their delightful boasts, their power plays, their delight at whatever the weather seems to present us with that day—it's a tonic and an education.

Soon, I'm back at the house. Lamps are low, and there's a sweet and rather private atmosphere settled. It doesn't always feel like that; the home has its procession of moods. This is pleasing, conducive to study. But there're still no stories about. No silk ladders to the moon, no hare erupting from a bag, no red-eared hound, no king's wine in my cup. So I do what tellers have always done—the *griot*, the *seannachai*, the *kalamakari*, the *gosan*, the *scop*, the *gleoman*, the *great rememberers*—the ones who sing across the blue ice for the good of their people, the old woman who croons while turning a stalk of barley slowly in her brown and ancient hands.

I call to the stories.

I am in the hut.
The warm hut of myself.

Where language is
a herding magic,
nine mares
galloping loose
on the tongue,
an equine flood.

Up in the crag-world
do you hear these whinnies?
Let the loom of my teeth
craft the wild bees furry speech.

Black clouds I am a-lightning;
I hurl rain-daggers into mud.
Black clouds I am a-shire,
loosening my muscle hoofed stomp.

The geese that flew for Parzival, I love.
The hawk that claimed three drops of their blood, I love.
The snow it fell upon, I love.

The hut is a rattle-house of sound.
A croft for wolves.
It stands in dark privacy.
Deep nested, wine briared
from the drifting snows.

Walls are the big trees
Siberian trunks, enormous
Irish voyaging stories.

Bark shines wet,

*the roots are mad
and deep,
I ramble under the
billowing skirts of
love's tall pines.*

*This twigged hump
holds the vastness
of a stag's breastbone,
a pirate's cathedral,
is a smoky den of gaudy leaps.*

*Gawain's bent head
in the green chapel, I love.
The heavy horse alone
in the orchard, I love.
The woman who lives at
the edge of the world, I love.*

*Grasses hum with beehive.
I break chunks of honeycomb
and offer them up to Dartmoor.*

*The hut shudders with foamy energy,
reaching northwards to coax the rivers—
the Tavy, the Plym, the Erme, the Avon,
the Dart, and the Teign.*

*Brittle gods are amok
in the tourists' sour heather.*

*I call the names
under the names*

*Broken Court—Breazle,
Dark Stream—Dawlish,
Great Wood—Cruwys Morchard,*

all shimmering in the gramarye
of this Kingdom of Dumnonia.

I carry green waves
from the bright girdle of the sea,
generous beer in a bronze cup
for the spit-wind.
I come in the old way.

I leave a hollowed-out hoof
filled with apple-blossom,
I haunch the dream path
up to Hay Tor, Lucky Tor,
Hound Tor, Benji Tor, Yal Tor.

The dry-stone wall, I love. The moon over corn, I love.
Branwen of the white breast, I love.

I bend my head.
I come in my father's boots,
and Alec's, and Leonard's, and Bryan's.
I carry dark bundles of my mother's hair,
and Christine's, and Monica's, and Jenny's.
The blood holds Shaw, Gibson,
Causer, Thackery, Vaughn, Bray.

I clamber flanks of bailing twine
and rusting tractor engine to get nearer
to your gurgled speech.

I break the hard crust of snow with blue paws.
I lace granite with whisky and milk.

Within the stag's bone there is a hawkish wine,
in the hare's print lies the old singing.

Let the tusks of Dermot's Boar
get soaked in the wine
of your education,
Let your milk-heavy udders
splash hot into our
story-parched mouth,
Let the wild swan at dawn
rise to meet Christ's dark fire

I ask for protection from the good powers.

Let all stories hold, heal, and nourish my small family. Let them be hazels

for our mouths. Nothing but goodness—

no fear, no meanness, no envy.

CHAPTER SEVEN

Elfrida of the Flowers

Wintering trees are always faerie tale trees; you get to witness their skeleton—the thin, bony fingers that beckon and poke as you pick your way through the half light of the woods. It's winter, and a comb of branch brings the old world closer. A land of twiggy huts and gusts of blue smoke, old ladies with bobbing heads leading you into enchantments, crows that a second later are elegant men with fine black cloaks and smokers' cackles. Magic's close.

I'm wandering through the boreal forest on the way to the shepherd's hut. Dawn. Grasses glitter, the dew is frozen. I'm laden with extra blankets and a tweed jacket whose pockets are stuffed with kindling. The temperature has dropped yet again overnight, and the radio promises snow for those of us a hundred feet above sea level.

The key turns the latch and I'm in. I don't waste time. My own breath steams out before me. My kindling's lobbed into a stack of twigs gathered back in late summer by the door, and I kneel by the small wood burner and start to scrunch newspaper. I glance up as I hear rain start its tap dance on the barrelled tin roof; in fact that's more emphatic than rain—that's sleet. Only one move away from the mooted snow.

The fire plays no tricks today and is soon furnacing the burner; I hear the pops and crackle of the wood and see little flicks of burgundy through the small air opening in the door.

There're heaps of books, a stack of lanterns, and a raised bed with a space underneath for any passing sheepdogs or lost lambs. Praise God, there's no internet signal and a distinctly erratic phone connection.

As I write, I have a curly sheepskin wrapped over my legs, two scarves round my neck, a defiantly battered trilby on head, and still the cold is resident in my hips. I get up and squeeze a large log into the grate of the burner. If this keeps up, I'll soon be up on that bed, where much of the warmth is gathering.

But I have only a little while; I will be following the trail of story for much of the day, so my dawn time must be spent singing it out into the hut. Otherwise, how will I track? I close my eyes and begin.

❀❀❀

Elfrida of the flowers

Far to the west lived a woman. There is always a woman far to the west.

Elfrida was her name. She had strong defenders. Her father was a big man, Earl of Devon, and her brother a giant, who some say built the original Tavistock Abbey.

In the east, King Edgar, the Saxon king, brooded for a wife. When word reached him of Elfrida, he sent his courtier Ethelwold to meet the woman—a dangerous journey, hoofing many miles. As the courtier wearily arrived, Elfrida met him in the doorway.

Her hair hung in two long black plaits over a tight green bodice, her eyes calm like speedwell flowers. All memory of his king's inquiry grew dim; the desire to even mention his lord became ashes on the tongue. Entranced with her swan-white skin, he was a-fever with desire for the lover's wrestle. A sophisticated courting took place, and she, dazzled by the exotic stranger, agreed to be his wife. Finally, he was to have something that even the King didn't have! His chest became puffed and his gestures inflated, his tongue positively loquacious.

> East courts the West,
> and cardinal directions
> get dizzy, just
> for the thought of
> one other.

> The evening star
> cannot help
> but pour the wine,
> when geese with
> their bales of dawn
> arrive.

But this eastern king
does not rove the lanes,
but sends a ferret
as his eye.

He should have let
his own fur
rustle the bracken.

On return to the King, the servant thought quickly. "Sire, it appears that travellers have overpraised this woman—she is fair, to be sure, but lacking the rapture that a man of your stature would befit. But she is wealthy, and for a plain man like me, she would suit. So, the journey was not . . . entirely . . . wasted." His hands were sticky as he thinned out the truth. The King swallowed the whole story, rose, and gave his blessing for his courtier to head out and live on remote Dartmoor with his new wife.

Having made his bed, Ethelwold knew that a large part of lying on it would require keeping Elfrida out of sight and making sure no one saw her true beauty. So in the castle she remained. Ethelwold would not have traded the comfort he now enjoyed for anything.

Occasionally a passing traveller would catch a glimpse of Elfrida, gazing out from behind the turrets or even turning her horse in the meadow. Even in such brief glimpses she was so magnificent that word cantered up through the country and finally got to the King's ear. Shocked and angered, the King proposed a hunting trip to the forest of Dartmoor and sent word on to Ethelwold. Cornered, the husband tearfully confessed all to a stunned Elfrida and begged her to disguise her beauty—twigs in hair, a bruised and muddy face, rough clothes—or the life they had shared would be utterly lost.

This was the first she had heard of a king. A king? She looked at him with a cold expression: "Oh, I will change my face, certainly."

Courtly knights
wander
Provencal villages
just for word
of her.

Fish wives
weave cloaks
to cover
grey puddles.

But she is a
dagger-maiden.

A lover to Saturn
and all those other
Old Men of the Night.

And all council a reckoning.

Rather than dirtying her body, she slow bathed it in milk and herbs. She washed her face with elderflowers. She wore her costliest gown and a necklace of delicate shells. Her skin was like cream, her eyes as deep as a moorland gully. Her hair was unbound and laced with Hexworthy wildflowers. Just as dawn was breaking, she rode out ahead to meet the King. When he beheld her, he loved her, this utterly untamed thing.

A hunt was arranged in a desolate stretch of the moor, and Ethelwold did not return that evening. Another union was arranged, and Elfrida and the King were married. Their son, Ethelred, became a king of England.

The woman from the far west lived a long time next to her husband in the east. But I cannot tell you that on long autumn nights she did not look up from the hearth and gaze wistfully homewards. But so it is when you marry a king.

Woman, you
galloped
to the big life.

Acres of sorrow
squeeze their mud
between your toes.

And that is just:
the hem of sovereignty

is blade and bone,
dog-rose and penny-royal.

Close your gate, and light the wick.

❋ ❋ ❋

As I crest the high moor, I am surrounded by soaking fog. Fog that obscures the purple-and-brown-scored valleys. The descent towards Tavistock always takes far longer than memory suggests, and the mere mention of the abbey is pretty much all I have to go on in terms of the story.

As I see a small gate on my right, just off the track with a rough little turning space for a car, I feel the hairs on my arm stand up. Proper spook. Just a mile or so up that track is Wistman's Wood—home of the antlered earth god Dyer, vegetative talisman of fierce pagan, black-blood consciousness, a deep chord in the great moor's music. When that rough god goes riding, it is best to fling yourself into the gorse and pelt across the bog, home to the twinkle lights of old Ashburton. Get a horseshoe above the door. But it's not the story of him and his hounds that I am tracing; at least I don't think so.

Even in this padded world, the mist breaks open as a whip-thin, Lycra-clad jogger suddenly lurches from behind a copse and then back into the wintery bank of gray, with barely a wobble. After a period of more icy-breath stomping I dimly see the small white cement blocks dappling the hillside, which tells me I am approaching the housing on the outskirts of Tavistock.

I arrive at school-run time. Mothers push, with tribal aggression, clusters of red-faced toddlers towards kindergarten; fathers crawl past in kiddie-seat Volvos, balancing scalding coffees on the steering wheel. The air is hooting with horns; lots of lurid colour flashes from the luminous cyclists and traffic wardens. After the soaking white world I have just emerged from, this scene is doubly gaudy. It is always wobbly to come down from the mountain.

I loiter around, trying to find the remains of the Abbey. Surely there is some cordoned area where a good and respectable citizen can gaze through the railings at some partitioned chunk of the past. I seem to be going in circles. I come to a sign listing some of Tavistock's high moments, including the creation of the abbey in 965, indicating that I am almost standing on it. But no luck; I just can't see it. I wander the high street, counting no fewer than four pastry shops and two soap shops. Tavistock must have a lot of very clean pie eaters. I notice several empty cafes and then the obligatory Costa coffee shop, gloating the legend: "We make it the way you like it." Well, it has worked. Through the half-shaded window, I can dimly make out surely the town's entire collection of over-seventies—sucking up hot chocolate from outsize mugs through children's straws, or nibbling on tiny Italian fancies. In an almost empty street, the one truly corporate emporium brings all the (elderly) chickens home to roost.

I'm desperate for a coffee myself, but won't go in. I'm turning all this around in my head when a man in his fifties, somehow browned by outdoor work even through this chilly winter, hands me his credit card. When he speaks, he gifts rare treasure: a deep Devonian accent. Clutching his card, I ask him what it is for. "Well, ees gawt all me savings onnit," he continues, pressing it again into my hand. It takes a moment to realise that this is not a wonderful, heaven-sent donation to a wandering storyteller but actually a request for help. He can't figure out how to use it. We get to a cash point, I put the card in, and soon he has his gold.

His openness is genuinely touching. I can't imagine there being many places in England where someone places their life savings in your hands and implicitly expects you to help them rather than cosh and run.

Minutes later, something similar happens again. I have now wandered down the same stretch several times, until a lady in early middle age emerges from next to a book stall, asking me what I am looking for. I explain that I am looking for the abbey and she gives some directions—I am, indeed, almost literally on top of it. She then goes off to get me a book about the town. Here we go. Obliged to buy the book because of the favour. An old keeper's trick. But no. She comes back, places the book in my hand and says: "A gift." A moment later she is gone, back behind her wobbly piles of Dickens, Dartmoor memoirs, and Rupert the Bear kiddies' books.

The Tavistock Abbey situation starts to become clear. It has become rhizomic, a multiplicity, a scattering. Some of the cloisters are across the road in the graveyard, to the left, and up several hundred feet is Betty Grimbal's tower—originally the west entrance. A few other stumps loiter sullenly by the Tavy—the river coursing dappled and vigorous through the centre of town, direct from the moor.

The abbey—something that must have seemed a *constant*, symbolically charged, a flame of the godly amongst the blaggard hills—now bashfully peeps up here and there, next to queues of traffic and coffeehouses ablaze with geriatrics. Friends, we are witnessing the altermodern—histories gossiping to each other, and rapidly. Mossy cloisters, somehow shrunken into the Devon turf, competing with a polyphonic blur of crow caw, exhaust rattle, and radio out of every car window.

Isn't this really a medieval scene? Just add pissing water rats, piles of excrement, hallucinating beggars, and we have the same car crash of sacred and profane. Anyone from Delhi knows this montage.

But still, there is a sense of loss. No circling cant of liturgy, no evensong: the centre is in fragments. And tell me, is everything really holy? Was Allen Ginsberg right? As early morning traffic charges like irritable ants over the corpse of the old abbey, it's hard to feel bathed in the luminous. It seems like just more of the same old crap. I find myself muttering lines from an old Welsh translation I've been working on just last night—it seems to nail just what I'm feeling as I weave the traffic.

> This eerie ruin among the alders,
> ghostly hump of bramble and thorn,
>
> was once the court of Ifor Hael.
>
> Boys don't make
> their stick-dens here.
>
> The thrush and badger
> are discreet visitors
>
> in a low-lying fog,
> or at dawn's yellow glitter.
>
> Where are the poets?
> the bard and storied-harp?
>
> or the generous lord,
> with a cup of wine at his arm?
>
> For Dafydd,
> chief of the skilled singers,

it was a bleak woe
to lay Ifor in the slick clay.

As he lit the red candles,
and the snow wetted his beard

then Dayfydd knew
that the game was up

This used to be a welcome ground,
a broad thoroughfare of song,

but is now an owl-court
for those lost in the forest.

For all fame's
beating of shields

there's no ramparts here
jutting through this ivy,

Just a moon-blue cry
from the thin, black branches.

EVAN EVANS (1731–88), ORIGINAL IN WELSH
VERSION BY MARTIN SHAW AND TONY HOAGLAND

I end up in the market. There is a working café, just tucked away in a corner. You can be sure their meat ain't organic. Still, I order the biggest breakfast I can find—eggs, fried bread, black pudding, bacon, sausages, extra bread and butter, and bucketfuls of instant, cheap, acidic, woefully bitter black coffee. The stone has been rolled away. I feel like a golden god. You won't get that nibbling on your Costa biscuit.

The café is run by "blown-ins"—newcomers to the town, a cheery couple of guys from the East End of London. They and the locals engage in true friendship—by hurling insults at each other. Each local gets and gives his or her dose; it's specific and emphatic. Maybe that's what we are missing in these corporate chains of coffeehouses: inventive insults.

But soon I'm not there. My imagination has been claimed. In my head I'm back at the small gate leading to Wistman's Wood, that remote copse of stunted oak, scattered with occasional rowan and holly. I am elsewhere.

The name is from *Wisht-man, wisht* meaning "haunted," or "faerie led." I've seen magpies—the "devil's bird"—gathered there at the entrance, carrying just a drop of old Nick's blood under its tongue. They say that at dusk the slate-gray rocks and green moss writhe with a host of adders, and that a small dog—named Jumbo—howls for an owner who will never come. Very near is the Lynch Way, the "Way of the Dead," where they used to drag corpses for burial at Lydford.

As I look around the strip-lit café, the ruddy faces slurping hot tea, the cut-out photos of eclairs stuck on the wall, the world of the old gods' wood seems far distant. But still it persists, hewing its entry point into this other story walk. Its tendrils curl around the rotund breakfast, the jolly insults, the sound of roadwork. Reluctantly I draw myself back from this otherwordly invasion—and wild Eric and his faerie wife, Godda, and "Old Crockern" and all the other antlered and bare-breasted gods of the British. But I get a sense of their import, of why they are banging on the thought-shield of my mind.

Regeneration.

So many town councils are caught up with the notion of *visual* regeneration of towns like Tavistock, but all these wild pagan spirits like Dyer have more to do with a regeneration of *spirit*, of vitality, of a good, lusting appetite. Without them, with an effective boarding-over of wildness, then the village loses its lustree and the sacred becomes so fragmented that it can no longer gather the spiral energy that this land has drawn upon for millennia. We replace the faerie glows spotted on the moor or the solitary chapel candle with the electrical promise of a coffee shop sign. That's no temple gate and no kind of trade.

I start to wonder about the faces and the scene I am in. Have I stepped back in time? Am I looking at the strong blond features of an Alan or some Anglo-Saxon from the eastern king's court? The atmosphere is a little coarse; I feel quite at home. Of this book's myth lines, this has been a lingering with the village mind. And yet the village has shown some of its better hand, its goodness.

Tavistock has not yet been remodelled, despite its council's protestations. I doubt the *Guardian* is flying off the shelves in the local corner shop. The town is gaudy, ancient, friendly, slightly boring. It's a good mix.

From now on I can't walk this story; there's no more trackable geography—
it flies away, hovers above the squabbling café folk, the chopped-up abbey, and
the tooting motors and waits for the right pair of ears and tongue to start its
telling again. It's in no kind of rush. I leave with a sense of unexpected trusts
and generosities, clear that some nobilities have nothing to do with kings and
queens.

The woman at the edge of the world

But what of the story? Right now the king wants a bride. The good king in a
story is always a hint of something divine, the tips of his crown tickling the
underside of the stars. But these men are not always characters that evoke a
strong response: the erotic charge of Gawain or the beguiling magic of Morgan
le Fay is somehow more engaging than the central but often lightly described
figure of Arthur. The more mythic a being, the less personal description the
being carries. Everything radiates from such beings, but, like the sun, they are
almost impossible to look at directly. We can't quite make them out.

In many myths there is a woman far to the west or a woman who lives at the
very edge of the world. She is beyond the setup of the sovereign's kingdom; she
is an untamed, ecstatic being but also has a regal bearing. She is a match. Just
the knowledge that a woman like that exists will send the normally staid king
utterly crazy with longing.

So the king sends the courtier west. The sovereign within us sets the
intention and we, with all our frailties, follow the impulse. The woman is
not always about a physical, earthy relationship—much of the emergent
thinking in the twelfth-century schools of courtly love was that some aspects needed to stay at a slight distance—it was distance, not erotic fulfill-
ment, that usually transfigured the attraction into delirious states of soulful
awakening. The woman at the edge of the world, whom they called "the far
distant lady," was a portal to dignified romantic consciousness, a honing of
eros into *amor*.

Equality did not come into it. The woman had to be of a rank superior
to that of the adorer, and so being her husband could not cut it. As it was,
the marriage often represented more of an economic arrangement and so was
hardly the ideal setting for the supercharged, adulterous spiritual reckoning
that was the longed-for pleasure. For many courtly liaisons, this remained a
tense game of poetics and manners, whilst others took it a little further with
discreet meetings in hay barns and loving abandon under a harvest moon.

A problem for many of us in the image of the far distant lady is passivity: Does she sit immobile, valued only for external beauty, whilst all the real adventure is had by the hungry men beating a track to her door? There is a kind of dishing out of roles and expectations that no longer feel appropriate to either women or men. And beauty as the sole source of power? That is a slow route to misery for anyone.

Of course we recall the trobairitz, female troubadours scattered over the south of France. Although there were only a few of them, their poems are earthy, gossipy, imaginative, and defiant. Viewing the school of love through their words finds a dynamic, less celestial scene. Recall Garsenda de Forcalquier:

> You're so well-suited as a lover,
> I wish you wouldn't be so hesitant;
> But I'm glad my love makes you the penitent,
> Otherwise I'd be the one to suffer (Bogin 1980, 109).

They seem to be watching their backs rather well and are not the mummified statues of male fantasy but real women enjoying the intrigues and stature of the role. But still, the role seems restricted to those of a youthful and pretty face.

Whilst a celebration of any aspect of the feminine is to be praised over a blanket repression, the sensation remains that this rarefied image could be inauthentic to a woman's wider personality. It could be dangerous to regard the feminine as "other," just another trap by beardy saboteurs to ostracise the experience of being a woman. A woman would have to feel deeply into her own nature to get a sense of the truth in that. I know women who are utterly exhausted, completely closed to the natural world, rage-fuelled, finger wagging, statistic-obsessed—what is the "archetype" for their disposition? Or for the many men in a similar position, weighed down with a kind of Hercules complex?

These days the language of the sensitive male "discovering his feminine side" is everywhere and a prime technique for attempting to convince a woman that you are a worthy candidate for sex. It's often a con. Many men are now nauseatingly adept at expressing emotion entirely from what *they* consider their "feminine side." This is often a combination of seduction and a stunted repression around mature male expression that we are all familiar with. If you haven't witnessed it, then how do you model it? I recall leading a workshop in

Ithaca, New York, with the poet Jay Leeming, when a man claimed that his testicles were really little "wombs." The women present were appalled at this handing over of his last remaining shred of maleness, and my own response is not appropriate for the confines of this book. This is not to attack crossgenders, just New Age chancers—which I will, every chance that I can get.

Who can claim definitively what is an "inner feminine" or "inner masculine"? Is there even much exploration left in the phrase? Much fertility? Why is a man drawing on the feminine if he wants to sit quietly in a forest? Writers scour their pages to find where energy crests in language and where it dips, and there appears to be a simple flatline when such exhausted phrases crawl sheepishly out from behind the couch.

A thought:

The image of Elfrida may feel one-dimensional. Where are the crusty-hoofed, foul-breathed, bloodied-thighed ruminations of this being? We know that we don't have to go far within myth to encounter the terrifying characters of Kali and Yaga, who have no wan young men with lutes serenading them at dusk, rather a bone pile of clumsy humans surrounding them in steamy heaps. The phrase *juicy*, which is often used for these beings, is very naïve. *Loaded, potent, vast*, or *terrible* may be better.

The woman at the edge of the world is not really about a human woman, and that very lack of roundedness is what makes this a myth, not a novel. Roundedness is what they call "characterisation." It's what makes certain characters relatable. The storyteller has to walk a line between sensing who within a story holds that roundedness and who is almost elemental in nature. Elfrida is a radiance, a woman of flowers, some say, the soul itself. And we just found out that the soul is tough, sometimes deceived, but will kill rather than marry falsehood.

It would be a useful discipline for all of us to refrain from trying to cram every single scene and character into the human experience. The stories are not just for us.

I have met many women who have simply given up on secondhand Jungian archetypes or inherited notions from books about who or what defines these impulses that move through them. These approaches have become unthinking, somehow. The women have chosen a more experiential route: the labour of a craft, relationship to wilderness, handling a business, raising red-faced and troubled kids, attention to dreams, delight in making clothes, unconventional lovers, bizarre and unharmonious opinions, or suddenly leaving the idyllic country for a big city.

In other words, they don't rely on the passivity of received opinion but let the energies that want to speak in their lives arise and be witnessed. To know the mythic ground you stand on is a very real desire. The longing for the living world—to reach out towards foaming wave, the yellow brightness of a wolf's tooth, or the lover's call of the nightingale—none of that is a patriarchal trap; it is a call to being a full human being. The key is to find its true resonance, not just vague platitudes.

A greater visibility of the feminine, woefully, is a very recent event. I would imagine that many more years of feeling our way into an embodied, rather than conceptual, sense of feminine and masculine is the right order of things. I know many women who are going deeper into their own mysteries, and men also. But their eyes are open: they are swallowing wholesale neither mainstream nor cultish dictates about what defines them. They, like the characters in these stories, are on a journey and will pick up the signs and boons as they go. They may well settle deep into the part of themselves that is indeed connected to the woman at the edge of the world, but the thread they hold comes *gut deep*.

Two streams from the dragon

Some do venture out into the world and track down the beauty but then cannot bear to give over what they set out to find. The "give away" required on instruction to Ethelwold, he cannot obey; he just cannot do it.

So this odd half-life begins, the radiant being cooped up and hidden away, herself never quite clear why this is or how this happened. The courtier, for all we know a good man, has betrayed his king and become a dragon-hoarder—a scaly one that ferrets away all that shines in the dark hill. This is no kind of life for him or his "beloved."

To deceive the king is to break a connection between soul and sovereign. To deceive the king is to have a "trophy spouse" but no real union. She has not been truly wedded. In our world this is like bringing home some extraordinary treasure but then not knowing what to do with it. A darkened basement filled with Buddha statues, dream catchers, and maps of Asia—not placing our treasure within the part of ourselves that knows how to organise ourselves around it. In the first flush of attraction, the woman would have had a glimpse of the courtier's nobility, but now that the dust has settled he cannot complete the task, he cannot bring her into the presence of true sovereignty. How many of us end up in shadowy castles of our partner's making? (It takes two to tango.) The deception is twofold when we realise that the woman has no idea about the king, that she is bonded not to the real thing but to an intermediate, a messenger boy who failed to relay the message.

To be a messenger boy is a noble tradition—a god stands behind the task, as we have seen: Hermes, who carries information between deities and the wider world. The nobility is lost when we recognise a kind of ethical collapse within the man, that he is capable of such deception to both his sovereign and his wife.

But let's own up a little. We can all understand that love's madness encourages many kinds of transgressions. We will do almost anything to stay in that lovely, woozy, inflated state. We have only to look over the parapet at Guinevere and Lancelot, or Tristan and Isolde, to see other examples of romance transgressing protocol. It is the essence of much courtly thought on love. However, this is not quite a love story—Elfrida is not in on the whole picture. She has been lied to.

The lie arises because the little man senses he could be the big man. Ethelwold, lacking the emotional discipline to complete his service to a higher cause (this is really what the good sovereign provokes), becomes a taker not a giver, a hoarder not a gifter. This sense of his becoming a dragon in his hoarding is mythologically interesting. Interesting because in parts of the world—mainly the East—the dragon is seen as a source of blessing, power, and abundance— in other words, kingly. But in many others we have this rather more typical image of the hidden treasure, the bound feminine, and a kind of impudence as to knowing what to do with it.

In his move to deception, Ethelwold makes the transition from service to the generative stream, to the hoarding stream. The dragon flips. It is up to us to decide which stream to follow—generative or hoarder—but we can't get far without raw dragon power in the first place.

I have a friend who has for many years trained as a ceremonial leader within a Native American tribal group. At a certain point in his preparation, he was told that it was time to make a choice and that the choice he made would dictate the kind of education he got from this point on. Was he to go down the route of personal gain or the route of service to the community? We have the two streams right there. He had gathered up large fistfuls of dragon power during his training—his body and mind stretched and toned—but he now had to decide what to do with it.

Ethelwold's decision is made alone. He sounds like many modern men—isolated, travels a lot, looking to get what he can from a cold world. Wants to feel big. All of us carry grandiosity—hidden or rampant. Either way, it's there. It's a tingling sensation of personal greatness, god juice in the veins. It can be hidden by depression, as a defense mechanism, or peacock large for all the world to revile. In *extremis*, we appear inflated and manic, or withdrawn and depressed. No one quite gets sophisticated enough to leave grandiosity alone entirely. Not monks, holy people, or shamans. If it is not conscious, if it is not adequately channeled in the life we lead, then it is possible that we start to entertain these kinds of betrayals in our own card games of life.

Why? Well, if we are a little bit like God, then surely we deserve more than the paltry servings that our time may or may not deign to give us. Surely we all want our name trumpeted through Rome, bathtubs of champagne and wildflowers, and sonnets painstakingly prepared on our birthday by wan-faced geniuses. We all get a little Genghis Khan sometimes. That may seem the last thing you would desire, but I would suggest that it languishes underneath all the worldly egalitarianism we pile on. The expression may differ, but it's in the mix.

The Sufis call it the *nafs*, the "greedy soul." If success comes to us with no semblance of a container, then a giant overstimulation of our grandiose energies follows, and many lofty stars will do anything they can to derail their own success—drugs, violence, theft. Robert Moore points out that the continual statistics over climate change can also cause this overstimulation. We must save the planet! Zealot overdrive kicks in, blue eyes shine even bluer, but some grounded dynamism is often missing from the message.

The whole point of chivalry was to take a brutish young knight, probably plumped up on some regional power—a feudal lord perhaps—and instill a value system that informed his emotional literacy and spiritual life. It revealed a world of meaning deeper than his own ambitions. This is really a psychological function for health. In the brokenness they would have seen scattered all around them, they would have had an intact cosmos, a goal of repair, a value system. It tempered them.

In a world that could be said to be greatly more fractured than the medieval regarding matters of the soul, when the gods are silent and the great tribes depleted, then what replaces the chivalrous viewpoint and creates anchoring for humans? Little, it seems. So we have either the wised-up believer in the gospel of nothing or the Semtex-laden religious fundamentalist.

I didn't quite understand prayer as a child. I was the son of a preacher and grew up in a lively but sometimes troubled house; prayer wasn't something I intended to take with me when I left home. But that has changed over the years. Not least, as I see it, as a kind of funnel for my own issues of grandeur. It orients us to more than our own narcissism. Any speaker will attest to the heady experience of praise and general excitement when you seem to be saying important things to a group of people attuned to the message. For a brief period, you take on something of their longings, fantasies, and projections. In other words, they send you something of their own grandiosity. Churches are often a place for the regulating of one's own importance by placing ambition into the wider orbit of the community. I saw it all the time as a kid.

So this is fine for the congregation, or audience. But the speaker is now dealing with both the speaker's own overstimulated grandeur and a mass offload by the audience. It's a hard comedown. Public figures wrestle for days trying to settle down to earth after a big success. If you stay in its fizzy orbit, it will make you ill.

Two pieces of advice. One is from Alastair McIntosh, who claimed that in the spiritual traditions of the Hebrides, when one stepped up to speak in a holy setting, all gathered knew that this was a prophetic, not a profane moment; the speaker just let something greater speak through that individual and then sat down and was quiet. There was an immediate understanding of a presence far larger than the speaker, and little expectancy of that individual after that moment of knowledge. The second comes from my friend the singing teacher and elder Doug von Koss, who claimed that every time he received rapturous applause he imagined it as nourishing rain for an enormous oak tree that stood just behind him, a world tree maybe. He didn't take more than a drop for himself. He did the same with a harsh dressing-down.

So, in both examples we have small ritual touches that regulate the flow of both projection and grandeur, that keep us active but sane. Make no mistake, the dragon is a constant in all our lives, but this tempering dictates the difference between the generative and hoarding streams.

Shelter verses comfort

Second, we might consider the trade of shelter for comfort. We do well to wince at Ethelwold's preservation of comfort at all odds. It's a move that takes us right back to the beginning of this book—the story of the fox-woman and her pelt. We could say that the West has been trading shelter for comfort ever since.

Do you remember the talk of nomads, a few chapters back? All nomads understand the need for shelter, for the black canvas to defend against the lively desert sand, or the life-giving flame that warms us against a Tuvan winter; without the ingenuity of shelter, we die. But that canvas breathes, is a porous door to the wider desert; you have only to step feet away from that fire to experience the reality of snow. Shelter gives us enough ground to behold a wider world. But as comfort becomes our highest aspiration, our peak religious experience, we must be aware that it is rapidly becoming a sedative. Comfort can dull us to merely seeing, but the porosity of shelter raises us to beholding.

The difference is never clearer than when we are huddled on the top of a hill during the wilderness vigil. A long sash of tarp deflects the majority of raindrops, but it's not the robust anesthetic of bricks and mortar most of us are used to. Bedding may be a sheepskin not a mattress; drink is water not wine. But friend, look at that rolling flank of smudge-gray cloud, the glitter-green tide below, the peregrine aloft in his ruminations—is that not a world in full disclosure?

It is dawn when Elfrida rides out to meet the king. Daylight: the end of shadows, of rumours, of the indistinct. Dawn is of great significance in the wilderness fast. After an all-night vigil on top of four days without food, the first budding pinks in the night sky are something never forgotten. You take the experience with you.

Dawn is also popular with poets and ecstatics. Within the troubadour tradition there is a small but significant strand of poems entitled Alba—dawn poems. By the thirteenth century these poems were being sung in several voices and often with music, in a recognised genre of their own. Common to all the poems—and there weren't many, possibly eighteen—was that they described the grief of lovers who, after a night together, separate as the sun rises, as it would be too dangerous for them to be caught together. The poems also have a triad of characters in the guise of a night watchman who will announce the coming dawn. Sometimes lurking in the hedgerow will be an irate lover or jealous husband. In Franklin Lewis's study of the poems, he draws relationship with these themes and their continuance into Shakespeare's *Romeo and Juliet*—in particular the scene of Juliet at the window as she talks down to Romeo about whether they can hear the call of the nightingale, "nightly she sings on yon pomegranate tree" or the lark, "herald of the morn" (Lewis 2000). Her nurse fills the ancient role of the watcher and announces the arrival of Juliet's mother. Romeo slips away. The long night of soul-filled union is over.

But I doubt that Elfrida feels such affections for the night just gone. She has been duped, not wooed. Dawn is a hinge: between dream and clarity, rest and labour, solitude and bustle, shadow and awakening. It is this awakening that seems to be the state of play. She is literally dressed to kill, resolutely stepping towards her rightful inheritance.

In her position, dawn is not heralding the pain of separation, rather the arrival of what could be the beloved. It is less the anxious watchman and far more the haunting lilt of the muezzin on his minaret calling all to prayer, to true "waking up." This is more in line with the psalmist: "Weeping may endure for a night, but joy comes in the morning."

If we have wondered about a certain lack of personality in Elfrida, we certainly experience a sea change in mood when the courtier confesses and insists she muddy her beauty. First she hears that she was meant for a king—another life entirely, one not hidden in paranoid shadows—and second, that she needs to disfigure her radiance for the good of her and Ethelwold's continued relationship.

At this Kali finally enters, the one with the blade. There is no passivity here. The knife knows when to cut blood-deep, sharply, emphatically, and finally. So change she does. She rides out more resplendent than *ever* to meet the king and the vertical world he carries with him. There will come a point in a woman's life, especially a woman who has learnt to hear, see, think, smell, and sense mythologically, when enough is enough. She would rather bite her own leg off than stay in the trapper's snare one moment longer. Elfrida knows she is inviting her husband's death as she does this. But when the marriage of sovereigns is occurring, there is no longer a need for the messenger boy.

It may be that a kind of sobriety enters at this stage in our life. The courtier can be perceived as a stage, a lightweight flirtation turned bad. The death is the end of that era. To enter the sovereign's marriage is to make soulful awareness paramount. Not to deny humour, goofiness, and just plain waywardness, but it is a move towards psychic health. We cannot hope for these riches without the inner king and queen. But to be in touch with soul can be uncomfortable, painful at times. We are as close to sorrow as we are to joy's upswing—all is amplified. It is that part of us that will look and wistfully dream of simpler times.

The nomad in the local (2): A Scythian Camelot

The story touches on the business of invasion—Anglo-Saxon in this case. But if we get too sentimental about some numinous, original breed of Englander, it is with broadening our commentary and addressing a controversial notion, one that goes to the very centre of English mythology—the Arthurian cycle. I cannot conceive of a greater conversation starter of the nomad in the local than this particular confluence.

C. Scott Littleton and Linda A. Malcor (2000), two scholars of folklore and anthropology, have made the case that the core of this tradition is not Celtic, but Iranian. Scythia was the western segment of the vast "sea of grass" that extended all the way from the Altai Mountains to the Hungarian Steppes. Everyone in this region spoke a variant of northeastern Iranian. The academic perception is that the changes in dialect were minimal and that tribal groups were bound in a common culture. They were fierce; unlike the Celts, who were still utilising horse-drawn chariots, they were on horseback, fighting with bow, lance, and sword. In a show of equality, women fought alongside. In fact, it was said that there was a marriage law that forbade a girl to marry until she had killed an enemy in battle.

This was the nomad culture of the ancient steppes: the Scythians, the Sarmatians, and then later the Alans of classical times. They adored art engraved with animals, often with great curling manes of gold, and interestingly were often blue-eyed and blond-haired. Part of the theory of Littleton and Malcor is that, as this culture followed migrational patterns to France and England, they carried a kernel of stories—their myths—with them.

In the year 175 C.E., the Roman emperor Marcus Aurelius sent a contingent of 5,500 Sarmatian cavalry to Britain. They were posted in groups of five hundred along Hadrian's Wall. When their fighting time was done, instead of returning overseas, they settled in a *vicus*, or veteran's colony. The post was very near the modern-day village of Ribchester, up in Lancashire. Their commander—practically hero-worshipped—was named Lucius *Artorius* Castus, prefect of the Legion VI Victrix, who was charged with the defense of northern Britain. During late antiquity there were numerous occasions for the steppe Iranians to have contact with Europeans and to permeate the stories that eventually became the fuller medieval picture.

The theory is that certain key motifs and characters in Scythian mythology fit unusually well with the Arthurian canon. There is a magical cup called the Nartamongae, a grail-like vessel that appears at feasts to the most worthy and never runs out of food and drink. It is not in the running as the chalice of the last supper (a later add-on), but certainly fits with earlier Welsh and wider Celtic images of a cauldron or stone.

There is also Arthur having Excalibur thrown back into a lake by faithful Sir Bedivere; the great Scythian mythical hero Batraz, when stricken with guilt over much destruction, also orders his sword to be thrown into water—this time, the sea. Both henchmen fail to accomplish the task several times, and both heroes know that their henchmen are lying because they are aware of magical occurrences that will take place when the sword is thrown. For Arthur, it is the hand of the lady of the lake reaching out; for Batraz, it is the waters turning wild and blood red.

Even the beginning of Arthur's work life—the drawing of the sword from the stone—bears resemblance to the old Scythian motif of a great warrior drawing a sword from the soil. The name Lancelot—never perceived as British in the first place—is suggested to be a derivative of Alan of Lot—the Alans being another well-travelled Scythian group. It's intriguing at the very least.

Nomads breed nomads

The Alans arrived several hundred years later, in the fifth century, and married into families in France. The Alans were serious business, carrying heavy reputation. They loved fighting, adored their wagons, and regarded it as an unutterable embarrassment to ever be caught on foot. Although they carried their heritage proudly, they assimilated well. Ageing was not encouraged, and killing your parents was seen as quite reasonable behaviour if you needed to spread your wings a little.

As consummate horsemen and warriors, the Alans enjoyed all sorts of privileges, continually intermarrying into the next invading force to the point where, when William the Conqueror took over England, many of the French-afforded English estates were in fact those of the Alans—feudal and landlords over the conquered English. It was partially these very knights who commissioned the medieval Arthurian romances that then fed back into France and had such an impact on troubadour culture and the courtly love ideal. Could it be such a stretch that their enthusiasms for the stories were partially a recognition of ancient tales surfacing again in their new home?

It is ironic in the extreme that those very Lords of William helped create a *new* nomadic culture—not of the steppes, but of the Greenwood—as a reaction against the brutality of their own regime change. As we will see later, these invaders forged a strong, marginal consciousness in the relegated, on-the-run lords, minstrels, and wolf's-heads, who took to the forest to form retaliatory strikes against the "Norman yoke." Funny how it all comes around. Up sprung Eadric the Wild, Brumannus, and Brave Hereward the Wake to combat the most recent set of invaders and ignite the oppressed imaginations.

> *In their lairs in the woods and waste places . . . they laid a thousand secret ambushes and traps for the Normans.*
> Flowers of History, thirteenth-century chronicle

The arrival of William was a great class leveller—*everyone* was in trouble. Even twenty years after his arrival, there was a trail of decimated villages and homesteads in the line marking his march to London. Soon there were only two English names in the Domesday Survey for tenants-in-chief of the King. There were Ailric of Marsh Gibbon, gripping his land "at rent, heavily and wretchedly," and Warwickshire Hereward, now in service to the charming-sounding Ogier the Breton. It was an unbelievably brutal period, the land and its people flattened against Norman might.

So we have this possibility that the roots of the Arthurian canon (perceived as the very greatest of English mythology) derive from ancient folktales of the foreign conquerors, from way back when. The Greenwood rebellion it invokes, although never a revolution, instates what I call a "leaf-bowed morality," something that Arthur and the whole courtly system have been greatly sympathetic to: the idea that the margins hold a clarity of ethics that call to account the centre for its indulgences.

Where else is it that the Knights of the Round Table ride again and again, for spiritual and ethical refreshment? The two strands of Arthur and Hood are in no way opposed but mystically entwined in Western mythology. So, it could be argued that Scythian culture is behind the two most vibrant threads of English story!

Scythia holds some of the most powerful myths that we in the West have encountered. That's a big statement. It is right and probable that research should be done to investigate the mythic migratory routes, and that this canon of Arthurian stories and Iranian images be amongst them. This is an exciting development. Or at least it will be, until they figure out that the Scythian stories originate in Africa or North Korea, and then it all begins again.

We see again and again and again that a story's origin is rarely its end. It rolls around like a sow in mud and picks up fragrant lumps of cultured soil and toddles on, drunk and frisky. We find Russian fairy tales in New Mexico—or is it the other way around? The Arthurian romances, Nart sagas, and Peublo love stories keep unfolding every time we gather round a fire and the mythteller begins.

This tugging at what we presume is fact has a tricksterish goodness to it—this emerging Scythian Camelot illustrates the collective commons perfectly. Who owns the story? The people of the Caucasus Mountains? The medieval scholar? The dreamy child in love with the romances? Where did it begin, where does it end, and where do we stamp copyright? Such it is with empire thinking. As Lewis Hyde notes, "If we go all the way back to the ancient world, to the old bardic and prophetic traditions, what we find is that men and women are not thought to be authors so much as vessels through which other forces act and speak" (Hyde 2010, 19).

To an extensively literate society, the long reach of the Arthurian stories can seem bewildering if one is trying to anchor a living tradition to the authorship of specific individuals. Of course there are beloved signposts: Geoffrey of Monmouth, Chretien de Troyes, Wolfram von Ecshenbach, Malory. But to emphatically nail down the coffin proves elusive when the origination and destination points of the story are wonderfully shrouded in the mysterious. Everyone is working out of someone else. And who's to say that the story is not "working" them?

This is not always a popular idea for a society focused on the mantra of the entirely original executor of brand-spanking-new ideas. Of course, to the archaic mode of thinking, if there was no historical precedent, then it is most likely the "new" notion directly arises from the Otherworld—rather than thrashed out in one individual's mind, entirely without supernatural assistance. That would be seen as a very unsophisticated idea. A kind of sorcery. There is some tang of selfishness without deference to the divine. Hyde, a man who has worked deeply into thoughts around originality and ownership, reminds us of this quote from Goethe:

> Everything I have seen, heard, and observed I have collected and exploited. My works have been nourished by countless different individuals, by innocent and wise ones, peoples of intelligence and dunces. . . . I have

often reaped what others have sowed. My work is the work of a collective being that bears the name of Goethe (Goethe, as quoted in Hyde 2010, 177–78).

So where is the copyright? Are we to be like Benjamin Franklin, refusing a patent on his wood stove, as he understood it to be a collective, the bringing to fruition of many individuals' ideas; or more contemporary—battling it out in the law courts for the merest shred of personal innovation? Of course, part of the genius of both Goethe and Franklin is the assembling of these others' ideas into a cohesive whole; that alone blows open the distinction between "I" and "the many." Both points of view are served within one individual and create art.

Within the storytelling traditions, a certain sense of handed-down-ness is actually a sign of authenticity—it is to be admired, not avoided; it indicates roots.

The Arthurian story is too big, too well travelled, too deep, too robust to have irate steppe Iranians claiming it back for the Caucasus. Elvis has long since left the building. And in the same way, Celtic scholars will have to suck on that same lemon as long-atrophied ideas suddenly leap thousands of miles to the east. This is a Commons of the Imagination now. The claims of diffusion through Europe, or even of Jung's rather exhausted *collective unconscious*, are but milky teats hanging on the magical belly of the stories as they amble through the known and unknown worlds.

> *It is difficult to begin without borrowing.*
> HENRY DAVID THOREAU

CHAPTER EIGHT

Liminal Culture (2)

IN THE LAND OF WESTERN DREAMING

The room was gently rocking. My throat was clogged with rusty nails and the prickly fleeces of a hundred furious rams, all charging deeper into my lower intestine. This is how storytellers announce they have flu.

That regardless, the room was still rocking. It took a minute or two of the sway before I could place myself. I wasn't in the tent or the caravan or the crumbling Victorian house on the edge of Ashburton I now called home. I was half a world away. On a boat.

I aimed my hot bones northwards, headed up the fuzzy nest that is my brain, and shakily peered out a window. Oakland harbor and the wider San Francisco bay leered back. This was a long way from what I knew. A long time had unfolded since those days in the tent.

In those passing days I had become reasonably known as a teacher of story, and it had become a tangible, demonstrable form of work that tied together my love of both the forest and the village. This gift gifted me too: always something of a diviner, I learnt by glancing at a burning candle—at its splutters and rasps or steady evenness of descent—just how a story was working its way into a room of people; or the moving wispiness then density of shadows on the back wall would whisper something astute of the particular ancestors that had rolled up to listen that night. Both would influence what I had to say. I was a diligent student of these things. Powerful moments happened when these old stories entered the hall, tapping their canes, adjusting their elaborate cloaks, and fluffing up their feathers. The way I was able to witness stories seemed to have become something of an event. Before I knew it, word was out, and the road opened up before me.

So I'm a week into an extended foray of American teaching, all the way from Santa Fe in New Mexico, up to Port Townsend in Washington State. Seven nights before, I'd flown through a red-skied lightning storm into Albuquerque and, not warned of the change in altitude, wondered why I was in a permanent state of mild breathlessness. Still, the land and the warm reception had acted as a stabiliser to my wooziness. Teaching on the bleached recesses of that antique ground felt like being on some cherished ridge of the moon, unutterably different.

As is so often the way, I was just beginning to find a little conversation—or at least a phrase or two—between the water snakes and mesas, before it was time to clamber back into a plane and be propelled over the simmering dust of Arizona to Northern California. I remember resting my head against the seat, squashed intimately and scent-close to a buzz-sawed young man with "I Love to Cage Fight" on his t-shirt. Beautiful.

It was around then that I'd felt the first tightening of the throat, the first dew-light bead of moisture on the forehead, the ache when I blinked that indicated the Lord and Ladies of Head Fever were plumping up the pillows and setting up residence in my skull. I rapidly closed my eyes as my neighbour cranked up Slayer on his earphones, grunted twice, and had a nice, slow scratch of his crotch.

As the plane tilted, I wandered through some recent memories. I found myself back in Santa Fe, the very day before. I had been wandering the market and ended up just off the main drag, waiting for a lift to the cabin a few miles out in semidesert that was providing a temporary home. I was feeling dislocated from the familiar and straight-up lonely, and the notion of weeks of teaching without the rough and tumble of my little family was weighing heavily on me. Too many trips away. I was feeling burdened.

I was sitting on a wall, admiring the low-slung quality of the town's adobe buildings, when I caught the scent: that same stuff that, years before and thousands of miles away, the medicine man had lit for his ceremonies—a very particular, especially fragrant sage. I jerked around and glanced up and down the street. Just normal stuff transpiring—the slow grunt of traffic, a heat haze crowning distant hills. But man, I could smell it.

I turned completely round now, and the scent grew acute. From between two buildings there was the tiniest of alleys, and walking steadily out from between them came an old Indian holding a lit bowl of the sage. Probably late middle age, mirror shades, baseball cap, Levis, skin resolute witness to a life led in the full glare of the sun.

He didn't look left or right, didn't indulge in conversation, didn't ask for change. He just produced an eagle feather, leant down, and wafted the smoke from my boots to my hat. When he got to the top, he tilted his head and finally spoke. But what came out was not everyday words but a song. Something traditional? Yes. Something stirring? Yes. Something from the depths of his people's tradition? Not exactly.

In the glaze of that spring day, with my own startled reflection mirrored back in his shades, the Indian cleared his throat and, in a gorgeous, tobacco-strewn timbre, sang:

> Amazing grace, how sweet the sound,
> that saved a wretch like me,
> I once was lost and now am found,
> was blind but now I see. . . .
> Through many dangers, toils and snares,
> I have already come;
> 'Tis grace hath brought me safe thus far,
> And grace will lead me home. . . .
> When we've been there ten thousand years,
> Bright shining as the sun,
> We've no less days to sing Gods praise,
> Than when we'd first begun.
>
> JOHN NEWTON

I'll never hear the hymn like that ever again; its quiver of blessings couldn't release its arrows with such mysterious lustre twice. It was like getting skewered on raw beauty. A sound made before Eden.

He tilted his head in that curious way again, like a fox, as if to make sure whatever had needed to land had landed, then turned around and disappeared down the alley. Astonished tears. Well, all right then, señor, I'll continue. There we have it.

America. Only a few hundred years ago the people of the boats had sailed from Plymouth docks, just a few miles down-country from me. Into the west. The dreamers, the rowdy adventurers, the slick entrepreneurs, the unutterably desperate, the pale-faced kiddies, the villains, the mystics, the mean ones with squint eyes and vast jaws, ready to tough out whatever was coming. They wanted a new story.

The New World. That's what they called it. But I want to give it another name. An older name. A name that, deep down in the barley dust of our bones, back in prehistory, we would have known. A word that squats firmly in the understory of the pagan imagination.

The Otherworld

A name that would have resided in the mythic memory of we who waved the boats away. The old belief that when you sailed west you sailed into the Otherworld. This is a belief with teeth, nerves, and vital organs. A belief that swishes its tail over all our literalist banter of acreage, start-overs, and opportunity. To the Welsh, even Ireland was *Dreaming Across the Waters*, the place our great heroes sailed with the wounds of a culture about them. All the wounded of Europe sail west. It's where they go to dream and to die.

So in some archaic way these pioneers sailed into the land of the dead whilst attempting to outrun their own. To outrun the fates. Somewhere in my fever, I realised that I had arrived in a kind of Otherworld.

Ever since I had started to teach over the waters, in that very dream time, the most sincerely delivered query had always been: How do I claim a relationship to the wild in a place I didn't, to all intents and purposes, come from? It would take someone with a darker skin than mine to start delivering authoritative statements about old America, so I could offer only wide-eyed and recently arrived musings.

Although the history books would have us believe that a mythos can be wiped out by annihilation of a human culture, that's still seeing things through the witchy eyes of the conqueror. A real mythology is held at least equally by the condor, doe, green river creek, and red-dirt dreaming. I had been overwhelmed by the mythos of Turtle Island since the moment I had arrived. It had gone no place.

What had gone somewhere, most tragically, were the age-old intricacies of a deep and splendid ceremonial, farming, village, and mythic relationship to the island. Not entirely, but for the main, the original peoples that had stood in the full flow of the land seemed scattered and adrift. I have no words for the degree of that tragedy.

But to anyone on that huge island: *get back out there*, was and is my council. Not as devourer, but one prepared to be devoured. The spiritual seeker who seeks nature "to get some healing from it" is, surely, a subtle manifestation twice removed of those who continually use it for financial gain. We have to give up "to get." No river creek responds to "to get." They've felt the lash of that tone before.

The point of the wilderness fast is the willing abdication of any kind of advantage. A visible loosening from food, wristwatch time, any of the normal "comforts" of modernity. So the manner in which one goes onto the hill is paramount. As an offering. It is usual that only when the odd buzzing of a human mind has been ground down into fine particles and released to the tireless winds do we maybe get an inkling of what the earth's thoughts may be. A newcomer will not recognise the local earth-speak as swiftly as will an old resident, but that's not to say that there isn't relationship attempting to reveal itself, whatever your skin. It's usually academics with all sorts invested who insist that a heart-sore white kid sitting alone on a badlands hill is some kind of racial travesty. The sickness of amnesia is moving through the reservations just as swiftly as it is the cities.

A mythos is a being constantly in development, in movement, an unruly cross-roads between tradition and innovation. The mythos of America is something here now, not something that was. It's strung out in the most peculiar transition, but it's here. It's really a question of a long-invested devotion to beholding it and the willingness to junk probably 95 percent of the detritus that is in the way of that beholding. It comes with a price. Your life would look different. Where it could be heading is a shape and constituency that we have never witnessed before. It would most likely look like disintegration to a jaded set of eyes.

I've almost never witnessed someone coming back from a deepening into wilderness without an enormous braid of grief enmeshed in the raptures that almost certainly arise. But grief is often the feeling they didn't quite expect, or if they did, it proves not a passing influx but a way of seeing.

So, gird yourself for sorrow was the council. But sorrow is not necessarily lostness. It's sanity. Waking up. You can go out and see America all you want, but until you behold it, there's no relationship to be had. And I'm not talking a perpetual poetic reverie but knowing the bones and vital organs of a small stretch, of digging in. Maps, sitting with the old folks, night vigils, wanderings (I'm English—I don't approve of the word *hike*) hedge knowledge and the assorted pragmatisms of attending to a land that may, one day, glimpse itself briefly through your eyes.

It was in America that I realised that, if we were in the Otherworld, then deep down many of us secretly suspected we were ghosts. What other reasoning could I find for the way so many seemed to glide through their lives, touching little? The media bleats its message that a substantial life is one viewed by thirty million, and when we don't receive that, the only conclusion is that we don't deserve it. And so begins the inelegant contortion of trying to fit in. Every layered numbness, every cryptic cloak disguising honest speech, is a step towards thinned-out ghoulishness and, ultimately, deep lostness. That's where despair lives.

There comes a point when a society in this kind of trance will consciously unwitness anyone that behaves differently. They will stare through you. Try to make you the ghost that they themselves are becoming. Damned if you do, damned if you don't.

Amongst the eco set, the premature intelligence and even strident wisdoms of many of the young people I met also disturbed me. They meant that in some way the youngsters' parents had let them down. It was as if twenty-year-olds were having to squeeze into the britches of elderhood because of a mass abdication of the task by their parents. They were adopting enormous spiritual attitudes that have always traditionally been held by much older folks. I just didn't hear enough about hell raising, unrequited love, and shitty jobs. I didn't smell enough life on them. Those polished little "I" statements just kept rolling off the tongue. Every time I heard the phrase "going to India," it meant their mythology was in pieces around their feet.

I spent a lot of time listening to people talk, and a large part of that was witnessing what stood behind them. Not in some psychological sense, but to literally witness the deities that crowded around the back end of their syntax. I wanted to see what temple they served in.

No matter how agile the speaker, how impassioned, how coherent, how current, I rarely caught that little crosswind flicker that meant their little story had a tributary way back, running to the big ocean. That's a whole other soak; the water is way deeper out there. So, over time I started to name whatever myths or folktales the speakers were unconsciously rubbing up against in their speech. Not as a diminishment but as ballast, as firmament, as real firepower, as confirmation, as the beginning of a mythos they could carry in their jaw. As soil.

A clear argument could be that these folk are in an accelerated time frame and don't have the luxury of a misspent youth, that they are facing complexities their parents never did. I'm prepared to absorb that, whilst not letting their parents off the hook. But advice, regardless, is the same: Your insights, though brilliant, cannot yet carry the chthonic weight of images that have trawled countless thousands of years to lay their treasure at your door. We could learn to bend our heads; otherwise we are just kids with laptops and a point to prove. Filled with spirit, but low on soul.

But I admire the intensity of the search. I really do. It's something that the English—still so constipated by history—would do well to consider. The notion of America as the orphan of Europe is a mythic one. It's always the orphans that become culture heroes in the old stories. Don't take too much inflation from that; just consider it awhile.

Ancestor worship won't carry us too far either. By all means find ways to authentically and sometimes imaginatively ground yourself in the traditions of your people, but don't fantasise too often that they had one foot on Mount Olympus. They are the ones that got us into this mix in the first place.

As has been said better by others, in the end *you* have to become some kind of nutrient-rich, many-boughed tree of splendid crookedness to the ones coming. If you achieve nothing else, create some shade for the seedlings to grow. Practice becoming an ancestor. Outrageous and maintained generosity, a degree of useful wiliness, and worker's hands are all identifying characteristics. Identity comes not from what you claim is your innermost self but from the myriad ways you reach out and touch the world. They are your tribal marks, your pirate banner, your relatedness; that is what will have you claimed at the gates of heaven as a proper human being, not the hundred times you put your own whims first.

And in all this, I still say, get out on the hill. *Before* you become farmers, activists, travelling circus people, reindeer herders, temple makers, green politicians, actors, silversmiths, writers: get your ears tuned in case it's just *yourself* that you're listening to.

I digress. Again. Back to the boat. A companion on this wandering was one Daniel Deardorff, out of Port Townsend. Consummate storyteller, musician, ritualist, writer, and holder of immense thoughts for the good of all, Danny was meeting up with me in San Francisco, and from then on in we were in it together, teaching all the way up the coast, to his hometown. Thousands of miles, bobbling along the roads towards the great forests of the north. There're few pleasures more honestly wonderful than watching this gorgeous, complicated man teach. Everybody falls a little in love with Danny; I don't know how he bears it.

On the face of it, little went right. The sickness got deep into my bones, and our events were woefully underadvertised and booked into way-too-big venues. Night after night we gazed out at barely heated churches, small theatres, and the graveyard teeth of several hundred empty seats. The joy of hearing Danny teaching was a little diminished by my flu and by the minuscule scatter of audience swimming in my vision.

The couples we would lodge with all appeared to be unravelling their relationships at dramatic speed. It was uncanny. We arrived at one place literally as the bed was being removed through the front door by furtive hippies; the windows were wide open, letting in blustering rain. The host had disappeared into the fields, his wife in the truck with the engine running. All was loosygoosy, hay bales untied and flying in the wind.

By the time we hit Oregon, workshops were being cancelled ahead of time; before foot even touched tarmac, we would be met by promoters already shaking their heads. Relentless dumps of bad news and nagging anxieties would crackle down phone lines from back in England as the weeks wore on, and we all were gradually borne down with seven shades of homesickness.

One morning I couldn't stand it a moment longer. To hell with it. As our small van trundled through yet another tract of endless West Coast forest, I resolved silently to quit. No more stories. Sick of the price tag, sick of the life.

The very second I had the resolve, a small bird flew directly into our closed window, right in my line of vision. A distant smack on the thick glass.

Blood specks. We pulled over about twenty yards later and I ran back through the light rain to the bird. Its heartbeat was a wild drum thump out of its chest that gradually slowed; it died a minute later in my hands. I crouched down in the early morning light and said the old prayers. Soon it was just bones and feathers. The air was sharp and golden.

When you stop telling the stories, precious things fall dead out of the sky. I stayed still for some time, the engine of the van idling a discreet distance. And then, out of the reverie I realised I could hear something over the low wind. A creaking. I looked to my right and saw there was a small home a little distance from the road, with a slowly rocking house sign. No one was about. The name of the residence was just two words:

Martin Home
Shamed in the best sense of that word, I got up, walked back to the van, and stopped complaining. I *was* home, with all the difficulty that ensues. There was nothing I could quit. This is what life looks like sometimes.

It would be a salve to say that those last few weeks got a Hollywood make-over, that Danny and I gazed in wonderment as the audience we deserved rolled in, waving books for us to sign. Can't do it. It didn't happen that time round. The moment with the bird showed us both that we had an audience all along, that we were witnessed doing our work, with or without humans about. The gatherings stayed resolutely minute, the venues still too large, although we attracted our first stalker. A bald, shadowed man who would appear mid-event at the back of the halls, a swinging pentagram round his neck, jerking spasmodically as if under the fists of an invisible puppet shaker in the gallery, as though he were at a rave with no music. No one, and I mean no one, would be claiming that as victory. Maybe he'd come over on the boat, all those hundreds of years before. Only Danny and I saw him.

Early one dawn after a thirteen-hour-straight trek with our valiant driver, we rolled into Danny's complex up in Washington State. Weeping with relief, steam rolling from our shoulders, we blessed each other, rested, and a few days later I was preparing to leave America. Exhausted and killing time in a book-store before the flight, I came across the growingly rare sight of a mythology section. Way up on the top row was a thick anthology of African folktales. I reached up to get it, and the book next door jutted out, something tiny and small. I pushed it back in and reached again for the exotic tome. Again it remained firm and the little book stuck its slender neck out. Irritated now, I shoved it back in and made a final grab for the bigger book. This final time, the small book squeezed itself out and fell to the floor in front of me.

I kneeled down and picked it up, glancing briefly at the cover. I was looking at a black and white photograph of an old blacksmith's forge that my father had played in as a child. The book? *Folktales of Devon.* I travel the world telling stories and am led to a photograph taken less than two miles away from where I'm born.

It would be easy to assume with these few stories that any underlying mes-sage could be surmised as: *Get out of America, you imbecile.* But it has proved more nuanced over the years. What I can state is that the experience eventually led to that hurling of a twenty-mile lasso round the hoof print of where I come from. It led to me digging in.

It also led to me returning over and over again to this Otherworld of the far West, but teaching more and more of what I knew from just outside my door, in all its ordinary grandeur. And sometimes at the request of Native folk as well as that of someone who looks like me. It's quite a thing to see an old

West Country story be recognised by a tribe and gleefully taken into their hoard of stories—without a blink, I tell you. It wasn't a call to hole up in the shire and never peep out again. That's called *hoarding the gifts,* and that's a dragon's thinking.

A Peculiar Social Position: The Cunning Man and the English Pagan Spirit

Five pounds, three maidenheads, and a broken shin.
The rogue wizard Joseph Heynes recounting his takings at Ware, Hertfordshire, in the year 1676

So, my "digging in" has led me into study of the English cunning man and hedge woman. These characters occupied a peculiar social position—as edge people—sometimes feared, spookily charismatic, maligned by the clergy, but offering immediate response to the magical reasoning of the medieval era. These folk were not often practitioners of hardcore witchcraft (although some could be persuaded) or high-end court magicians, but men and women with a broad mix of gifts and sincerity: those with hedgerow knowledge, many with a bent towards smoke and mirrors, and the occasional genuine seer. Court records of the time relate that, although frowned upon from the pulpit, these characters rarely did long terms in prison. Necromancy and ritual murder would get you there, but these rarely constituted the daily trade of the cunning man.

If you were the unhappy victim of nose bleeds, cramps, aches, inflammations, or unsightly swellings, it is likely you would go to the hut at the very edge of the village. If you desired divination in order to see if you would outlive your husband (a popular choice), then you headed in the same direction. Magic often involved recourse to the oral tradition—here is an old Devonian incant for a scald:

> *Two angels came from the west*
> *The one brought fire, the other brought frost,*
> *Out fire! In frost!*
>
> *In the name of the Father, Son, and Holy Ghost*

We note a jolly amalgamation of Christian language and pagan magic, a mix encountered all over the world. Although there were public tuttings and proclamations, many edge folk merrily hurled biblical language entwined with Tudor magic at the client and were quite genuine in the intent.

When the Anglican Church did away with the holy water, sign of the cross, and fecundity of image the Catholics possessed, it replaced them with a rather stark agenda—prayer in cold pews and the baleful cry for repentance. As Keith Thomas (1971) writes, they had little symbology sufficiently rich to root the concerns of the public, many of whom were caught up with all sorts of magical combats with neighbours and enemies.

Whilst the church maintained a clear acknowledgement of magic's power, they had abandoned what Thomas calls "ecclesiastical counter-magic," which had many citizens feeling they no longer had a protection to draw on. To those out in the lonely fen and isolated moors, this was a disaster. They needed a more visual and less abstract approach to their psychic battling. As Reginald Scott points out, the empty spaces left by the departing medieval saints were swiftly occupied by the wise women of the Tudor countryside. Indeed, a hedgerow conjurer of the time, Robert Allen, wandered the green lanes with the jaunty title "the God of Norfolk."

Despite the robustness of the church's position, ordinary men and women saw edge people as generally decent, divinely inspired folk, creative in a fix. The cunning men themselves generally left the source of their gifts specifically vague—a few claimed the spirit of a familiar for guidance and honing of technical gifts, whilst others claimed they were simply doing God's blessing.

The English pagan spirit, for thousands of years fed by images and ornate mythologies, may have just about been able to tolerate Catholicism with its pantheon of angelic and saintly wanderers, but when it was so diligently pruned, when the instinctual magical thinking of the people was given such heavy penalty, then the church inadvertently opened a door back to animism.

Sir Thomas Moore lamented: "In such wise witches, have many fools more faith a great deal than in God." God's inscrutable visage peering down on the chilly-pewed churchgoer was far less attractive than the attentive ear and the healing poultice of a hedge woman. In time, relentless promotion concerning the values of hard work and prayer would pay dividends, and this older form of magical bartering would be regarded as primitive. Even so, it has never quite died out completely.

It is always a mistake to set up religion and magic as opposed forces. We recall Sir Walter Raleigh: "The art of magic is the art of worshipping God." The famed magician John Dee, known for his conjuring of angelic beings and excitable occult leanings, would have been horrified to have been regarded as wandering beyond the ken of the Christian god. His search for celestial knowledge was not a grubby end-of-pier divining but an attempt to experience the very consciousness of the Holy Maker. A dangerous enterprise but one perceived as a noble quest.

Of course, there are sticking points, but the emphasis is that magical formula rubbed closely against certain Roman Catholic creeds and Latin paternosters; both involved an invoking of keenly felt but usually invisible dimensions. Carefully thinking through this situation, the church made a subtle argument that to rely too heavily on prayer was tantamount to superstition, and one should seek natural cures before supernatural ones. Speedily heading to the witch's hut with a bout of toothache was indecent and heretical. Of course, the irony is that the herbs contained in many suggested cures could not be more natural—and who created the herbs in the first place?

Some reverends went rogue. Robert Burton furiously wrote: "Poor country vicars are given to turn mountebacks, quacksalvers, empirics." The Devonian parson Hugh Atwell acquired a rather tricky reputation as a magician because his prayers actually seemed to work. Another cleric, John Bell, was caught attempting to cure fevers by writing words on paper and giving them to anxious parishioners, and the Reverend Joseph Harrison went down for the "charming of pigs." A cunning man of power and regard, a "big man," Nicolas Gretton crossed over entirely and led an independent congregation near Lichfield in the 1650s. The poor Cambridgeshire vicar of Gildon Morden protested vehemently in 1599 that he had been absolutely acquitted of sorcery by no less than the archdeacon of Ely, but his parishioners *would not let it lie* for years afterwards. We have the unlikely (but not as rare as you may think) appearance of the *sorcerer-parson*. Some of these wild-haired old clerics had a look in their eyes that was frankly Panish.

Other techniques of the cunning man included burying animals alive to assist an ailing patient, drenching the individual in south-flowing water, or even a boisterous drag through nettles and thorny bushes. Others again boiled eggs in urine whilst weaving herbs into the tails of the cows. To ascertain if magic was being practiced against you, the task was to somehow procure a sample of the assailant's urine and boil it up, or to burn a strand of hay from the potential witch's roof, both to see if the purported offender would come running out of the house in distress. These almost pythonesque routines were not part of an overriding cosmology; they were inherited and intuited systems of local folk magic. In the neutered logic of modernity, they seem utterly mad.

A really sick client was seen as being beset by the "three bitters—heart, tongue, and eye." This belief indicted malice in the heart, bitterness and spell casting on the tongue, and the focusing of the evil eye on the individual—a malevolent brew.

It is naïve to assume that this magical thinking went on only within the working-class community. Samuel Pepys loyally carried a hare foot around his neck for colic, and Runce wore a magical ring for fortune's sake. Even Charles II was regarded as a healer—the placing of his florid hand on a citizen was meant to confer a kind of royal, hands-on healing; records insist that, in twenty years, he doctored ninety thousand people in this way.

This hands-on approach slipped under the royal nose (its only "legitimate" vehicle) and was found to be a central tenet in the healing work of five-year-old Richard Gilbert from the green hills of Somerset. Gilbert was revered as beginning his practice as a "stroker" when he was but one day old. As a slightly older infant healer, he would gather the infirm on a Monday and set about their swellings and general discomfort. When asked about his powers, the little cherub would sniff: "I touch; God heals." Another practice, grotesquely wonderful, was the hoisting up of the sufferers of wasting diseases to grasp the still-twitching hand of a freshly hung villain.

The upsurge of popularity for edge magic coincided with the wider tide of Neoplatonism that swept through Europe at that time. A clear invoking of the old pagan worldview—that the world was not dead matter but animate and utterly open to myriad communications—made the seemingly "mad" descriptions of potential cures less crazy, even in the minds of England's intellectuals. It was a world beset less by evil than by an absence of light, a world soul of immense sophistication intertwined with the inner life of all. This road of thought, initiated largely by the Greek Ammonius but brought to fullness in the work of a Roman, Plotinus, has had a profound impact on the thinking and cultural life of the West: from its revival through Nicholas of Cusa and then the Italian Marsilio Ficino, it blazed a trail in the minds of Blake, Hegel, Wordsworth, Keats, and Jung.

Aspiring magi swiftly divided up three magical pursuits to employ in this responsive cosmos: *natural magic*—accessing the elemental, druidic consciousness of the land itself; *celestial magic*—the astrological fortunes of the heavens; and *ceremonial magic*—plea bargaining to any number of assorted entities, minor league spirits, and great big angelic powerhouses. Thomas describes this as "the doctrine of correspondences," or what Cornelius Agrippa calls "the harmoniacal correspondency of all parts of the body." A plant, the moon, a menstrual cycle are all delicately and infinitely connected. Suddenly, those strange women at the edge of the village are not so mad after all.

A decent cunning man was able to both liberate imagination in the mind of the client and peer around the corners of the prophetic world. They were link people between very human issues—health, money, or love—and their correspondence with seemingly random magical happenings from seemingly different spheres of awareness. It is clear that most of them were not studying Plotinus by candlelight and would certainly have had more in common with tribal medicine people than with the rarefied apprentice magi of London.

Like the old oral storytellers, the cunning men would have to draw from the recesses of their knowledge and sense which remedy fitted which client, just like discerning which story suits which mood or which season of a tribal group. These were figures weighed down with the projection of the village or tribe, which was often an advantage, sometimes disastrous. We have moved from the ancient mythteller loosened wild with buffalo speech, to the later cunning woman dragging wisdoms like rooster blood from the hidden side of the moon. They smell different. The wayward consciousness that the cunning men represented was just as important a revelation as the fact that the world was not flat. To the witching people, that consciousness was porous, mighty, and always thinking.

Despite the many quacks and loons, the best of the cunning people reenchanted us and rebartered us to magical relationship. They, despite or because of their seeming waywardness, pointed us back towards finding our ancient mind. These characters quietly and doggedly survive, even in cramped up modern England; they are *natural* people, tuned slow to the occult form of wintering crows over a Somerset field.

In the takeover of the Americas, a potent technique to disorient tribal groups was to herd them away from their indigenous ground and replant them as far away as possible—to cut away the churning tones of the animate world their ears had beheld all their lives, to remove them from the sacred ground of their fasting spots and divorce them from the waterholes, great prairie, and local herbal medicines. To a culture that did not recognise any separation from their place, this was to literally drive them "out of their mind," their local being, their wild psyche, their place. It is a grief from which many have never recovered.

Animal call words

We like to trace the evolution of modern English through the growingly elevated traces of our conquerors' favoured dialects. Before the conquerors arrived, a Devonian would have spoken Brythonic—divided into Cornish, Breton, Welsh, and Cumbric. Devon is a word of Brythonic origin, meaning "People of the Deep Valley." After the initial push of the Anglo-Saxon tongue into the country in the fifth century, we witness three major game changes in the march to modern times.

First are the Viking invasions from around 787, bringing Old Norse, already closely related linguistically, into the mix, but bringing words like *blunder, cake, freckle, die,* and *husband,* whilst also blending with the Anglo-Saxon in words such as *awkward.* Second is a more abrupt leap with the Norman invasion of 1066 and three centuries of French as the language of power. Suddenly we have another enormous wave of beautifully sculpted sound—*forest, castle, vessel, dandelion.* An estimated 30 percent of modern English comes from this enforced vacation on Brutus's soil (himself an immigrant invader, of course). When English finally returns as the predominant language of England, we have a third burst crashing in on the nervous shores of this mutable tongue, Latin. Now we start to sound really sophisticated with the like of *belicose, equality, procrastinate,* and *foliage.* The linguist John McWhorter (2008) illustrates the ascension of the three waves with the example of the humble Anglo-Saxon *ask,* then sharpening up with the French *question,* to the clearly intimidating Latin *interrogate.*

English is a language of immigration and flat-out invasion, immune to any claims of racial purity. It bends with the aggressive winds of the conquerors, then sleeps around, acquires some elegant new phrases, and saunters on into a new century. It's not exactly sentimental. This language so associated with the genteel is a barbarous montage of power moves and bartering.

But it is not with the dainty language of parliament and tea parties that I wish to stay. In keeping with the wider book's inquiry of the rebel edge, I want to keep our gaze close to the soil, close to some oral remnant, some cunning tongue. To stay with the unlettered. And so we come to the tradition of animal call words.

Call words for animals have very rarely been taught in a formal manner, rather heard orally and then repeated for hundreds, if not thousands, of years. Less on the tongue of the gentry, more from the shepherd or horseman. Call words give us, by their linguistic roots, a map of migratory patterns into England, both before the three influxes previously listed and from a far wider degree of ethnicity.

The Welsh author David Thomas (1939), from the earlier half of the twentieth century, made it a vocational quest to gather hundreds of examples of call words and, with a prodigious knowledge of history and anthropology, traced their slow migration across Europe and into England over the last five thousand years.

Thomas draws on a distinct Arabic strand found in certain call words across England, in these cases not found in central Europe, indicating arrival by way of the Atlantic: (1) In North Arabia we find *hoit, hoit* as a call to camels; in Wiltshire we have *hoit, hoit* as a call to birds. (2) North Arabia has *heik, heik* for driving animals; Wiltshire has *haik, haik* for driving young pigs.

Rustic terms such as *derry, thurr, goosh, quishoo, hutch,* and *hillick* are not French, Anglo-Saxon, or Latin, but from the great culture of the Arabs—words that have evaded change by being channelled through the animal call words and other dialectal phrases used by working people for thousands of years. So, down in the Combes and green lanes of rural Devon, far from the candlelit table of the gentry, the farmers and shepherds were daily speakers of Arabic. Even the Arabic calling of a cat—*qsh, qsh*—is of the same origin as the Devonian call for a cat—*kaash, kaash.* A word we use daily—*shoo!*—to send away a troublesome animal, is western Mediterranean.

Thomas claimed evidence for a Neolithic emigration from Arabia, extending to the west of Britain and out in a broad band from Egypt to Finland, Scandinavia, and even the Shetland Islands in the far north. He traces this wave by the distribution of the terms *sak, sek, sok, suk,* and *sook,* all being call words to lambs, goats, horses, pigs, dogs, and cats. In these we see an oral onomatopoeic—that is, a human dialect deliberately imitating the suckling sounds of young animals when feeding. The Arabian call *saq* becomes *saak* in Galloway, *sek* in Wiltshire, and *zeck* by the time it gets to Devon.

Amongst many oral peoples—villagers, storytellers, cunning men—there would have remained this ancient strain of calling that invoked kinship with the far-off Middle East. Lost in most history books and ignored at table as guttural phrases not worth the teaching, animal call words are a secret history, a threaded field that contains the footfall of epic migrations and the urging cry of human speech renewing itself in the expression of a wider animal sphere. More scholarship is needed to frame Thomas's work in clearer light, but the possibilities are exhilarating. I have cradled hot tea on an early summer's morning and heard Devon farmers use language that seemed eerie to a human ear, but watched sheep eagerly flood the lanes of Berry Pomeroy to follow the call. And to that we now turn.

Yan tan tethera

A Brythonic remnant can be found in the sheep-counting techniques of shepherds from northern England down to the west. To prevent animals from straying, to keep some record of births and deaths, shepherds had to keep a frequent headcount of their flock. In general the count would be made at dawn and again as the last duty of the day before the shepherd's return to the cottage. This old system didn't get past the count of twenty, and so the shepherd might count up that number as often as needed, whilst moving his hand rapidly to a series of marks on his crook, placing a mark on the earth, or dropping a pebble in his pocket with each twenty.

The crook of a shepherd is a kind of animal wand—for steering, protecting, and rescuing the shaggy herd; it is also grooved, nobbled, and nicked to allow the counting methods mentioned. The stick was a companion, relief up the rutted banks on a hot day, and an aid through the icy lanes on a wintery dusk.

The call varies in different regions—the West Country count to twenty being:

> hant, tant, tothery, forthery, fant, sahny, dahny, downy, dominy, dik, haindik, taindick, totherydik, fotherydik, jiggin, hain jiggen, tain jiggen, tother jiggen, fother jiggen, full score.

Note that the *hant, tant, tothery* is the West Country slant on the *yan, tan, tethera* more northern phrasing that this wider counting is now listed under. Up in Lincolnshire, where my parents now live, the count is:

> yan, tan, tethera, pethera, pimp, sethera, lethera, hovera, covera, dik, yan-a-dik, tan-a-dik, tethera-dik, pethera-dik, bum-fit, yan-a-bumfit, tan-a-bumfit, tethera-a-bumfit, pethora-bumfit, fidget.

To actually hear this language being used by some old boy wandering the lanes is deeply moving, almost unreal to the ear, a chattering burr delivered sometimes tenderly, sometimes with full voice to the gathered herd.

As the insides of nearby cottages glow queasily to the trance of reality TV, out on the lanes in the gloom, just feet away, ancient tongue is incanted. It is a tribal enterprise to the animals, counting them all home—wrestling their curly thatches from the perils of a barbed wire fence, striding the dew to find the lamb astray in the misty copse. There is a lot of love embedded in these old words.

Place names

Rather like the animal call words, a seeded core that has evaded the three major adjustments to the English language can be found simply by studying the place names of a region, and suddenly a Celtic undertow is found across the moors and scored fields.

Devon is filled with combes: Widdicombe, Babbacombe, Combe Martin, and Staddiscombe are just a few. *Combe* has the same Celtic root as the Welsh *cwm* and Cornish *cum*, meaning "valley." As we can see, it is more often than not tagged onto other words to flesh out the description.

Celtic place names include Breazle, meaning "Broken Court"; Carley, "Fort Place"; Crowdy Mill, "Pig Sty"; Dawlish, "Dark Stream"; Maverick, "Goat-like"; Duvale Barton, "Dark Peak"; Cruwys Morchard, "Great Wood"; Poltimore, "Pool by the Large House"; Whimple, "White Pool"; and Hemyock, "Summer-like." When we factor in the number of churches named after Celtic saints—St. Urith, St. Brannock, St. Budoc, St. Necton, St. Petroc, and on—we realise that the Saxon influence is nothing like as embedded in the west as in the midlands and east.

The local dialect still carries Celtic traces; it is also there that we find a greater Anglo-Saxon route to all sorts of phrases. Just a few riches are:

- axwaddler: a peddler of ash, one who collected ash to use, when strained with water, as "lie" for washing clothes, before the common use of soap
- baastins: the first milk when a calf is born, extremely rich and very desirable to local folk
- blimmer: a mild swear word
- champeen: a champion
- cryin the neck: ancient pagan ceremony on completion of the harvest,

in which a "neck of straw" was twisted and kept safe, talismanically, till the next harvest
- gaw sparkin: to go courting
- kerping: finding fault
- musicker: musician
- tacker: a small boy

Among the people

I heard localspeak growing up in the 1970s, trailing around with my father as he first cut his teeth as a local Devon preacher. This was still a time of the heavy horses—the *gypsy cobs*, the *clydesdale*, the *percheron*—that would sometimes block the tiny lanes we drove along. There were still horse fairs, red beer, and young men and women getting sunburnt romping on the hay bales. I would peer out at them from the back window, on the way to some remote chapel, and wonder.

We would borrow my grandparents' car and take to the lanes, occasionally stopping because of the nausea invoked by the twists and high hedges. We would arrive at the church and be greeted by some positively ancient keeper of the keys. There would be a gas bottle fire spluttering in the corner, trying to persuade the damp to briefly vacate the premises. After a while, maybe ten to fifteen folks would shuffle in and settle in the hard wooden rows, some smiling benignly at the young man with the long hair and the Bible, others less so. These were often straightforward farming folk or retired teachers, all working people with faces marked deep with joy and loss.

As Clement Marten (1973) points out in his study of the Devonshire dialect, much of the county is "chapel"—meaning Wesleyan or Methodist. They show up in the wildest, shaggiest, most remote of locations. The "laukel praicher" or "Methody praicher" was a subject of keen interest.

As should be clear, these weren't the superchurches of the American Midwest or with developed outreach programmes for bringing in new converts. These were rural community gatherings and, to the outside eye, would have seemed to be in decline. Dad's style was pretty straight-line evangelical, not much metaphor, but theologically sound and always engaging. And why engaging? Because he was a natural storyteller and never made a scholarly point without warming its embers with an anecdote. I've never seen him use smoke and mirrors—he always works hard to be understood.

A major factor is the willingness to turn up and do the work, regardless of pay or the size payoff the congregation. My father has dreams just like anyone else, but he tries not to let those dreams drip like a poison into the sanctity of his vocation. Only six years ago, I drove him out to yet another rural Methodist congregation amongst the cabbage fields of Lincolnshire. Thirty years on, we parked up and were greeted by yet another beaming geriatric and let into the church. Look, there's our friend the heater, spluttering away, and the tea and instant coffee, poised and ready for after the hymns. Maybe twelve showed up.

With a smile, my father began a sermon that he may have rehearsed a couple of hundred times. Relaxed, self-deprecating, and always with an ear to the arrival of the holy, he did good service to his god. As they pressed the pay into his hand, possibly enough for gas money, I was proud to be his boy. A local rural audience is hard to impress. They have buried loved ones with their own hands, been diminished by recession, and witnessed their world change almost utterly over the decades. Dainty illusions to metaphor and ambiguous religious leanings would have caught short shrift in their eyes.

And there they sit, some of them still using the very animal call words invoked in the Middle East three thousand years ago; others bidding their sheep with *yan, tan, tethera*; others still with memories suffused with the old Dartmoor stories. I remember shiny, strange-fitting suits, hearing aids, very brown skin, small eyes blinking occasionally. Some would be the great-great-granddaughters of cunning men, and others sons of the right and proper women of chapel. A flank of Devon history gazed levelly on him most Sundays. He must have been pretty good; he survived.

CHAPTER NINE

What Price to Lay an Eye?

The Church House Inn stands firm at the crossroads of Holne as a silver torrent churns past its solid oak door. Everything I survey is dripping, soaking, and has had any possible shred of warmth drained from it. Through a sopping mist plods one horse rider, replete with luminous top; other than that the hamlet is utterly contracted.

It does not seem, I admit, the perfect beginning to a great Dartmoor spirit story. The story begins in an old cottage at the edge of the village, but as I glance round, all I'm seeing is an array of satellite dishes racked precariously up on small, shuttered-up, modern houses on the road out of here.

I start up the road from the village, past the old red phone box, past the barn that briefly held the trellis, ribs, roof, and graying canvas of my yurt when I could no longer find a quiet place for it.

It is always a longer journey than expected up to the cattle grid that is really the guardian stone for that entry point onto the moor. That slight tightness to the thigh, the gulping of oxygen-fat air—you feel that you have earned the unfolding views. The yellow of the western gorse pokes through the mists. To the right arches valley after valley, tor after tor, a rippled blur like a buzzard's wings skimming the surface of a gray pool, all feathered browns and cool teal. Punk-rock sheep wander around looking miserable, fur sprayed blue as identification for farmers. It's really cold. Again. And I have many miles to go. So, as I walk I begin the story, speaking its myth line to underneath the tarmac. The occasional car passes, school kids pointing and laughing at the muttering man with his odd gestures to buzzards and far-off hills.

THE MIDWIFE AND THE BENJI

Night. A storm on the moors. Rain battered a harsh tune on cottage windows, cattle sheds shuddered as if needing rope. The old midwife, Morada, had stoked the embers, had crawled under blankets, was settling to sleep. It was then she was disturbed by a knock at the door of her Holne cottage.

She pottered down through the flickered shadows of the creaking house and opened the door. Peering into bright rain and flooding track, she was greeted by what she recognised as an earth soul, a benji, a faerie. A slim figure on horseback, he leant down—a murmur in the agitated night—and offered her ten gold guineas to deliver his child. His voice was strange, like water passing over stones.

She swiftly agreed. That was a great deal of money. He bound her eyes in a handkerchief and they took to the green lanes, up to the high moor and into mighty gusts of wind and rain. Past Vennford Lake, over the bridge at Hexworthy, past the old chapel and then on in the general direction of Bellever Tor.

> *Old arms grip*
> *a slim waist,*
> *alive in the surge.*
>
> *This old oak*
> *now hugs tight*
> *her fey chauffeur.*
>
> *A girl again*
> *straddling the rain-horse,*
> *the glitter bright track,*
> *this clattering night.*

Somewhere out in the fusty acres of weather they got to the benji's cave. A few waxy candles spluttered next to pools of brackish water; indeed the entrance was little more than a small hole, deep ridged with brambles.

Inside was utterly different, like the longhouse of some ancient moorland king—ornate patterning skillfully hewn into thick pillars, the floor cosy with animal skins, a fire glowing, its smoke sweet like dried herbs. And there was music, music so tender it would have pricked tears from your eyes. Morada crouched by the faerie-wife and settled to her task. Faerie or not, this ritual she knew. By candlelight she delivered the baby, wind screeching through the sodden branches outside. The whole moor was a-shake that night.

Part of her instructions was to rub an ointment—a kind of mud—on the baby's eyes. She did so but, of course, got antsy to try a little herself. Just the one eye. What could be the harm? Well, it stung a little but that's it. After a time, she was delivered home to her door, pockets heavy with gold.

> *Hard to forget*
> *such a meeting*
> *with the*
> *hidden dignitaries*
> *of Dartmoor.*
>
> *Fairy.*
> *Sometimes in the*
> *farthest stable,*
> *or*
> *the last field*
> *between the farm*
> *and the forest.*
>
> *Whose horses never tire,*
> *whose musics never cease,*
> *whose food must not be tasted.*
>
> *Quite a secret.*
> *Like tasting the king's wine.*

A day or two later she wandered down the lanes and into the market town of Ashburton, and everything was different. The stars were visible in the daylight, cats were as large as hounds, salmon leapt from the River Ashburn with the faces of foxes—the whole world was rocked, luminous, awake. She tried to steady herself with a whisky in the snug at the Exeter Inn, just off the market, but even that didn't work. Maybe buying supplies would sober her eye. But at the bustling market she, of a horror, spotted the faerie rider ambling slow and unseen through the throng. In a fraction of a second he turned his attention to her. She almost stopped breathing. He cantered forward and leant down on his saddle, his face obscured by a battered old hat. "Which of your eyes can see me?" he breathed. When she slowly pointed to the left, he, in a flash, scooped it out with an icy blade.

For the rest of her life she carried a dark pit where her left eye should be.

Children would run to the door of her cottage and then away again, just to say they had. When she finally died of old age, they cleared her house and found those ten gold guineas under her pillow. As the villagers gleefully picked them up, they became oak leaves, withered, and fell apart.

What price to lay an eye?

✿✿✿

As soon as I've finished, there's a response. Wind rushes in. Over decades I have heard many voices in the air up here, high ended and almost hysterical, serene, and, like today, a low ceremonial breath, yards of chanting settling on my burning ears.

The tors are heroic—ice-nippled paps jutting out from strong, horizontal lines of granite. On a day of mist and below-freezing temperature, the land seems defiantly unscored by agriculture.

This rain ruins the fields, turns the hedge to vertical slurry, tips the thresher into the mire, pushes cows flat to the lichen-covered boulders, piss-wet and numbed. The big-handed sons of bailing twine, the farmers, are washed clean away, sloshed across the bruise-flecked downs. The land grapples with the some distant possibility of spring. Wet branches hold such budding fast.

In the distance, the north moor. There is a nordic band of light—clear, thin gold, framing maybe twenty miles of treeless upland on the very horizon line. Underneath, the more familiar Prussian blues and endlessly varying heathers. It is almost like a Rothko painting still drying, with linseed sluiced through it—the wonky gold, blue, green strips—every colour utterly translucent with moisture.

I put my back into travel. On a day like this I find myself drifting into imaginings of the pilgrims' route they would have taken between abbeys, and stories of locals having to carry bodies across freezing streams to be buried in specific parishes. Blue limbs under rough robes, coffins wobbling on raw shoulders. Still, the bracing talk-back of the wind keeps bringing me back to what is right in front of me. On this last day of January, I meet no fellow travellers.

I cross down into Hexworthy, past the Forest Inn and many houses being worked on or modernised. I am touched to see a damp cardboard box of fresh farm eggs, donations tin, and glass jar of snowdrops outside an older house.

Standing on the bridge, I take stock of the frantically chugging West Dart River. To its left bank are small churns of nothing but foam, whilst most is a hurtling blur of icy waters, passing in a second from my eye. On this handsome, two-arched bridge, I imagine the satisfying clunk and clatter of the great horse from our story passing over with its two passengers. Some bit of gossip tangles this reverie in my mind—apparently it will be minus six tonight. Indeed, indeed. Rain is starting to lick my beard.

When Hexworthy Chapel rears up on my right it seems harsh: granite black, steep-roofed, small bell, a severe overlooker on all these organic curves and moss. It seems like some Dickensian character wrought in stone—bah humbug. This building has unforgiving sight, a hawk nose, cold fingers, and thin lips in all this pagan, sensuous nature unfurling that surrounds it. First impressions.

Although I mean to keep walking, I notice a sign on the gate encouraging visitors to come into the chapel's small garden and enjoy the snowdrops. I do like a snowdrop. I enter. From this side of the tiny chapel it seems utterly different. Scrubbed walls, lots of care and attention, handwritten notes of welcome, a pearly speckled flank of flowers. It's delightful.

In these recession-heavy times, most church doors are locked for fear of thieving. I never came across a locked church door as kid growing up here. I try it. Wow. It opens with a push. The chapel is minute and freezing, but after the long haul from Holne, it is a shelter from the coming rains.

I am astonished to see a wood-burning stove, a stack of kindling, and dry ash. I've never seen that in a church before. Even unlit, the stove cheers me. I imagine some other poor soul, wetter and colder than me, working that kindling to a blaze, warming up in this devotional shelter in the heart of the moor.

Saint Raphael is saint to all healers and travellers, so it says on the wall. Well, this traveller feels heartened by the welcome note, the unlocked door, the burner. After some time in its restful quiet, I get up to leave. I can see some books by the door, and another donation tin. Peering over to see what I imagine will be theological literature, I find two books: one on Aboriginal song lines and the other on the legacy and philosophy of the Robin Hood ballads. Well, I'll be. I feel strengthened, confirmed somehow. I place coin in the box and head out into the rain, tattered books under my coat.

Another long stretch of track up to the cut-through road towards Princetown and Bellever Tor. It's here that the story of the faeiried midwife lifts entirely from geography and into the Commons of the Imagination. Somewhere out, just beyond this stretch is that faerie's dwelling, somewhere out in the rough acres of weather. I know Bellever, have wandered its coniferous forests, have stumbled upon its old tombs and many secrets, have fasted there, have sat with my brother on the very top of the tor and talked of love's impossibilities. I would throw a hunch and venture to suppose there's an opening or two to the Seelie Court of Faerie up there, even now.

But standing at the T-junction outside Hexworthy, I feel a robust charge in my bones that the story has up and taken flight, is no longer traceable by my pilgrim's feet, but has broken through to faerie. It's walked into the Other-world. As with grail searching, it would be inappropriate to place geography on such a dwelling. However, there is one last place for me to visit.

The pint of Badger's Ale expertly poured in Ashburton's Exeter Inn is a thing of beauty. The reddish ale glints in the heavy glass. The pub is legitimately old, even ancient. It was here they arrested Sir Walter Raleigh and took him off to the Tower of London and his company of ravens. The pub is snug against the dark and the cold, low ceiling and welcoming to a mud-flecked and starving traveller. Round the back, they rustle up fish and chips. In my mind I see Morada, there in a corner, strange-eyed and holy in the bustle of a town pub, unable to halt all that was now unfolding.

It was a walk of distance, this one. Of obscuration and sudden twists, of thinking one way and then seeing entirely from another, of confirmation in a ghostly chapel, of a story leaping from soil to stars. All the momentum on the walk was for the route of the horse and the riders, the excitement of night, the mad weather. But now, comfortable and feeling that old beery joy, I feel grief for Morada and the one-eyed life she led after her impossible return. A hard task, beholding.

Night as taboo

So to be claimed by a place, to behold a place, involves etiquette to the spirits that may already be there. Faerie belief in Britain has remained strong for many thousands of years. Although in modernity these stories may mistakenly seem whimsical, it wasn't always this way. As recently as the nineteenth century, hair-raising accounts of encounters on lonely lanes with such beings were commonplace. For a recent account of such energies, read Malidome Somé's *Of Water and the Spirit* (1995), a startling account of initiation within the Dagara people of West Africa. It quickly becomes apparent that to tribal cultures worldwide there are windows to immensely powerful spirits that have been knocking around on earth forever. It's a crowded scene.

Earlier in this book, we addressed the notion that inside every house there is a hut, hidden in the being of the dweller. Houses are thick with memory: the structure of family time, loneliness, felt securities, habitual reveries that grow more pronounced by the stability of the surroundings. Our house can help us forget about fascism, starving Ethiopians, or birds falling stone dead out of the sky. We stomp around down below in the musty cellar of reflection, or we pad circular stairs at night, with candle and nightcap, to our celestial dream tower. Faerie tales tell us that in such a tower—which lives within us—is a tiny old woman, ancient, who weaves on a spindle by moonlight. All little girls understand this. But these dream ascensions or cellar nostalgias are familiar, daily. It is quite another thing to have the courage to suddenly open the door to the bright rain and the faerie rider.

The Fay Ones, Seelie Court, Gentry, Other Crowd, whatever name a county or country gives them, arouse many opinions about what exactly they might be. Some claim them as the dead walking, some a kind of earthed angel, others (spurred on by Puritanism) claim they can only be demonic in origin. Probably the widest claim is of powerful denizens that have abided in the natural world for as long as anyone can remember. Within many communities there will often be one or more sensitives who appear to have some contact with them.

Victorian etchings of quaint little creatures with wings do not always cut it for preparing someone for the experience of meeting one of these beings. Seneca Indian medicine men and West African shamans take them extremely seriously. Indeed, their doctoring skills are often reliant on bartering and assistance from those very beings.

Humans are not the only ones with song lines. In Ireland, an old cottage may have a corner knocked out if it is thought to interfere with one of the faerie procession lines. It's simply not worth the ensuing trouble to leave it. Folklore insists the faeries will nip babies away and place changelings in the cot, leave gold that is worthless, draw you into endless revelry whilst you gradually lose your senses.

Our story begins at night. Night always carries its liminal invitation. Edges become blurred, routes home we swore we knew suddenly lead our feet some other way. Many have experienced this up on the moor. We remember that night used to be regarded as the ending of clock time altogether. It was another kind of thing completely—a time when the spirits took full advantage of those blurred edges and created all sorts of mischief.

In Tuscan culture, to wander alone at night indicated you were either a sorcerer or a prostitute. In their farming communities, even into the twentieth century, the world of minute time was a distant notion. Time was dictated by the village bell, heard in the distant fields, at noon for lunch or ringing the hour before sundown to bring all home to the hearth fire. To linger would have been *Chi va di notte cerca la morte*, "Who goes out at night looks for death." Although the family would often leave for work at different times, as darkness arrived the group would almost always be situated around the table for supper. This "hinge" time, with its strange textures, would be met by the dishing out of food, drink, and general conversation. When night's grip became inescapable, the desire for human companionship became even more pronounced with the *veglia*, the gathering by the fire, the telling of stories, the singing of songs, the setting of riddles. Whilst family cleaned the dishes and emptied the table, the grandmother would be coaxed into telling a story, even though mildly protesting at first. This is good protocol, as all storytellers like to be asked. But as the folklorist Alessandro Falassi (1980) reminds us, no one wants a reputation as the kind of storyteller who "needs a coin to start, and ten to stop," taking things to the point that an invitation becomes an imposition.

But the busyness of table, the pleading with the storyteller, the stoking of the fire, the collective settling for the tale, all were protective devices, familiar rhythms for warding off the swift shadowing of the cornfield and the stables. Out just beyond the farm were sometimes abandoned fields or pig pens in disrepair; these were soon seen to have fallen into the atmosphere of the forest and not to be lingered in.

The whole situation with darkness was much edgier than we imagine. There was not the wholehearted exorcism of the dark that a strip light offers; the storytelling time by lantern or candle was dappled, shaded, a back-and-forth. The real brightness was to be held in the liveliness of table and the warmth of the assembled group. There were still dark corners. Whether in Tuscany or a village off the Norwich Road, occasionally an eye would nervously go to the chimney—an entry point for witches. Often the hearth fire was loaded with secret magic devices to keep such beings out, the story being such a device. The hearth and the scene I described, seen in variety all over the world, were truly an *axis mundi* for the small group surrounding it. In the poem "The Stars" by Dafydd ap Gwilym (c. 1325–c. 1380), we encounter a young man getting unstuck on his night journey across the moors, with the Otherworld materialising all around him:

I staggered about in mud-ridged fields,
nine thickets caught my finger and jacket.

I gripped an ancient wall
like a sailor grips his oar
when he sees the storm coming

Ahead was the brow of some terrible mountain,
thick with goblin, amok with caves;
a dungeon of my own making.

"Holy maker, I ask for bail;
In the speech of my people, I barter tonight

If brought safe to my lover's Hall,
that I will pilgrimage to far Llanddwyn.

"I am Ap Gwilym:
Bring me bright path

and I will lower my head
to the babe that was born in the glow of animals."

The stars came out then,
brilliant and holy,
a gold foam to one without shelter.

FROM *DAFYDD AP GWILYM*,
VERSION BY MARTIN SHAW AND TONY HOAGLAND

An opening into the night's many jujus began when I was little more than a kid. At around thirteen, I made my way home down a small path next to a stagnant stream overhung occasionally by willow trees. The name of this old pathway was Melancholy Walk. At night it was not a walk I enjoyed, but I was keen to visit my friend Oliver Hibble, whose family lived at the end of it. This night was particularly dark. As I walked I looked firmly ahead, at the first distant street lamp; I clearly remember singing songs under my breath to keep my nerves at bay.

I had just reached the part where willows overhung the path and dangled into the sludgy, brown waters of the stream. The wet branches blocked out the distant light. What I remember next was a kind of low, almost wet, gurgling laugh right in both my ears, loud, and then being lifted by my shoulders several inches—so that I was on the balls of my feet. The grip was crazy strong. There was no one else on the path.

I shot forward faster than I have ever run, instantly out of the grip of whatever it was, past that first street light, up the cobbled hill, past St. Gilbert's primary school, past the Green Man pub, up the narrow alley that led onto Radcliffe road, and up to home. Oddly, I don't think I spoke to my parents about it at the time. I just couldn't bear it. To speak it was to incant it all over again. To keep making it real.

At that young age I became aware that things happened when the day darkened. The movement from fevered imaginings into a direct experience was real, very tangible. It didn't *feel* like something was out there; there *was* something out there, and I got nailed by it. It is a strand of Western arrogance to believe that everything "unnatural" that occurs is somehow a psychological response to some shift in the human mind, as if that were the centre of all the action.

It's illuminating that the faerie requires a human midwife. We hear from many cultures that the Otherworld is as interested in us as we are in it, and we detect the scent of that here—that we have a skill that is of real use to them. And what a skill: to guide a being from the watery realm of the belly out into spluttering life. We often pray for a celestial or divine intervention; could it be that we occupy the dreams and concerns of the gods, spirits, and devas? Do we have something to offer them? Are we a dream of the gods?

Mud

There would have been a time when we knew a lot more about that mud, when we knew an exposure to nature as more than just the ploughing of the soil, timber for the house, or slate for the roof. To be rubbed with the mud is the realisation that you are part of a fibered cosmos, that you are related to the sleek-bellied otter and the rich thinking of the Renaissance, that we are receivers of a vast inheritance. Some great energy is knocking at our door with astonishing news. It is the opposite of feeling miserable, unseen, depleted, disconnected, despairing, too fragile, ungrounded, lost, and prone to delusion. It is visionary at its heart.

W. B. Yeats and Hildegard von Bingen certainly responded to the mid-night rider at the cottage door. God knows how many unearthly children they delivered to get such a potent supply of mud. We are witnessing a seeker of mud when we witness the graceful turns of a Sufi dervish, or the steady pound of a Miwok earth-drum during a longhouse ritual, or a young woman from Detroit finding her place on a forested mountain and settling down to fast.

The faerie mud *marks* you. Once you have been there, you are different, wrenched open. Now, in a spiritually literate culture this is a scene of cele-bration. You return from the wilderness to a sensitised community ready to help you live out your insights from the edge. It is clearly understood that the tribal soul is strengthened by going beyond the everyday—like the midwife accepting the strange midnight knocking and following the adventure.

When you have the experience, but without the holding, of the return to human community, the world you come back to does indeed look like a world turned upside down. Salmon do indeed have the heads of foxes; stars do come out in the daylight. Without real holding and understanding from the village, we mistake the *prophet* for the *lunatic*. The quickest way to lose any tangible insight is to be placed back into the humdrum without any sense of the sacredness of what just happened.

Suddenly the mud is not a gift but a very real problem. It is deeply un-ruly—both to the daubed and in the ripples of disquiet it causes for all those who did not take the journey themselves. I had a Ghanaian friend whose brother one day disappeared suddenly from the field he was working in. He didn't come back, and they mourned him. About five years later a thin, ema-ciated man appeared at the gates of the village. It was my friend's brother. He claimed to have been taken by bush spirits, to somewhere else entirely. It was clear that he believed he was telling the truth. After many vigorous cleansing rituals, he was allowed a small hut at the edge of the village. He disappeared inside and was rarely seen after that. This wasn't the first time such a thing had happened.

In the end, the situation is resolved by the faerie's cutting away the mid-wife's visionary eye. The ancient belief was that those in possession of such beholding had to *do* something with it—honour the waterfall, teach the young women, be a bridge person. When the old understanding of the visionary is not crafted into some expression that edifies the wider world, then some great power takes the gift away again.

Many of the people I have met over the years who have fasted on the mountain have had the experience of the marketplace. They too have not found support or any understanding for what they experienced. And little by little it drifts away, until they awake one morning missing an eye for that wild world entirely.

Experiences like that cannot be easily compounded into worldly terms. They will rarely make you rich. When the greedy come for your inheritance they find crumbling leaves, not heavy coin. But for the ones with the seeing it could all "appear as it is, infinite" (William Blake). The Otherworld looks very carefully at our concerns before deciding whether to grace/bother us with an encounter. For most of us, money lust is absolutely magnetic, so it is often something we need to be shaken free from if we are truly to go deeper. Like the wood shavings gathered behind a door in a faerie tale, those leaves show real experience.

Those tent years were, for me, a collecting of wood shavings. I even went seven years without putting scissors to my hair; I could tuck it into my belt. Another faerie tale image. The black tent, the door facing away from people, the remote location, all was a kind of underground brooding. My experiences within wilderness vigils had claimed something in me and I could not go back. I remember seeing a photograph of a Lakota medicine man in mourning for his wife. He had ripped loose one of his long plaits, and it flapped uncombed in the wind to show his grief, the other tight and bound. I remember feeling not like the man but like that loose plait.

One day, several years later, feeling too edgy, straight-up lonely, I collected all the spare change I had and from my tent took the long walk to a public pay phone to ring a man in America who I thought might be able to help. He couldn't, but blessed me nonetheless. As I walked home—grounded, tearful—a crow swooped low, landed, and launched itself off my left shoulder. Hard. I felt *owned*. It was not entirely reassuring.

So I have a feeling about this whole one-eye business. We are led to believe these openings happen only on the steppes, or on Bear Butte, or hanging in the darkness of the Plains Indian vision pit, or to "special people." Not so. This is not the road of a slick guru, just one rocked by mysterious forces. I was not planning to write books about it, or franchise it, or workshop it. I was just trying to *survive* it.

To live a soulful life is going to involve openness to certain strains of grief, a recalibration of your being, regardless of what society is trying to hammer it into. But here's the thing that self-help books and spiritual pamphlets generally forget to tell you: soul without eros will eventually drive you crazy. Think of the Greek myth of Psyche and Eros—the watery depths of Psyche and the fire-sparked arrows of Eros—only when the two are in relation does life in its ramshackle fullness reveal itself.

So, in the plainest language I can find: to attend to depth without a communicable art form is the difference between drowning and swimming. Eros is what reaches out and touches the world, demonstrates itself, shows up for duty, riddles the most mundane of tasks with an invigorating, generative warmth. Eros is the sparkling bay of fiery light for soul to settle its vast, green waves in. In other words, it becomes a container. If there's no communication, then the Psyche person just swims round and round with their oceanic insights but never reaches shore. It really doesn't matter how many Mary Oliver poems you know if you're not sharing their essence with others.

It's in relatedness that you get the real, and yes, it's that word again, *indigenous* shape of who you are. Character is revealed in your relationships to others. It's not what you *tell* others you are; your true hand is revealed in your myriad dealings with a hundred different things.

Wandering around in a poncho quoting George Monbiot is absolutely without meaning unless it's *your* face serving at the counter at the 3:00 a.m. soup kitchen. There comes a moment when it really doesn't matter if your chackras are balanced or not. Life's not going to wait anymore.

The earthy map of the face

As in so many of these Dartmoor stories, the mood in this one is cautionary. The stories hint at something lost or leaving, a vivid interaction between human and animal and spirit. Again and again, greed, laziness, or simple ignorance wrecks the arrangement. So we ask ourselves, could it have been different for the midwife, had she had soul friends to communicate her beholdings to? With that in place, maybe the encounter with the ice knife and the coal-black steed would have been unnecessary. As it stands, I wonder how many of us wander, one eyed, through this world, trying to find our way back to some glimpse of soulful things and needing that third step to fertilise our fistfuls of wild seeds.

People going through deep openings often get it marked on their appearance. Shakespeare says: "For by his face straight shall you know his heart" (*Richard III*)—that the canopy of wrinkles, frown ditches, crinkles, brittle taughtness, and jowly abandon form a ridged history across our blinking skull.

That to the right eyes, a face can be read like a landscape: it reveals a vivid story of disappointment and triumph, sadism and grace, as varied as weather patterns. It is a natural legacy, piled on incrementally by how we think, food we eat, how much sun we get. Roland Barthes (1972) talks of the *chronos* of biology and the *chronos* of passion; so we see in late photographs of artist Georgia O'Keeffe not just the result of the New Mexico sun, but something under that skin radiating through. Photos of Howlin' Wolf reveal the same thing. We note a degree of dignity to ageing in these seventeenth-century Welsh verses:

> *Past forty,*
> *a man can carry*
>
> *the flush*
> *of a tree in leaf,*
>
> *or shoulder a*
> *quiver of speech.*
>
> *He can laugh quietly*
> *over his scars.*
>
> *But the sound of*
> *a vault being opened,*
>
> *Lets the*
> *crow settle*
>
> *on the soft acres*
> *of his face.*
>
> VERSION BY MARTIN SHAW AND TONY HOAGLAND

It's said we should never trust a teacher without a crow on his or her shoulder. The ascendance of cosmetic surgery is another result of our wholesale inability to deal with the wild's ravages. Just as we razor-cut an old-growth forest, we mangle and bleach our own faces in an attempt to place a fabricated montage over the persistent fructification of our cheeks and brow.

When rough-and-tumble wisdom is not cultivated, then something in the personality remains thin. The unexamined life. All that remains is this exterior jumble of flesh on the top. When that starts to resemble a hag rather than a crone (important distinction), we grow self-conscious—but not in the best sense of that phrase. This one-eyed-ness, this "plucked out" feeling, may contribute needing to the knife's fabrications, to distract from the growing deficit of what has been lost inside.

Oh England, my lion heart

Humanity has taken to monoculture once and for all, and is preparing to produce civilisation in bulk, as if it were sugar-beet. The same dish is to be served to us every day.
CLAUDE LEVI-STRAUSS

Cosmetic surgery gives primacy to the generic over the characterful. Peeled-back faces create a sort of new race all their own. No matter how sophisticated the procedure, even an untrained eye can usually make out the surgeon's work. The personal story is gone, as well as all kinds of familial traits, biologically inherited. The saga has been scrubbed away. The ancestral symbology through the skin is akimbo; the old signal is scrambled. In its place is this kind of look-alike new breed, all with expressions of mild surprise on their faces. Yet another blast from the trumpet of monoculturalism.

In his book *Real England* (2008), the writer Paul Kingsnorth traces another kind of facelift—this time going on amongst the villages, towns, and cities of England. The motivation is the same, a kind of consensually approved sea of Starbucks and Subways moving like a glutinous wave into every high street in the country. I will be halfway down Stamford High Street and suddenly think I am in Winchester; all the references are the same.

Kingsnorth takes on the standardising of English pubs by "pub corporations," no longer related or showing any loyalty to brewers such as Ruddles (1857), Brakspear (1799), Morrels (1782), or Redruth (1742), all of which have disappeared in the last decade. These corporations take their tips for expansion from pizza chains and are slick with loans from Japanese banks. The kind of large-capacity "drinking shed" we now see in all town centres is tactically constructed—no chairs (sitting slows consumption), no flat surfaces (can't place a drink down, so you speed intake), loud volume (destroys conversations so you just get back to drinking). To long-term lovers of the pub, this is a subtle form of violence. The drinks glow blue, thick with sugar and prohibitive alcohol content; and the inevitable fisticuffs this will later produce, well, the police can deal with that.

Again, the enemy of this corporate attitude is *intimacy*, for centuries a hallmark of the tavern. A quiet corner, a napping dog, a good fire, an old friend. The poet Hilaire Belloc, a French man who spent much time in the traditional pub, warned almost a century ago: "Change your heart or you will lose your inns, and you will deserve to lose them. But when you have lost your inns, drown your empty selves, for you will have lost the last of England" (Belloc 1948,119).

Something passes from soul to soul in good conversation, especially when folks are lingering over a pint. The pub is a gentle liminality, a suspension of time from labour and obligation. In those conversations, we touch sometimes on something deep; we can remember a little of who we are. Since the Romans first rolled in with the *taverna*, our earliest ancestor of the pub, in the first century C.E., we've had a protracted love affair with it. A community meeting place, a gossipy stew, a lovers' rendezvous, a hotbed of informal storytelling. It is too easy to chastise pubs with talk of brawling and drunkenness—there were often quiet spots, cosy corners with a dozing hound and coal fire. There's none of this in the strip-lit, piss-up shed of our modern high streets. Intimacy is willfully banished as an interference with the task of emptying our pockets as swiftly as possible.

Everywhere I go I meet people seeking a life of greater depth and intensity. But they also want speed, immediacy, stability, insurance. It may be that we cannot have all of both, that real compromise is at hand—that life must slow, that possibilities are not indeed endless, that we must be willfully political in an attempt to wrestle power back to the local. And to handle that power well, we need to know what local is, what we stand for.

Kingsnorth, while building up an inspired head of steam at the end of his book, reminds us that, actually, England no longer exists. That in 1707, due to the Acts of the Union, both England and Scotland removed the constitutional identities of both countries. They became, and remain, along with Wales and Northern Ireland, Great Britain.

In a kind of ghastly twist, England is now the only British nation without democratic devolution. The British government fairly bristles with ministers for Wales, Scotland, and Northern Ireland, but ministers for England? Not one. Whilst I absolutely celebrate the growing independence of these three nations, it is growingly clear how badly served the English are by British democracy. It's in a weakened state.

As Kingsnorth states:

> Local councils were denuded of much of their power by the Thatcher government. The Blair regime continued the process of centralisation, crowning it with the setting up of the unelected, anti-democratic 'regional assemblies'. The Brown government took even this fig leaf, handing power to the corporate placelings of the Regional Development Agencies, which now make many of our decisions for us, in the shadows (2008, 278).

When our own sovereign is weak, we all the more eagerly hand power to a Herod. When we don't have the energy to vote, then there will always be someone out there more than happy to do it for us. Local councils won't do; local communities just might.

CHAPTER TEN

Applegarth's Rose

Folks warned me. Pleaded, in one case. Said it was the most haunted stretch of land in all Britain. No place for a boy and his tent. Of course, all of this was a red rag to a bull. Irresistible. Berry Pomeroy Woods, home to the ruins of a castle and thick with any number of spooks. I'd been hearing about it since I was a kid, down the road in Torbay. Everyone over the age of forty seemed to have a story. It brought out the raconteur in the most unlikely of grownups. Standing outside church on a Sunday morning, respected members of the Baptist community would lean in, hands gesturing grandly at the sheer ghostliness of the place. I, as an infant, gazed up at the storytellers, ablaze with the eeriness of it all. I loved every word.

This was wandering through my head twenty-five years later, as I tied sections of the trellis together to stabilise the tent. I was moving into the gardens of the lodge house of that very castle, at the edge of those very woods. Cara was busy doing the same on the other side of the creaking beast, whilst Jonny squatted on a rickety chair surrounded by near-swamp mud, holding the yurt wheel steady to start assembling the roof poles. This is always when it feels most precarious, as if a strong wind would instantly end the whole endeavour.

Only minutes later the great wraps of felt begin their slow and heavy shouldering of the tent—wrapped around the ash skeleton before my ever more thinning canvas is finally put in place. There's a slight bow to the sides, as if the tent had been gaining weight, and suddenly it appears robust and settled, as if it had always been there.

But of course, it hadn't. Even though it was a move of only several miles, it was a different land to negotiate. Different streams and birdsong, infinitely more damp, another terrain to break bread with, to be tutored by. Soon the trunks groaning with deer and goat skins, wine goblets, cords of rope, paraffin, billhooks, coffee, extra blankets and oil paints were unloaded and smoke was merrily puffing out of the flue.

So everything was the same and not the same. The soundscape around the tent was quite different, would require a retuning of my ears. The woods were telling tales of a nature other than the ones whispered over the open hills towards Stoke Gabriel. Darker, odder, bleaker. Over a couple of years, those stories would break open another dimension again in my carrying of stories, in the way I slowly allowed all aspects of my own nature to show up in a telling. It was the way that Berry Pomeroy wore its shadow like a cloak—without shame—that helped me to the same ambition. I needed swampy ground and swift-gathering shadows for that part of my education. The woods brought my darkness out. It's that simple.

Saffy, my cat, rescued after being abandoned by travellers, would be glimpsed as a white dot heading into the tree line, unperturbed by any ghost stories. To follow her solitary trail would always lead somewhere trouble-filled and intriguing.

Twelve years later still, I find myself back on the old ground to tell this coming story. There's fast-moving sky, blade-sharp air, and the ironed rump of Hay Tor in the far distance. I peer over a half-fallen wall and into the old garden. No trace the tent was ever there. Like a dream. That's fitting. And Saffy too—now beloved and gone—no more white dot in the tree line, no more leading me on.

Ah, you funny old cat. Tears nestle my lashes. I begin.

❋ ❋ ❋

Sally Applegarth's Rose

Sally Applegarth was in love. She was no good for peeling fruit, folding linen, or weeding the garden. Her father, working in their fields, had given up worrying about her. She was caught in whimsy—by affection for a certain young man. But she was not sure of his feelings for her. Her mother pointed in the direction of the cottage of her grandmother; maybe she could help her daughter break this state.

Sally wandered from the hamlet of Little Hempston, along shady lanes, over a small bridge, and up through the forest surrounding old Berry Pomeroy Castle, already ruinous, already beset by ghosts. As she briskly strode past the ruin, she remembered the old tale of the lord's daughter falling in love with the son of one of his enemies. Found in the arbour where the honeysuckle climbed, both were cut down, brutally slain. Many swore that on a moonlit night, the two lovers could still be seen gazing down, luminous, from the castle walls. She drew her cloak around her and hurried on, not looking back.

> *Through bleak wood*
> *with the candle of*
> *her heart,*
> *many eyes*
> *watch her stroll*
> *to the hut*
> *of the strong door.*

Her parents wished her to marry for money, a man called Simon Moon, but she refused; it was love or nothing. She muttered an old chant to keep her spirits up.

> *An even-leaved ash,*
> *And a four-leaved clover,*
> *You'll see your true love,*
> *'Fore the day is over.*

Her old granny was in no mood for talk of weddings, having just recently buried her husband in the red turf. The cottage was ancient—almost a lean-to. Bundles of dried herbs hung from the ceiling, and your eyes had to adjust to the smoky light. They drank black tea and the old woman told Sally: "I should have trusted the story the beans told me. When I pulled a row of beans up, one was white and four green. Never thought 'twas him to go." Still, her advice to her granddaughter was this: "Plant yarrow on your grandfather's grave, and when it grows, take the very first sprig and set it under your pillow, and I tell thee, your true love will appear in the dreaming. Use these words:

> *Yarrow, sweet yarrow, the first I have found,*
> *In the name of Jesus I pluck it from the ground.*
> *As Jesus loved sweet Mary, and took her for his*
> *dear, so in a dream this night, I hope, my true love shall*
> *appear.*

With that the cunning woman stretched, straightened, and then lovingly ushered Sally out of the cottage. As she started down the track, the girl considered the advice. That whole process that granny recommended would take way too long. Typical grandparent and their long-term goals. So at dusk she went to the edge of the woods and spoke even older words than her grandmother's, straight from the pagan world.

> *All hail, new moon, all hail to thee!*
> *I prithee, good moon, reveal to me*
> *This night who my true love be,*
> *Who he is, what he wears,*
> *And what he does all the months and years.*

On the way home, in the dimpsy light, she saw old Silas Garland, the cowman, trudging the lane behind a dozen cows. His peg leg scraped the track and he tipped his battered hat as he limped past. A rook cawed nearby. A chill surged Sally. Surely not! She was so caught in terror of his being her suitor that she barely noticed a figure on the hay cart, riding the elder-scented lane. She then caught sight and ran after him, all the way to the small stream at the bottom of the Berry Hill, but he was gone. Was it sweet Will, or just the little farmer lad, George?

No clear answer there, then. It appeared her granny's insistence on time might be more important than she realised. In the dusk light, an image placed itself hard in her thinking. That night, the summer solstice, at midnight, she went to the rosebush outside the cottage, bound her eyes with a handkerchief, and plucked the rose as the parish clock chimed the bells. She pressed the rose between the pages of the oldest book she could find. Then she waited.

On Christmas morning she opened the book, and there was the flower, a reminder of summer in its fullness. She took a silver pin, attached the rose to her jacket, and the family headed off to Berry Pomeroy Church. The service was joyful and all sang with full voice: "O come let us adore him, Christ the Lord."

As the family walked out of the chapel into the glass-sharp air, calm-eyed Will Tremayne, the farmer's son—the one who rode the hay bale so many months before—bashfully approached, a shy smile on his face. "Sally, 'tis a fine rose you're wearing! How did you come to wear a summer rose on a Christmas morn?" Quietly he asked, "Would you let me wear it as a token?"

The promise of the midsummer rose had come to pass. The flower Sally pressed so long ago had been claimed by her love. Will was her sweetheart, defender, and companion through good times, hard times, squabbles, long silences, and laughter all the many long years of her life.

> *Mice drag their tails*
> *through dust,*
> *crows wait in the high tree.*
> *In the lanterned kitchen,*
> *two lean in*
> *by the small table.*

❋ ❋ ❋

Little Hempston is very old Devon—thatched, white-washed cottages, small bridges, tiny rivers just begging to have stick races down. In the spring, every available stretch of public soil erupts yellow with daffodils.

Walking from it towards Berry Pomeroy, you soon come to the fast-moving road between Totnes and Newton Abbott. Left at the pub and on for another few hundred yards, until a swift crossing over and down into Berry. Not that our Sally would have been negotiating the seemingly endless sweep of 4x4s and horse boxes.

Past a few houses and the road widens, the castle's surrounding forest on the left and onwards to the village itself. On the right is a green lane—once beloved of a motley assortment of travellers who lived quietly at the top. There were trucks, caravans, hastily assembled benders, folks coming and going. Some settled for as long as the law allowed, others—what locals call "blow-ins"—just passing through. Cara and I have known a few people up there, and as I passed I remembered dusk visits, clutching wine and cakes firmly whilst negotiating the slippery, rutted track, settling comfortably by a wood burner for an evening of music and story.

Still, that is many years past, and I don't have the time or inclination to wander up to see the thin trails of smoke through the green that used to indicate occupancy. Just past the travellers' turning is a swift cut to the left, into the greenwood. There is much-felled conifer, two great banks of it, but behind, in the shadows, stand old-growth forest, badger dens, and a bluebell patch. In the years that I was at the castle's lodge house, these rough routes through the woods were a kind of open secret to the locals—there were dog walking and surprise meetings in the most unlikely of places. But today they are cordoned-off no-goes; keep out.

Down at the ruins I produce coins and let them fly over the ravine that protects a good half of the castle. The original owner, Ralph de Pomeroy, apparently willfully picked the most inaccessible keep he could find, on a ghostly knoll high above a low-sunk tributary of the Dart. I like his style. The coins don't make the tributary today but simply disappear into the abundant ferns gripping the steep drop.

I turn towards the ruins. I have two streams of imagining—side by side. One is the young woman, Sally, picking her route through the dark woods, head blooming with love thoughts. The other is of a small blond boy with an oversized bike—my father—with the flash of torches and excited swearing from his friends. The intersecting lines of this particular story place—of Sally, of my father's trip, of my own time living here—all seem activated at once; there seems a kind of intermingling of emotion and scene. The walking is clearly not just physical, but psychoactive; not just a goodly stomp, but a gathering up—a tightened inner seeing.

Scattering proudly across the wintering banks is the plant "lords and ladies," what the scholars call *Arum maculatum*. This robust little plant is many-named in England: the cuckoo-pint, naked boys, starch-root, devils and angels, bobbins, and wake-robin. In autumn, it cheers the grasses with resilient clusters of bright red berries, but take heed, they are not for eating. The root, when roasted well, is edible and was even once traded under the name Portland Sago. It was a working-folks' drink before the introduction of tea and coffee, but prepared incorrectly it's highly toxic. I doff my hat and leave it alone.

I see something I had long forgotten about. The Wishing Tree. A tall, wide-spreading beech. They say that three peregrinations around it in the sun direction, and then three times backwards, always thinking of a wish, will lead the wish surely to come true. Surely Sally stopped at this tree? Despite some vicious pruning, even across the trunk itself, I can make out carved names of old lovers from other generations. In the three massive branches, I find, to my delight, lace ties, symbols of wishes. Unable to restrain myself, I am soon clambering the slippery roots and holding a dear wish.

I am leaving the castle behind, with its attendant human dramas, and following the story's path. I am heading up and out of the ruins' aura. There is a small teahouse settled in by the track side, and I try to keep my mouth clear of the lust for dark roast French coffee. It doesn't work but I trudge on, nonetheless. It's not hugely steep, this track up to the lodge house, but long enough for a little ache to move into the thighs.

Everything is tall. The trees, either old growth or conifer, seem vast, and the path's crumbled leaves blow up for seconds in front of me in glyph-like patterns and then settle. The steep banks bring back the very familiar sensation of being watched. Indigenous folks say that every forest is thick with calmly assessing eyes; we are always being watched. To my right, two crow couples seem to play on brisk currents of air way out over a sharp dip, two above the other. There's no violence and no jostling. It's sweet to hear the caw.

I reach out to touch the rough bark of the older trees. Moss lies thick like drifts on the northern flanks. A white pheasant is seen for a second, to the left of the path, just as it opens out of the tree line.

I decide to break the law and vault the *Do Not Enter!* sign that halts entry to the lodge house or farther fields. The signs are there for good reason—years of carloads of Torbay youth congregating at the gates at midnight, dealing, brawling, and generally getting a kick out of being so near a scene of dark power somehow mirroring their own turbulence. The old initiations were a way of sacralising this kind of death wrestling; as we know, when the rites of passage disappear, the longing remains but turns feral.

There is a view to end views just beyond this forbidden track. A pine forest, and then a panoramic opening—of patchwork fields, budding tumps of woodland, glints of dusk light in nearby Totnes and Dartington, and then more forest and field before hints, just hints, of Buckfastleigh and Ashburton. And beyond them? Haytor and the moor, caught in shadows, and bleary, forbidding lumps in the distance. To the right, just out of view but salt-scented in the air, is the ocean.

It's like a Ravilious painting. Cara and I often ate supper underneath the dry stone wall, or she would take her guitar and disappear into the field. One form or another of that view had held my attention my whole life. But Sally's story doesn't end there. That's my layer of the story. Hers is still to be walked.

St. Mary the Virgin is on the edge of the village. Lovely to behold, intricate architecture, stone well cleaned, but, as a symbol of our recession times, resolutely locked. Too much stolen. With that traditional pagan flourish, two yew trees add a dash of the old religion to the graveyard. But times have moved on in little England: I glance up at the notice board and see that the reverend is called Deborah.

The birdsong is more playful here; clusters of starlings chatter noisily to each other before taking short, direct flights into other trees. In the distance a solo Mr. Magpie passes. Catching its flight, I notice a sturdy stone hut between fields. In a second, I have a mad desiring of that hut. That looks like a writer's hut. I can see Dylan Thomas, shirt crumbled with pasty flakes and balancing a couple of Guinnesses, making his way across the rutted field before delicately producing a secret key and entering. After a minute, we would see kindling smoke from its discreet chimney. I am getting distracted.

I take in gravestone names—Henry Fletcher, William Jordan—almost expecting to find a Sally and a Will. I'm about to leave when I notice one finely carved thick stone, all swirls and baroque showboating. It's been erected by a John and Mary Ann Hawkins. They lost three children in one month in June 1832. Elizabeth and John Home, both five years and six months, and little Sophia, just seven months old. There must have been some sickness that just passed through the district; I am somehow resistant to digging up more information about it. Suddenly my eyes are filled with tears at the thought of the little bones underneath the soil and also for the utter heartbreak of John and Mary. I realise that this time my coins are for them. The walk has been leading here. I crouch in the dirt and place silver for each of their heads, and lay some simple prayers over the site.

So a myth line takes me to the grave of a flesh-and-blood family, and my flesh-and-blood experience of living in Berry leads me to the telling of the story. It's a raw affair. That wind has got up again. I look around at the dive-bombing starlings and the church steps where Sally met her true love, and I say goodbye. Minutes later I pass the old red phone box where my father would ring my mother in Berry village on breaks from rehearsing with his band in the local hall. All part of the courting. Only then do I burst out laughing—her name? *Sally*.

Love's forests

This charming little tale contains, maybe unexpectedly, an infusion of themes common to the wider book. Love also reappears.

Sally is insistent that she will marry for love and nothing else. In this regard, she falls in line with the romantic tradition. Although literature had continued the powerful sentiment of *amor*, amongst rural communities court-ing was still much more pragmatic. Through delicate inference we can sense that this story is set in the eighteenth or nineteenth century, although its roots are most likely earlier. There is already a sense of *looking back*—the mother sends her daughter back to *her* mother for uncovering the secrets of the heart. The message is for us to look back. For the soul, nostalgia is not an indulgence but a considered turning things over, a slowing of the pace.

This is clearly not the era of sun gods or of a moor thick with giants and immortal ravens, but a period of history that is preparing to rub up against our own. We are immediately drawn to another walk through a forest to a grandmother's house: Red Riding Hood. We know from our childhood tellings that the forest is a-teeming with fright—in both supernatural and slathering animal presences. It is resolutely *not* the cheery market square of collective certainties. It is oppressive, ghoulish, otherly. The trails between settlements were scenes of both robbery and epiphany, empty saddlebags or revelation, depending on your motivation for travel. For the aspiring cunning man or witch, it was a testing ground for growth and spiritual expertise, but to the working farmer or weaver, it could be a place beyond the edge of reason, unruly and rammed thick with woeful energies.

Red Riding Hood's encounter with wolves could have been very real. The Saxon King Edgar, who reigned from 959 to 975, used to receive a yearly payment in wolf skins from Welsh hunters, from the "walds" themselves—woods that harboured wolves and foxes. The term *forest* was originally a juridical phrase, indicating a designated area outside the castle walls, most likely meaning "outside," from the Latin *foris*. This also clarified the difference between walled but spacious royal gardens that were, on occasion, referred to as *silva*, meaning "wood." To a working-class Englishman, the forests were off limits on pain of all sorts of nastiness.

These noble glades teemed with coney, pheasant, partridge, grouse, hind, hart, buck, doe, and fox. They were in a state of both preservation and pursuit: the peasants were kept out, so woodland creatures enjoyed primacy until the nobles took the saddle and went mad for roving the copses. It was a kind of early conservation act, Robert Pogue Harrison (1992) arguing that these very enclosures could have prolonged the life of extended woodland in an ever more industrial Europe. In this light, William the Conqueror is a kind of rough ecologist. In this way not every wood was a forest—it needed this royal designation—but almost every forest had woods within it. The writer John Manwood (Harrison 1992), who in the Elizabethan era was a gamekeeper of Waltham Forest, gathered and laid out this system of wilderness preservation in what he called the "Forest Law." It was no secret that Manwood hankered after an earlier era, when the law was kept firm with a dread fist for poachers. By his time, the great royal forests were erupting into hiding places and leafy refuge for all variants of wolfshead and bandit. In Manwood's Arcadian reverie, we are back in the time of the *saltus sacrosanctus*, the "sacrosanct wood." Any den of ne'er-do-wells would be viciously plucked from the byres and lonely wains of the deep green. To become an outlaw—a "wolf's-head" (the price of your head was equivalent to that of a wolf)—was to be *civiliter mortuus*, or civilly dead.

It was a banishment that could be undone only by suing for pardon from whoever condemned you in the first place. This would prove difficult if your only hope of survival was staying uncaught and out of sight. And the best place for that was the greenwood.

> What critics of the royal hunting privilege refused to accept, is that an essential part of the king's personhood belonged to the forest. The wilderness beyond the walls of his court belonged every bit to his nature as the civilised world within those same walls. . . . The hunt ritualises and reaffirms the king's ancient nature as civiliser and conqueror of the land. . . . As sovereign of the land, the king overcomes the wilderness because he is the wildest of all by nature (Harrison 1992, 74).

So Harrison implies that the king must be aligned *to* and leader *of* all wildness, and so these royal swathes of greenwood were ritual quadrants of the ancient, magical hunt. The hunt was a nod back to an era before refined manners, four-poster beds, and foreign policy; it was to fill the king's head with hot blood, to remind him that he was a darkling king of the animals.

Without this leafy machismo the worry would be that the king was an effete man entirely of court, and that the land underneath his feet was actually out of his control. So these vigorous charges into the green were a remnant of a pagan cosmology. And this is not to presume that it was just an empty gesture to archaic concerns; a poem from the *Peterborough Chronicle* reports that William the Conqueror "loved the stags as much / as if he were their father." William certainly kept such paternal instincts entirely within the forests, slaughtering, decimating, and terrifying the English inhabitants of his new country for decades to come. It is an irony that the very forests he established became rugged homes for on-the-run nobles who became furious guerrilla bandits and would set the scene for the likes of real-life outlaws Fulk

Fitzwarin and Eustace the Monk, as well as for the move over several centuries into the folk mind of the Robin Hood ballads. The association between woods and a certain rebel English spirit was established for good.

Leaf-bowed morality

This sense of injustice creates a curious dynamic in that rebel spirit—the idea that it represents the true conscience of the English, an essence not seduced entirely by greed. So, true nobility takes a dwelling place in the margins rather than the centre. In this light, the forest represents not the opposition of the steady village but actually a mirror of accountability: of right doing, justice, fairness, equality. While I admit this has rarely been demonstrated by a flesh-and-blood wildwood bandit, it nonetheless is rooted in the dream-consciousness of England, a central tenet. In a dangerous kind of way it can be trusted. There seems to be a regeneration of soul available by taking to the woods. A freshening, a taking stock, a starting anew.

The forest that Sally would have wandered was the remains of a deer park once owned by Henry Pomeroy, of the de La Pomeroy family, installed in the district shortly after the Norman conquest—they were in favour with William. The remains of the castle to this day are haunted by two female spirits (amongst a whole gang)—the White Lady and the Blue Lady. The Blue Lady is a victim of Norman incest and murdered her own baby. She implores wanderers of the woods to come up to the top of the tower she perches on, and when they do, they have a nasty habit of taking a tumble to their deaths. The White Lady is farther down, in the dungeon, a woman called Margaret Pomeroy, imprisoned by her own sister, Eleanor, who was driven mad by her sister's luminescent beauty. Through a thin vertical slash of window in the dungeon wall, it is still possible to peer in from the outside, and several folk I know claim to have seen cold white light emanate from the crack. None of them have peered in.

For some, it is not the castle that spooks but the surrounding forest. Forty-five years ago, as a young boy (after fortifying himself by watching the Small Faces on the TV show *Ready Steady Go*), my father cycled up the lanes from nearby Torbay with some pals, to spend a night in the ruinous keep. They passed the lodge house whose rambling gardens would, three decades later, contain my tent. Deeper and deeper they descended into the fanged expanse of tree and bramble.

Conversation that began bold grew steadily muted. After a decline of about ten minutes, they climbed into the ruins. As they settled in the remains of the kitchen, the cold quickly rose through the soil and ivy-woven walls. Several older boys wandered out into the forest to look for kindling for a small fire. When they returned they were visibly agitated, a-feared. Sensing the weakening spirit in the older boys, young Robert was flooded with anxiety. When the twigs failed to catch light and cook up the boys' burgers, my father and his friend Mark Walton took courage and wandered the immediate forest themselves—hunger temporarily overcoming fear is a theme in the family.

Almost immediately, a sense of something utterly ghastly gripped them both. Not of a specific entity, but of a general atmosphere. The forest was alive, pressured thick with ancient presences. Sensing a frontier they were not prepared to transgress, they sensibly gathered the twigs around them and headed swiftly back to their large-eyed and edgy companions.

Admirably, but sadly without vitals, the small lads made it through the slow hours huddled together in the haunted kitchen, whilst bleak night made merry with their rattled imaginations. Come the first hints of dawn, the frozen band made their way back down Nut Bush Lane to the warmth of their still-awakening family homes. Soon there would be generously cut bacon, farm eggs, mugs of hot tea, thick toast, and marmalade, and the ears of admiring siblings to hear tall tales of the ghostly woods. Such heroes—Arthur himself would have blushed to have been in such company.

So, like my father, I have a personal connection to this story—that little stream at the bottom of Berry Hill? I have had many early morning dips in it—never less than freezing, I tell thee. The lodge house was at the top of a mile-long descent through heavy forest to the ruined castle—the most haunted castle in Europe, they say. A Buddhist Lama tried to exorcise the place years ago and fled the scene, never to return. This gives me tremendous pleasure; we should leave the old ghosts alone to wander the forest and the ruins—it gives the place a little style.

The long married

Waiting for Sally is the grandmother, the elder, the one-with-wit. It is she who evokes this notion of prophetic ground—that the picking of the white pea had information for her, a forewarning. She also brings in the notion of patience and the presence of an even older elder—an ancestor—her dead husband. So, for the grandmother, an issue as deep as one concerning true love involves a spacious questioning, one involving ancestor assistance, a magically evoked yarrow, and the dream world that amalgamates these elements and provides an answer. In this light, the grandmother is acting like a cunning woman.

In modern life we tend to celebrate the beginnings of things, none more so than in love. Sally's emphatic stance is attractive. We see love as a full bloom, an endless seasonal riff between spring and summer; it's all connections, support, giddy leaning in, eye contact, once-in-a-lifetime imaginings. If there is much in the way of autumn's bare trees or the iron ground of winter, then surely love has died, we were mistaken, we must seek out the giddy feeling of newness again. And again. We expect relationship to be *mono*—the unchanging characteristics we societally approve, rather than myth's *poly*—changeable, distant at times, suddenly wildly intense. Love is not just one spring tree but an entire scrubland of elms, muddy rivulets, silent deserts, and ghoulish owls. Because love rarely sustains the dynamic of the earlier, celebrated stage, we are often adrift at this deepening. What's this? Where are the giddy heights? The long married have no glamour; their stories do not litter the tabloids. We prefer to see them as stuck or codependent, as we shuffle wistfully on to the next honey-gorged flower.

So Sally's grandmother, in the light of modernity, is that increasingly rare phenomenon—the long married. What grit is required for this decades-spanning experience? The writer John Welwood (2006) talks about two kinds of love—absolute love and relative love. Absolute love is that which stands beyond human relations but occasionally, fleetingly, shines through. When caught in its radiance we feel accepted, connected, at peace, part of the wider turning of stars and seasons. It's wonderful. Spiritual characters will spend large amounts of their time trying to get tuned up to this, but for the wider world, we often experience it in the early stages of falling in love. So affirming is its presence that we decide that this must be love's only essence. Maybe it has more than one.

The problem is that, if we experience this through the temporary gaze of another human, we have to then realise the frailty of the human heart. Although the outpouring is majestic, it is also finite. We are so littered with defenses and hurts that this absolute acceptance cannot be maintained by a human indefinitely; our very life history will cause this divine light to fluctuate. It is here that we find relative love.

The very openness that love engenders will awaken the ravenous hounds of unfinished business, damage, and general misery that always hunt close to the lover's garden. There will be an equally strong *counter* intention to the intention of a fulfilling love relationship. These hounds sprinkle distortions, age-old hurts, and defense mechanisms into the mix. That one clear blue sky is now dappled with fast-moving clouds. Relative love, as Welwood reminds us, is dependent on time and circumstance. It is changeable, dependent on which gods stand behind us that day, the invisible inner balcony of family members, how much sleep we got the night before. With all this in the mix, the notion of love as a steady, unchanging state is naïve, even laughable.

We are constantly being hurled from delicious oneness back to a relative two-ness, usually without warning. We reach tenderly to the resting lover and are faced by a teeth-snapping ogre.

Welwood points to openness to these moments of the absolute but not an unreal expectancy that is ever available. It almost never is. For every wave of euphoric connection he advises acceptance of the salty crash that will surely follow as *a wider aspect of love*, not as something "outside" the experience or a sign that it has failed in some way.

But this is sounding way to sensible to me. I may be changing my mind. Because I also feel we have become overly suspicious, even skeptical, of romantic love. That's horrible. I'm not having it. Gawain and Mirabai please draw closer, I am your servant. And why? Because such intensities feed a world beyond the desires of the lovers. Handled well, it is an enormous gift to powerful beings that receive it like clear wine. Don't let anyone tell you that it isn't the greatest thing.

I mean, c'mon. Let's own up. We live for it. We really, truly, live for it. Would you really want to live without the call of the nightingale at your window? There are significant wisdoms emerging towards a psychology of love but at a grievous cost to the mythological. And that's no kind of trade, It can be an attempt to pay off the fiery angels, to reduce a great blaze to a simmer. In that reduction, we make small what is holy. Falling in love renders us open to a world in full disclosure, ensures we dance on the tips of the spears of grievous vulnerability, dream big, understand risk as an aching tang in our heart, not just a distant concept.

Love educates, it deepens, it calls us forth. Falling in love is what gives us our stories. It's what calls down the deities to dance with us awhile. Here's the thing. The problem is not the experience; it's that we have forgotten the dance steps to *approach* such an invitation. It is an attempt to make us bigger, not smaller. Trying to deal with its arrival without the mysteries of art and soul can lead to indigestion, due to its sheer derailing power; but we should temper ourselves for its magnificence, not attempt to neuter it. We cannot fully understand love any more than we can the motivations of the gods. We catch glimpses, sure, but the strange gallop of love's arrival is one of the few initiations still left to us. Rather than blunt ourselves to it or suck on the harsh pipe of cynicism, we should treat falling in love like the arrival of a rare, spark-feathered bird. It is metaphysical courtship we should get to know, not a terrified reduction of its power. We need to increase our listening to what this divine entry is trying to call forth in our life. There is a Russian tale of a firebird that every dawn flies low through the forest because it remembers a time when humans used to offer sweet words to it. It flies low to catch just a moment of such gorgeousness in its fine and praiseworthy feathers. As the years go by, its heart aches at the absence of such love speech. Somewhere we remember the same. How many of us are sweeping through lonely glades for just an echo of that old coo-call?

We could apply ourselves to become a sound house of sincere and great language again, to not cut off magic at its hilt; no goddess will come to your aid when you announce angrily to your partner that you both need to "work on your stuff." This is the danger of psychological reduction for fear of romantic love's transformational power. We are not to compartmentalise it but to forge a body robust and deep enough to absorb it. It's that absence that turns us to dust. It's an educational amnesia towards true, maintained deliciousness of heart, rather than the arrival of the love itself. But that education takes time.

Elders know patience. The seasonal wait for the yarrow to grow, the etiquette of both the question and the growing on an ancestor's bones, the reliance on dream as the link place between the murky worlds. Sally, like so many of us, grows impatient with this steady but slow turtle pace and demands evidence that night but then grows confused with the possible result.

However, her trip through the haunted forest to her grandmother's has emboldened some trust in her own intuition. Binding her eyes—an ancient sign of submission to occult revelations—she stands in a doorway between innovation and tradition. Without that earlier journey and grandmotherly advice, would she have had the grounding in the elements of nature, night, and waiting that she displays? She seems to be a good student but also a *bricoleur*—binding the handed-down with the intelligence of the moment, neither blocking the other.

In this, Sally is something inspirational—a bridge woman. Her seemingly tenuous folk tale has surprising depth to it. Willfully spirited, she utilises a whole cosmology to bring to clarity a common concern: Who will be my great love? She reaches out from the village into the liminal forest, gets advice from a wise woman, trusts inner prompts, and learns how to wait. Although the external costume of these stories has changed through this book, the prophetic energies remain close. Out in the green lanes, rutted fields, and hawk-heavy forest, up on the wet-flaked snow hills of the high moor, the ancient earth still has an ear for those who come with questions of love.

The storied tongue

No one had told me that the language that was the real glory of English literature was still being used in the field by unlettered men like these.
THE NOVELIST ADRIAN BELL,
ON THE FARM WORKERS OF THE SUFFOLK COUNTRYSIDE

As a young man, Adrian Bell was taken on for a farm apprenticeship— much the same atmosphere that young Sally would have grown up in. Although having received a public school education, in the eyes of the farmworkers he lacked real knowledge, barely able to handle a hoe. What he did possess were an ear for poetry and an open attitude. One day he had to lead a horse between the rows of young plants, still tender. When he asked for advice, the horseman looked him in the eye and said: "You lead that mare as slowly as ever foot can fall." In the literalness of the image—a direct observation from the horseman's world—Bell also immediately sensed an earthy poetry, in its taut rhythm and true substance. For Bell that was the beginning of a lifetime's admiration and learning from such men. Indeed he says: "I didn't begin my true education until I had the privilege of listening to the powers of expression of Suffolk farm-men who had left school when they were twelve years of age."

The great collector of oral accounts of England's old rural communities, George Ewart Evans (1970) agreed with Bell. He claims that the sweet observation, but also poetry, of the horseman's advice was very typical of many men he met in the field. They rarely spoke in abstract language but let the image lead the talking. He describes how rare it would be to hear a phrase like "early summer"—far more likely "beet-singling time," or autumn would be "sowing the winter corn." He recalls showing some healthy apples to an old woman who replied, "Those apples will keep till apples come again." The rhythm is pronounced, the thinking keeps close to the apple itself but also lends a kind of wistfulness to the wider thought—"till apples come again." The increasing lack of image in much language and a growing montage of abstraction (this is several generations on) saw Evans declaring that English has lost much of its "tactile nature"; it was simply less enjoyable to listen to. He made a clear distinction of the generation born between 1880 and 1890 as the last to generally speak with this deep, descriptive cadence, what I would call a "storied tongue."

A place where a little clarity was lost was when very direct questions were asked. Then the questioned individual used all skill in his or her formidable arsenal to avoid coming down strongly on either side of an argument. This was partially due to a generational buildup of caution around sticking your neck out in a small community. It simply meant vulnerability, and when you were living on the breadline, that is something you could ill afford. This reached amusing proportions when, after a day in the fields, a worker nursing a pint, rather than give an opinion directly, would give it as if describing a previous conversation in which the same subject arose. So you would say "I said" in the past tense, rather than "I think" in the present. This defused the intensity of the opinion somewhat, despite the fact that everyone knew that this other "conversation" was fictitious, because everyone used the same mechanism. So if it caused too much of an adverse reaction, you could always say you had reconsidered since.

These escape clauses also had to do with a certain kind of manners. You didn't want to apply pressure on your neighbours or leave them without the possibility of a graceful retreat. Evans describes the borrowing of a scythe between old friends; this had been going on for decades but the borrower never asked straight, he always offered a verbal "out" for the other by asking: "I suppose you ain't got an old carborundrum, Charlie?" (Carborundrum is a kind of rub for the blade.)

A flat-out error would be met by a gentle "I fare [incline] to think you've made a mistake, Bor." If under intense questioning, the farmhand could resort to either of two standards: "I don't fare to recollect anything about thet," or "Thet were afore ma time." This is very similar etiquette to that of tribal groups I have enjoyed meeting across the Americas. Direct questions are simply seen as a little unsophisticated, a little gauche; everything gets answered, but in a longer, roundabout, and certainly more elegant way.

When the farming system truly changed, around a hundred years ago, the hub of families working in close proximity to one another also started to alter. And when that changes, language changes, aspirations change. My daughter goes to a tiny rural school, only half a dozen lanes away from the ground of this story, a school full of farmers' children. So far I have not heard one Devonian accent, and these are Devon children! Not only is the phrasing identical to that of children all over southern England, the actual accent itself seems to be leaving the mouths of her generation. You'll catch it in a local pub or between two old boys at the greengrocer's, but all now speak a language of American and Australian soap operas. The accent is a kind of generic south English, the north holding on to more regional flavours for now. As is always the case, it has taken only years to dissolve something that took hundreds of years to build. It's not happening; it has happened.

The elegance of old-culture farming language is another example of cadence slipping under the net of official changes within English diction. The unlettered tongue retained all sorts of delicious, concrete, descriptive, ingenious phrases and descriptions—true wealth. As Evans rightly claims: "And a sympathetic, although not sentimental listener, has the feeling that some of the speech of Chaucer, of Spenser, of Shakespeare, or Tussar and of Clare kept wonderfully alive into the twentieth century" (Evans 1970, 168).

In the continuing questions that arise around the revival of storytelling, I cannot stress highly enough my belief in a return to the storied tongue of these earth folk. Of the apples that returned and the winter corn, of the dusk as wine red as the beloved's cheek. This is soul language, rooted in things.

CHAPTER ELEVEN

Wudu-Wasa

A friend of mine claims he saw him once. As a boy. Walking in autumn with his mother. They glanced to the edge of a Dartmoor field and they saw him. A hairy man. Not big like Sasquatch, but crouched up against the dry stone wall. Swift too, he picked himself up in a second and bounded over the stones and into a new-seeded pine forest. It bent my friend's head a little, and his mother didn't want to talk about it. Ever. But it marked him nonetheless. Gave him deep spook. Changed the trajectory of his life, that ten-second beholding of something impossible.

Another mate told me of lovers up near Boggle Hole in Yorkshire. It was Sunday, raining, and they'd driven out to the coast. As they sat in the car staring out at the ocean, they realised they were being watched. They looked up into the steep fields around them and saw, to their left, a naked, hairy man looking down at them. As soon as their eyes locked, he fell to all fours and started to leap down the hill towards them. The being made no pretense at running; he bounded. Like a hound. Like a wolf. Towards the car.

These little stories may give us something of a shiver, but in the north of the country and out on the surrounding islands, they carry infinitely more weight. These are not anecdotal yarns to make children behave; these are stories of young men in the fifties going out to the privy and glimpsing a little, gnomic being squatting in the low branches of a tree, a woman going to the cowshed and a creature made of cobwebs lurching past her for the open door and disappearing. These are firsthand accounts. Island people are pretty sober in their recounting. The ancestor that actually began our book, the Moo Roa Man—Mr. Symes—worried the villagers of Dartmoor as being a descendent of such original peoples.

So this little chapter gives some space and attention to a collection of characters that have hung round the edges of not just Dartmoor but wider English villages for a goodly stretch of time: the *wodwo*, the *wudu-wasa*, the *wild man and woman*.

The wonderful (and historic) Henry Hastings was one of the last to be—nobly or ignobly—compared to these beings. Throughout this book we see how communities struggle or thrive with the notion of otherness—and here we receive an image of it in its fullness. Tho' not quite a Dartmoor story, more of the wider West Country, Hastings invokes a deep note in our inquiry. And, like Moo Roa Man, he is calling us to sup at his table. To remember something almost everyone wishes you to forget.

❋ ❋ ❋

Only you know where you'll be when it happens. Drifting through a Wednesday counting emails in the office, bent over kale at the allotment, gearing up for the school-run dash through the rain.

Today is different. Today little Jacob, Nessie, and Ruby will wait by the gates. You've gone somewhere else. Something beckoned, called you by your name, bundled you into a large black car. No one looked up from their desk. You don't quite know where you are going, but by God you have to go. Now. You travel some distance, but finally, the car—which is now a carriage—has stopped.

As your feet descend to the earth, the driver mutters that you are a guest of Henry Hastings himself, the great Wudu-Wasa of the West Country of England. Wild man. One of the last. A royal keeper of the forest. You can't help but look around; I mean, he sounds so grand. Are there ornate turrets, crimson carpets, a table crammed with dainties? Servants attending to your every need? Not so much.

A greeting chamber has been carved into the hollow of an oak. And striding towards you is a man dressed entirely in green broadcloth. Squat and muscled, glint in his eye, cheek as red as a spanked arse, he beckons that you enter the heart of the tree with him. It is here he takes your measure.

If the stink of the city is not too much with you, he leads you farther into his maze. Past the stacked woodsheds, fishponds, and deer-thick copses, to his home. The man has a reputation, like a lusty tree spirit or woodland khan; every female for twenty miles has sought him out.

Hastings' great hall seems to have long reneged on the notion of outside and inside. In the high sconces of the walls you behold both falcon and hawk, roosting like emperors. The floor is thick with both their droppings and a scattering of hunting dogs—shuddering with terriers, hounds, spaniels. Peering through the smoke you see the upper end of the room converted into a hanging wall of fox and polecat pelts, two seasons thick.

You hold your courage and advance, encountering litters of kittens pawing for their master's plate, avoiding the long white wand he thrashes in their direction. But friend, by God, you eat. Fresh oysters from Poole, woodcock, hare, and venison—steaming on the plate or groaning tight within pastry. When you try to match him drink to drink, you find yourself sipping beer flavoured with rosemary, or wine strong with gillyflower.

Hastings' great treat is to bellow at his servants: "Bastards and cuckoldry knaves." They know his rhythms, his temperament, and grin broadly. What pleasure to allow full volley to the tongue. If you require further feeding he will shuffle into a smoky corner, where lies a disused pulpit. Reaching into its unconsecrated depths he may produce an apple pie—long baked, plump and sweet, thick crusted. If meat's still pressing he will procure chunks of gammon or even a chine of deep-cured beef.

The one that peers at us curiously over dinner—this Enkidu, this rooster, this Wodwo, lived a full hundred years, as the gentry fell like minnows around him. His hall is a strange Arcadia, the man a lord of misrule. His tapestries candle-flicker like cave paintings. You settle by the fire.

No one has ever told you stories like he tells you stories.

Speech so sweet and broad that starlings nestle in his vowels, the moon craning her elegant neck to catch just a whisper of his antlered language. Your heart hurts, and your throat is tight like when you ran fast as a kid. Please God, don't ever stop your telling, we're done for—all of us—if you do. And then suddenly it is over: you are outside—bundled up and under the stars, awaiting your carriage back to polite society.

The cell phone starts to pulse madly in your pocket; you know you've missed parents' evening for sure. You'll have to Skype the headmaster. But that's not the reason you find yourself biting back tears, blinking in the dark. The oak door is pulled slowly shut on the scene: the pipe smoke, yipping dogs, larders of ale, tables thick with hawk's hoods, fishing poles, dice, and cards.

As the ale claims residence to your tongue, as your belly groans with beef, you stand in the dark and you wonder:

Which of us is really the richer?

And how has this tragedy come about?

❉ ❉ ❉

In the medieval era, we find literary accounts of hairy men and women, often tremendously strong, with animal and elemental attributes—as cunning as a fox, fierce as a bear, swift as the wind—living outside the village. The women carried pendulous breasts that they slung over their shoulders, and the men had vast beards; both were often entirely covered with hair.

As Hayden White points out (Dudley and Novak 1972, 25), these shaggy characters live surprisingly close to our own world, just over the hill, in a forest, by a deep pool everyone knows but dares not visit. They are not entirely remote. The distant desert or far-off mountain is the place of a more malignant being: the monster.

These wild people are known for a loose, erotic nature; they are not bound by the labour-heavy, chapel-spun existence of the villagers. The wild man and woman are not regarded as being exactly sinful or wicked, rather innocent; their lifestyle is all they have ever known.

Most medieval villagers clung pretty rigidly to what have been called the three securities:

1. Sex (enjoyed and given rein within the sanctity of marriage)
2. Sustenance (you will be provided for within the structures of social, political, and economic institutions)
3. Salvation (through the church)

From the tree line, the wild couple see this and will have none of it. Stability is not high on the hairy one's agenda. One day they feast to excess on a haunch of venison, the next it is watercress and rainwater. There is no call to the plough, no cold pew on a Sunday, no combing of little Jed's tresses. They live just out of earshot of the crowing cockerel, make love in the sun-heavy meadow, crawl belly down through the grass to wrestle the musty stag. They are not blessed by the dainty water of the priest; their manners are not pruned for the neighbours. There is no insurance, no afterlife, no restraint—at least no restraint that the villagers can detect. To notch up the outrage still further, they are not even regarded as responsible parents. Legend persists that babies drop from the vulva of the wild women onto the forest floor. If the little one survives, then so be it; if not, so be it.

But they are not barbarians. They are not bringing apocalypse with them; all will not be put to the sword. They are not the three-eyed giant of the terrible desert. They are not quite evil, even to the thin interpretation of the villagers.

The relationship between village and forest is nebulous, with the wild ones as mediators and transgressors. They whisk away the occasional sheep or chicken, can outfox the gamekeeper, and carry off well-fed cherubs into the emerald boughs. Anything unexplained becomes explained by blaming them. To the villagers, everything beyond the tree line is subject to their imaginations. Orgiastic scenes, pagan rituals, the free pillaging of the king's deer—these activities could all be going on just over the hill. And the exhausted washer-woman, on her way home to thin-lipped Elias and his rough hands, wonders just who is the better off. Not something to repeat at chapel, but she wonders.

So we detect in the locality of the wild people, and in their nature imagined by the villagers, a fairly straightforward case of suppression having to have an outlet: if we're all being good subjects then somebody, or *something* near, is doing things we barely admit we might love to do. They're taking a walk on the wild side. All the natural impulses that are being repressed rise like agitated bees and descend onto the frolicking meadows and copses. So the wild men and women from this way are still working within the function of the community. They are not utterly other; they are being good scapegoats.

This is a very simplistic picture of the wild man and woman, ladled heavily with an incomplete Christianity. Around the twelfth century, something very interesting happens: the picture becomes an image—it deepens, develops nuance. Folklore around this time begins to shift emphasis. These seemingly base creatures start to become associated with a certain ethical ground. They start to become *wise*. They come to represent the preservation of animals and a strand of knowledge that can be found only beyond the gatekeeper's gaze. They are seen as connected to seasonal turns and weather patterns, as protecting denizens, genius loki—they are keepers of an earthy magic.

By this time, agricultural advances had begun the slow taming of the vast European forests; the human hand was forging a new shape onto a previously nature-dictated landscape. It could be that this handling diffused the intense fears that many felt about travel into wilderness. It could also be that it coincided with a revival of classical, Aristotelian thought or could be a peasant reaction to heavy-handed evangelising, but from this point onwards the wild couple start to grow in sophistication. Within time they will transmute into the "noble savage," a kind of variant of the Robin Hood theme: there to act as a kind of leafy reminder to civilisation about what we could be losing. So the wild couple become a reminder of Eden rather than licentious. They are before the Fall.

In his essay "The Forms of Wildness" (1972), White makes an important distinction between the word *primitivism* and the word *archaism*:

- *Primitivism*: the raising up of any group as yet unbroken to civilisational discipline.
- *Archaism*: the idealisation of real or legendary remote ancestors.

The latter of the two is the more popular, the more constant. It can appeal to both the conservative and the revolutionary. It is a harking back, a nostalgia, for a time before time, when the world was simply less corrupt. We see this as a constant in both political agendas and the creation of new cults. It pulls on an impulse that stirs us; once upon a time, life wasn't so complicated. In a conservative society archaism can mask revolution as reformation, a reaching back to a golden age rather than a complete kicking over of the feasting table.

The first, primitivism, is more complex. It is similar in its amplification of old-world values, but the idea also persists that this lost world can still be found amongst the detritus of modernity. Primitivism is not about a superior form of human being but an unshackling of ways that have become too unwieldy to carry any longer. In short, we have gone down the wrong road. Nature people, past and present, represent a wisdom that we desperately need. The views of nature within the two conceptualisations are very different: for archaism, think of Dante's *vico*—the terrible, mutable forest, or the "dark wood" of Lucretius. It's all about life feasting on life—claws, steaming entrails, treacherous paths shrouded in mist, lurching shadows. It's a macho scene, and only those adept at conflict will survive. It's heroic, basically. It is viewing wilderness through village eyes, as epic but treacherous.

The primitivist view brings more serenity with it, more of the lovers' garden. It is the move from the rapacious screw in a lighting storm to Provencal poetry read together under a linden tree. As White reminds us, this is the place where the virgin tames the unicorn, where the wild couple step forward as wise teachers, not enemies of culture.

By the time of Hans Sachss *Lament of the Wild Man about the Unfaithful World* (1530), this secondary position is gaining strength. The wild man is occupying the kind of conscience-pricking eco role of the headdressed Native American on a modern-day greeting card. Sach's text encourages a wild learning, that those bogged down by city life would do well to recharge their inner nobility, to take to the green wood, to see the world afresh. The old association with virility is never quite lost, either. From Sachs, it is only fifty years till a true flowering of European primitivism reveals itself in Montaigne's essay "Of Cannibals" (Dudley and Novak 1972). By 1719 some of these notions go viral in Daniel Defoe's *The Surprising Adventures of Robinson Crusoe*—a book that radiates the charm of bucolic existence to a citified England. As this education continues, we still occasionally hear rumours and scurrilous tales of villagers who have wandered "over the hill" to the revels of the shaggy couple.

Reconciliation

For most, the wild couple have never quite been reconciled. If civilisation is elevated from nature, then they are still lecherous, ignorant beast-people; if you draw inspiration from the earth then they are vivid prompts to wholeness, to spontaneity, to true stewarding of the land.

It appears that once we feel settled, we rather enjoy a frisson of wildness. Once wilderness is not quite the threat it once was, roll out the sentiment. But when we are truly buffeted by otherness, there is often a reversion to hostility and suspicion. We don't like change, and a vast element of wildness is change. When the wild is no longer wholly in the hands of the romantic and the forest ranger, when it is treacherous, up close and personal, it's tempting to revert. To tolerate, even embrace, otherness is a sophisticated idea. But it's an idea, despite the upsets and abuse, that has made England the country it is today. We are a good nest of immigrants.

Wilderness is in decline, but the wild is everywhere. How we honour the wild will dictate how we respond to wilderness. This catalogue of liminal culture—from the bardic schools to the dream poem, to the cunning man and wise woman, to the animal call words—is not casually offered. These examples are within these pages because I believe they are clues to this kind of right living. The people involved are prophetic, troubled, rural, opinionated, marginal. Just right for a moment like now, say the storytellers.

CHAPTER TWELVE
Liminal Culture (3)

THE REVOLUTION THAT NEVER HAPPENED

In the beginning of time God made the earth. Not one word was
spoken at the beginning that one branch of mankind should rule
over another, but selfish imaginations did set up one man
to teach and rule over another.
GERRARD WINSTANLEY
(*THE NEW LAW OF RIGHTEOUSNESS*, 1649)

In this final musing on England's liminal edge, we find ourselves swept up with the mystical politics of Gerrard Winstanley, journeying west with the gypsies, on a remote mountain in Snowdonia with two car thieves and locked inside one of the country's most notorious prisons.

It is tempting to view the seventeenth century only from a viewpoint of rapid expansion—the American colonies were being founded; the flag was being vigorously plunged into native soils all over the earth. For such a tiny continent, Europe's delusions of grandeur were swiftly becoming realities of grandeur. But when we turn our gaze to the old turf itself, we find all kinds of trouble brewing.

Groups like the Grindletonians, Fifth Monarchists, Diggers, Levellers, Seekers, Ranters, and Muggletonians embodied a strident cry from the people to disassemble the existing social, economic, political, even religious order of the day. Their arguments had teeth: these were confident, strident men and women willing to put their very lives on the line. This is not so unusual. As Christopher Hill reminds us: "Popular revolt was for many years an essential feature of the English tradition" (1972, 13).

The historian Hill writes about two revolutions in the era. One is the successful establishing of the "sacred rights of property"—power to Parliament and the wealthy, reducing all hindrances to their continued abundance; and second, what he calls "the revolution that never happened." This is the dissenting dream of the Diggers, a dream of communal property, a clear democracy within politics, a sharp examination of religious creed. Some claimed that the church was living far from the ideal of Christ, whilst other radicals claimed indifference to the holy book altogether. Although some of these groups' ideas seem jumbled or obscure, Hill rightly claims that their rebel spirit is unfolding over time: that Digger energy is in the mix of today's socialism, that the Levellers' position gains in clarity as democracy rises in the late nineteenth century.

Sound the trumpets: from the north comes Gerrard Winstanley, from the good parish of Wigan, sloshed clean with holy water in the year 1609. In his late twenties he moved to London and married the daughter of a surgeon—something we can only imagine as a move upwards. He then watched aghast as the English Civil War disrupted, and finally wiped out, his business as an apprentice clothier. Destitute, he took refuge with his father-in-law and moved to Cobham in Surrey, where he initially took up work as a cowherd. Back bent by labour and pockets emptied by war, Winstanley daily wrestled his soul, staring balefully out over the black fields. The poverty he witnessed and, to an extent, endured shook him profoundly, and the constant threat of eviction of the poor by landlords angered him. Something must be done. Had to be done.

He produced a pamphlet entitled *The New Laws of Righteousness*, which was clear in its advocacy of a kind of Christian communism. He drew from Acts 2:44–45: "All who believed were together and had all things in common; they would sell their possessions and goods and distribute the proceeds to all, as any had need." Winstanley fuelled his thinking with a vigorous reading of biblical texts—especially noting the book of Samuel's ambivalence to kingship. The brew became especially heady when he chucked in a large dose of old English radicalism going as far back as Wat Tyler's Peasants' Revolt of 1381. His pen grew hot: "Seeing the common people of England by joynt consent of person and purse have caste out Charles our Norman oppressour, wee have by this victory recovered ourselves from under his Norman yoake." This issue of the "Norman yoake" I have noted for the rise of noblemen involved in greenwood banditry in an earlier chapter. So there is the double rub of society going against the essence of biblical doctrine, and the wealthy sucking on the sour tit of the oppressors. We can practically see the water start to bubble around this man.

Come 1649, really a brief time after his arrival in Cobham, Winstanley had started to put his beliefs into practice. He and his followers started to cultivate common land in four counties—Surrey, Buckinghamshire, Northamptonshire, and Kent. There was an immediate response to his message, due to roughly a century of unauthorised squatting in the forests and wastelands because of land shortage. What Winstanley did was give it *shape*, a certain ecstatic dignity. The ecstatic came from the trances he claimed brought on his musings, the dignity from the biblical undertow to his community message. This is another form of English liminal culture—insights drawn from the rippled edge of consciousness and, as usual, causing trouble within the status quo.

As soon as crops grew, they were distributed without charge, as his message dictated. Not a good example. This kind of generosity always rattles cages, and local landowners got edgy. Only one year later, the colonies were destroyed and all involved endured a beating by hired hard men. Crops were destroyed; houses and tools, too.

Lesser men would have taken the kicking, doffed their caps, and retreated into the tree line. Winstanley got busy. Another fiery pamphlet appeared: *The Laws of Freedom in a Platform* (1652), in which he argues that the right and proper Christian basis of right living is to abolish property and wages altogether:

> If any man or family want corn or other provision, they may go to the storehouses and fetch without money. If they want a horse to ride, go to the common fields in summer, or to the common stables in winter, and receive one from the keepers, and when your journey is performed, bring him where you had him, without money.

Winstanley pushes the Anabaptist view that all institutions are by their very nature corrupt: "Nature tells us that if water stands still long enough it corrupts; whereas running water keeps sweet and is fit for common use." This is just a warm-up for then regaling Oliver Cromwell to fulfill the scriptures and hand the land over to the oppressed. It must have been a heartbreak to witness the toppling of royalty and the next devious agenda be hurriedly put in place. In its day, *The Laws of Freedom* was quite the seller.

What really stuck in Winstanley's craw was the notion of private property (specifically land); it is this that he regarded as the true fall of man. He believed that the Creator made the world as a "common treasury" and that to divide that by hierarchy was actually a satanic enterprise. Wage labour, buying and selling, all reeked of sulphur. Surely this is the greenwood spirit wrought anew?

Certainly, much of the clergy got it in the neck too. He rages:"Yet the clergy tell the poor people to be content with poverty now and heaven hereafter. Why may people not have a comfortable maintenance here and heaven hereafter too. We gave no consent to acknowledge crown and royalist land, our purchased inheritance being sold."

The later part of Winstanley's life is obscured. Someone of his name died in 1676 as a Quaker in London. A quiet fame has grown for him and an admiration, not just for his ideas, but also for his eloquence, his particular style of prose. Many of his beliefs of equality, love for love's sake, and a free medical service, for example, have a very contemporary resonance. His is another kind of Englishness; he is a kind of pragmatic visionary, a lion at table with sheep. Like Robin Hood, this marginal seer is not oppositional to order, not a representative of chaos, but a reminder of an ancient value system, a glimpse of way back, a myth line, a walking cosmology. He embodies a kind of remembering.

People of the roads

If Winstanley represented a strand of otherness to the life of seventeenth-century England, then how much greater is the outrage when your very skin, clothes, even spiritual persuasions seemed so utterly different from the climate of the times?

It was 1505 when a genuinely nomadic group arrived in the shape of "exotically attired Egyptians" (Simpson, quoted in Levinson and Silk 2007). Any brief fascination with the gypsies turned cold when Edward VI ordered all gypsies living in Britain to be rounded up and branded with a V for "vagabond" on their chests and then thrown into slavery for two years. Gypsy children were seized at an Englishman's discretion and put into service to save them from an environment of "rogues and beggars." For a culture that had travelled through Byzantium and Greece ,through the Ukraine and Spain, from Persia and Transylvania, this was a not entirely unfamiliar welcome to a certain type of English temperament.

The gypsies brought plenty of spook with them. The reading of hands, the sallow skin, narrow-headed lurchers, the wagons, the rouged cheek and dark plait, the bare-knuckle etiquette, not to mention "tigress eyes," according to Henry Williamson in his *Life in a Devon Village* (Levison and Silk 2007, 7).

Gypsies soon became the largest migratory group of travellers in the West Country.

They became kings and queens of fairs and revels; Stow, Bampton, and Bridgewater all had fairs that featured the grand tents and wild fiddle tunes of the travelling Roma. For the men, coats were long and black, with plush, brightly coloured waistcoats, velvet knee breeches, and brogues. Come the evening, the women turned the volume up still further, with amber feathers tucked into turbans, white satin dresses, and bare shoulders covered by multi-coloured shawls. Bottles were uncorked, howls thrown at the moon, and the gutsy dancing ached the feet but thrilled the soul.

As long as the gypsies remained travelling exotics, symbols of a kind of freedom that many secretly coveted, then they enjoyed an uneasy peace. Problems would deepen with a kind of quasi settling on the edges of town—due to agricultural depression from the 1880s—which meant it was more efficient to stay put in edgy times. The glamour fades a little when the occasional chicken gets stolen or wallet relieved of its bragging owner. You start to notice the tattered edges on those grand tents. Everyone loves a scapegoat, and who better than those dark-eyed, strange-tongued travellers at the edge of town?

To be gypsy was to watch your myths travel five paces ahead of you. A strong look. Being a gypsy could fill the tent on a Saturday night's dancing, get young women paying over the odds to have their cards read, but it could also have you picking your teeth out of the cobbles or have your children pulled right from your grasp. The open road was like a plump vein to these people, a trail full of nourishing blood, but also a duende vocation carrying sorrow and pride alongside. Maps were not used; rather one was guided by a nomadic homing instinct, looking for the old resting places, *Dannal's Basin* in the Mendips, or *Ember Pond* farther west. To the locals it was hard to make out a pattern to the wandering, but they had their own kind of song lines, their own way of getting where they needed to get to. Much of the movement was seasonal and had to do with hop picking, fruit picking, and on to the horse fairs.

The language is delicious; it's an honour to have it spoken in England or enjoyed on the page:

Wusto-mengresky tem: Wrestler's country, Devonshire
Lil-engresky gav: Book fellows' town, Oxford
Rokrengreskey gav: Talking fellows' town, Norwich
Mi-develskey gav: My God's town, Canterbury

I spent the latter half of my twenties frequently around travelling people. My tent was originally situated near a stopping-off point for travellers coming down from Wales and into England. My experience of the travellers could be as simple as seeing a horse-drawn cart arriving at dusk or waking up to find a vast array of trucks, children, and hastily erected benders filling the lane in the early dawn light. Within hours the music would begin, the relentless thump of techno rather than the lilt of the fiddle, and frequently a kind of chaos that was not edifying. This had nothing to do with "back to the land"; it was a kind of *truck* life, an occasionally nightmarish mirror to the very straight-laced environment of the Cotswolds they saw stretched out in front of them. They kind of suited each other. With each hotheaded police clash, both sides lumbered out for battle, each needing the other in some way. This was not Roma culture, not Irish traveller, but a kind of dilapidated council estate on wheels. That sounds harsh, but anyone who has been in close contact with this element of the travelling community knows the truth of what I'm writing. For every quiet and reasonably sober traveller that came through, these occasional terror hordes were the ones who would amp up the locals, pitch up for battle, and leave a toxic atmosphere that anyone living outdoors would have to weather for years to come.

When a society rejects something, it invites that something to turn ugly. If the concept of people living under canvas or on the road is unacceptable, then myth tells us it will regress—what was once beautifully wild turns savage. This is what I am describing. Any culture worthy of the name positions initiations, fairs, art, and music as conduits between the margins and the centre. This is an old truth. It is a way of handling and being edified by wildness but keeping the kids safe and healthy. It is mediation of the spontaneous, the unexpected, the liminal, back into the place of the village. In a time like this, is it any surprise we get the Viking masses at the Roman gates ready to play out this scene again and again?

It is too easy to label the earlier descriptions of the Roma as nostalgia. It is more than that. It is a recognition. It is a longing. They are beset by just as many issues as the English, but they have become emblematic, mythically tuned to represent a certain kind of liveliness and unshackled freedom.

The gypsies came to this country at an auspicious moment, in part to remind us of something that we were losing. This kind of grotesque mimic that I have just described makes me wonder whether that something has now gone. Gypsies have been a vivid mirror of otherness in this country for over four hundred years, and our resolute failure to engage reasonably with them has helped create this cartoon junkie-on-wheels caricature that this small but noisy set of travellers represent. They're us; we made them. The feral have replaced the wild.

The thirst for initiation

The question of when wildness goes feral has been a seat of much learning for me. And as this brief appraisal of liminal culture emerges finally into the present, we find ourselves at its burning edge: youth.

✿ ✿ ✿

As the kids sloped into the room, their reluctance to be there was tangible. Fidgeting, hoods resolutely up, sniggering, these were just a few of the at-risk youth in my local town. My old wilderness-rites-of-passage mentor David and I were facing down another group of profoundly uninterested teenagers, presenting the possibility of a trip up to Snowdonia for a four-day fast in the mountains. That is a hard sell, believe me, to this group of kids-trying-to-become-adults. They were all to themselves, the language blunt and filled with code. Eyes would look anywhere but directly into yours. For some, David and I were last chance saloon—it was this trip or a swift car ride to a detention centre or jail.

So, we tried. Sage was lit, which briefly interested the drug-savvy crowd; the drum I carried in to accompany the story got a few whistles of mocking interest. David talked about his experience of the poverty on Native American reservations, I told an old Russian story, and together we started to lay out the basic ideas behind a rite of passage in a wild place: that it was quite proper to feel disappointment and rage at the way life knocks us around; and the ancient belief that, without a grounding in nature and story, we were all woefully unprepared for the increasing blind alleys and failure-heavy opportunities that life offered. We held little back; we cracked dirty jokes, made fun of ourselves, challenged them to take this seriously. We just, only just, sustained their interest. The story was met with blank silence. Despite David's hilarious raps about his woeful youth and gentle questions about the walk of their own lives, there was almost no response. It was clear we were a mildly interesting distraction. No afternoon in a confined, domestic space was going to needle out the damage embedded in these kids' guts. No way. We had frequently been approached by local councils keen to see if the wilderness's transformative effects could perhaps be replicated in an afternoon, or a nature walk, or a session like the one we had just had. Our answer was *no*. We would come and work if there truly was the opportunity of the fast for these youth, if it was really on the table. No red tape.

Well, crunch time. The day arrives. Our phones pulse endlessly in our pockets with news of cancellation after cancellation. After several months of preparation, almost all of the group had pulled out by the morning of pickup. Gone on their own walkabout—to the local smack house or disappeared into the tired recesses of Gloucester's estates. Two turned up.

And the two were surprising. Jeff and Paul had not been particularly vocal or seemingly interested in the preparatory sessions, but here they were. One carjacker, one petty thief who had stolen out of that smack house in the early dawn light to meet with us. The eyes were, of course, guarded, hoods up, lots of spitting on the ground. One rucksack between them, loaded predictably with skunk and various drug equipment. No thought of tent, food, socks— they guessed the hippies would sort them out.

The long drive to Snowdonia is always significant. Clouds tumbled in and rain started to spit at the screen of David's Audi as we passed Newtown and turned farther into the lanes of Wales. This thrilled the boys, as you can imagine—gazing, bored, out on deep, forested hills. We just made camp before dusk, helping them erect the tents that we had brought for them. To say that they were out of their comfort zone is understatement.

Below was the mixed-growth forest of Norway spruce, Douglas fir, and several oak groves. Behind them and patterned wonderfully by the scudding clouds were the opening mountains of Snowdonia. The heather twitched now and then with grouse; an estuary led out on our right to the mighty Irish sea, ablaze with dusk light catching its ripples. The air was the freshest I have ever breathed. Even the buzzard seemed giddy on the breeze. The soil fairly bounced beneath our feet and a gentle fog started to roll down the hills into the valley. "Merlin's breath," David would always say. With the fire cooking nicely, we all sat on a farmer's wall and breathed in the air.

"What is this shit?" croaked Jeff, almost under his breath. Neither boy had been anywhere like this, ever. That, they were clear about. Checking out the early evening fog and the very first owl hoots, they were also both clear that they could die here.

We sat in silence for a long time. I had to confiscate the rucksack. I can neither confirm nor deny that the two of them had one final jazz cigarette before
the gear and equipment was handed over. Next morning, both boys claimed
they had never slept so badly, that this was a mistake, that they wanted their
gear back and would steal it if they could.

After three more days of counselling, preparation, and finding their spots,
the two boys-becoming-men set out with their borrowed rucksacks. Into that
Arthurian breath they went, saged from top to toe, laden heavy with prayers
both long and very heartfelt. These two streetwise kids, knocked from pillar
to post every day of their childhoods, drug addicts from ten years old, walked
away from us looking for all the world like broken little children in grown-up
clothes. Both of us wept for them, for their whole story, for every hard hand,
for every abuse that had gradually wiped hope from them. That morning, that
valley looked immense, I tell you. Dew-rimmed grass, sky thick with crows
and gloom; those boys, to use an old expression, were shitting bricks.

In truth, David and I were almost laying bets to see who would be back up
the hill first, and whether before lunchtime. Days pass. No return. We spent
many hours perched on little rocky outcrops far above them, just sensing the
psychic labour going on below. It felt like they were getting worked good.
Those buzzards would sweep by on the wind currents, occasionally there was
a half-heard note or two of fragile singing, and then nothing again. It was as if
the earth had just swallowed them up.

I never heard the valley so silent as when they were out. Watches had been
handed in on leaving, so these lads who spent half their lives working computer games were faced with the endless experience of a summer day outside
of clock time; no junk food—no food, period—within easy walking distance;
and the final challenge, to stay awake on the last night in vigil. Notes had been
written to loved ones explaining why they were doing it, as surely something
was going to die out there on the mountain.

On sunrise on the allotted day, two frail young men, arms supporting
each other, made their way back to us, tottering slightly. Empty belly, guts
stuck to spine, face muddy and tribal, hair almost limed into thick braids,
multicoloured pheasant feathers tucked behind ears. But that's not really what
I remember. It's the eyes that I remember. It's not even a look that was exactly
joyful—it was deeper than that—it was truly, utterly raw. They looked us
straight in the eye, hot tears leaping from both theirs and ours. "What is this
shit?" said Jeff, and we all burst out laughing.

Both men's lives changed profoundly afterwards, as we have witnessed not dozens but, in David's case especially, hundreds of times. Not all aggression left their body, but it did get a great deal more sophisticated. After some months of noting profound change in them, the local council rang us in shock—they had found weaponry under Jeff's bed. Well, knowing his old longing for a gun, we were concerned—had the whole experience imploded? We visited and found a beautifully whittled spear: ornate, polished, intricate—the weapon of a young warrior. When we reminded them of his previous obsessions, they began to realise the level of creativity and straight-up skill that had gone into it. It turned out to be a courting gift. Last I heard, Jeff was talking of becoming a carpenter. And Paul, well skinny Paul, who had crept out of the smack house early one morning to stalk his battered soul, Paul is now a fully paid-up Outward Bound instructor.

The teaching that the two men got was from a different place—the non-human. It had little to do with me and David. We just got them to the hill. True elders waited out there, in the form of mountains and forest. Elders who could absorb every racking sob, accusation, hurt, and shoulder-turning indifference. Elders who, if they were not respected, would most likely kill you. The teaching of freezing rain, the teaching of ground-down prayer in a dark gully, out of your mind with fear, the teaching of helping your buddy up the hill that last moment, when his legs are buckling, the teaching of what it truly, really means to see the sun rise on the final morning.

In the midst of what we villagers imagine is deprivation and some hard suffering, is the return from exile—the calm, gasping, horny, furious, grief-heavy, laughing-like-a-mad-crow part of ourselves that is us as *animal*. We may have some hard yards to sweat off all this sugary disappointment that's so addictive these days, but the reward is, well, clear. Only this creates the ear with which to truly hear the old stories, to whittle beauty from wood, to recognise the cosmos you are. This whole business with youth and initiation will not have a human teaching at its centre. That is important material but comes after the event. *The event is wilderness.*

Into the labyrinth

Years later I find myself working in a maximum security prison, one of England's most well known, proper heavy. I am led down a labyrinth of old tunnels and through gate upon heavy gate. It has a booming echo, like being at a swimming pool. After maybe ten minutes descending, I arrive in a small room. My session has been wildly oversubscribed by the inmates, and swiftly the room is full to bursting. And these aren't kids. These are men in their thirties and forties doing long stretches. Gang members. And some gang members who have not laid eyes on each other for awhile, with good reason.

There are Polish skinheads, Ghanaian street fighters, Triad members, several Londoners from major football firms—serious people. Before too long they have to start filling in behind me, so I find myself encircled. I glance round to note an albino skinhead gazing impassively down at me. Still, I have to turn round and address the wider group. Fifteen minutes into the story I take a break to hear how the men are responding. At some point in the last moments I have closed my eyes—maybe aware of the coming silence and the potential awkwardness of no response. When I open them, the intensity of the men's eyes is overwhelming. Almost instantly the room is filled with opinion: accents, both sharp and broad, filling the room, from Jamaican patois to Russian drawl, all describing the moment in the story that they have found the most compelling, the moment that they have found themselves drawn back to.

The next two hours were some of the most intense of my working life. Condensation was cascading down the walls as we journeyed, together, deeper into the story. Metaphor was appreciated, humour at a minimum; there was a sense of some real heavy lifting being done. For a brief time we travelled on the broad back of that story, got past the thick iron bars and out onto the snow-crisp tundra of image. Deep understanding of this initiatory tale was displayed at every turn; all sorts of nuance was raised by the assembled men.

Finally, exhausted, I talked at length about initiation, about Jeff and Paul and others, and some of the men—so much older now—openly expressed grief that they had never tasted something so sweet. When we witnessed their stories—of gangs, enforcers, crime, addictions—it was easy for them to suddenly detect the desire for a kind of initiation underneath much of it. It was like a snaking cord of electricity rippling around the room. There were the beginnings of a mythic framework for their own lives—the beginning of a refinding of their own story. In the centre of this labyrinth, I suddenly saw potential elders. As it stood, many of those men would never see the outside of the jail again. But they listened; by God, they listened. To stories of two young boys wandering down from the mountain, of a firebird's feathers, of women that live at the edge of the world. That day I saw many storytellers. That day I glimpsed the Moo Roa Man standing by some of them, Winstanley behind others, a coal-eyed gypsy behind a thoughtful Romanian—the place was alive with spirits.

CHAPTER THIRTEEN

Twelfth Night Wassail

The engine of the car is running as we bundle Dulcie into her car seat and wrap her in blankets. The temperature has dipped since twilight, and that heightens our excitement. The reason for this nocturnal trip is to head up onto the moor for the wassailing of a local orchard. This archaic ritual can still be found if you look hard enough. So on this early January night we follow scribbled directions until we draw up to what slightly resembles a rustic car park before the trees begin. As we leave the car, I hear the steady pulse of the bodhran and can see flickering lanterns up ahead—indeed we start to catch the strong whiff of paraffin. What was an imagined group of forty turns out to be over three times that number. Something is afoot.

Lots of chatter, laughter, kids, a growing feeling of wayward but good-natured chaos. I can see mums and dads from Dulcie's school, and children with holly crowns, clutching saucepans they are gleefully bashing. I spot Gus, an old neighbour from Scoriton, grinning by firelight and being an exemplary guide to the massed throng.

Before the gathering sweeps us all entirely, I pull back from the crowds awhile and stand in the dark amongst a small cluster of silver birch trees. The bark is cold and rough against my hands. The trees are like white fingers pushed out from a dark glove of soil. I stand in their palm as I begin this final telling.

TWELFTH NIGHT WASSAIL

Father coaxed the embers with an ash log and gazed ruefully at his son, peering through the window. The winter night was a blue-black cloak, and snow covered the granite soil. Utterly still. Turning from the frozen pane, the boy asked his father if he knew a winter story. The man scratched his dark beard and spoke up.

"Well, my father says, and his father Silas before him, that if you visited the cattle shed at midnight on Christmas Eve, you would see a holy thing.

Those beasts would stand utterly quiet in the shadows and wait. Sure enough, on the chimes of midnight from the church bell, the oxen sunk to their knees in honour of their little Savior King. Every year this happened; it seems hard to remember things like that these days."

With that, father took a slurp of strong tea, ruffled the lad's hair, and wandered out of the room, down to the kitchen. The light from the lantern was low, the air thick with the scent of pine. Well, Christmas Eve was come and gone, it was Twelfth Night tonight, and the walk to the cattle shed would have to wait another year.

The boy tried to sleep, drifting in and out for an hour or two. But before long he found himself peering through another window, dragged from the bed, wrapped in a heavy blanket, hypnotised. Who knows how long he sat there, moon light patterning the rowan trees, the grasses glittering knife-sharp?

We children sit
at this window,
no poverty tonight,
but feasting.

Friend:
Take your place there,
and behold with Blake's eye:

No thistle, but a
small grey man,
who beckons and
tells us to
forget our
lean-pelt-life.

To follow
crooked trails
in snow,

Left by the
vixen of the
hundred battles.

He saw a flash of lantern and the creak of the kitchen door opening, and a small procession emerging. Father led, his dark mop and broad shoulders still visible in the mottled darkness. Behind him a group of fathers and sons. They seemed to be heading to the apple orchard. The boy strained as far as he could to take in the scene.

In the centre of the orchard the group formed a circle. The men joined hands, as if part of a children's game. All laughing stopped, the smokers' hacking ceased. Suddenly, as one, they started to sing. It was a single voice, melodius and deep, like a great river. It was as if the boy had known the words his whole life, and he found tears pricked his eyes.

> Here's to thee, old apple tree,
> Whence you mayst bud, and whenst thou mayst blow,
> And whence thou mayst bear apples enough,
> Hats full, caps full,
> Baskets, bushels, sacks full,
> And my pockets full too, and my pockets full too!

Father produced a heavy jug of cider, and it was passed from mouth to mouth. Fingers gripped the cold handle as it circled. Three times the jug moved round the circle.

As the boy stared down, rapt by the unfolding, it seemed he stepped out of normal time altogether. No clock could measure what happened down there. It seemed that behind the fathers and sons stood others. Fathers beyond fathers. And beyond them all the old ones of Dartmoor. The Chaw Gully Raven watched from the black frozen branches, and bright Brutus too, and a woman in the shadows with a bow and arrow. And it seemed, as the men drank, that their wassail, their singing, was caught by the seeds within future summering apples, breeding life.

The moon stood resolute behind scudding clouds; stars threw out their frost light. When the small orchard was properly glowing with praise, the procession made its way back towards the warmth of the kitchen. As their feet crunched the grass, the boy padded down the stairs and peered through the keyhole. He spied husbands cuddling wives, he heard laughter, and his nose caught the scent of a large roasted chicken being lifted onto an oak table, sizzling in its juices. He saw a fiddle being tuned on his grandmother's lap. Jugs were taken from shelves and filled with farm cider. He hadn't realised how hungry he was till that moment.

Suddenly, as if sensing he was there, the door was flung open and he gazed shyly at the candlelit scene. There were smiles and ruddy cheeks, and the boy was scooped up and passed from lap to lap before resting on his aunt's. A plate of steaming meat and roast potatoes was placed in front of him. The music and laughter of that night would be with him always.

And around this Scoriton farmhouse lay the moor, that bruised land that holds its thinking in starling and trembling foal, its deep quarries of sacred language, that is in turn a sullen thunder and then as delicate as the otter's ripple on calm water. As they feast, it dreams its mighty dreams.

Friend:

The wind-bitten tower
has a candle lit
in every window
for your dark path
through the woods.

Red embers
curl the hearth,
there's bright wine
for your cup,
and fresh hay
for the thousand horses.

❖ ❖ ❖

The reverie of speech is broken by a mighty sound. A horn is bellowed, raspy and insistent, and a group of men step forward. I hurry back to my entranced family. Blacked-out faces, undertaker's hats rimmed with pheasant feathers and shades, some with long silver ponytails. They look like a morris group on loan from a Hell's Angels rally. This suspicion is raised again as they actually light the tips of the heavy wooden staffs they are dancing with. This is not the hanky-waving, ankle-bell-wearing, common-garden-variety morris, but the Grimspound group. They take up some space. The dancing is vigorous, masculine, the supporting music played by both women and men who are also ebony-painted and fierce in costume. Whilst humour is present, there is a sense of something ancient in the dance—less gentile village fete, more cave painting. The dance is to set the scene for the pilgrimage around the orchard.

The Grimspound horde seem utterly authentic—but handed down? Rigidly following some immaculate tradition? Actually, they are a group that want to mix it up a little. To take the essence of the morris form but clothe it in a costume that feels right to them, and to maybe add a note or two to the existing canon. As I watch their shufflings and leaps, absorb the purple sashes and feathered hats, enjoy the leathered pummelling of the drums, I realise I am witnessing something that we have trailed all the way through this book—the English imagination.

By actually breaking rank, using intuition, bringing their own imaginings and general desire for something earthy and a little pagan, they are making the morris a living tradition again, not engaging in a self-conscious reenactment. Some purists would sniff, turn their noses up, but the Grimspound dancers are in step with figures like Iolo Morgannwg. In the *doing* of the thing—the dance, the translation—something unexpected may happen that takes you far nearer to the spirit of the art than you could ever access in the cautious transcript. You may—just may—taste the *awen*, the living energy that stands behind the form. At a certain point caution has to drop away. We would be wise to remind ourselves that these dances or stories have nothing to do with a long time ago but with a certain kind of eternal present. With this in mind, that heretical imagination we have trailed can push open a way into a spring of nonlogical knowledge that ensures survival for that year, that decade, that century of liminal culture. Morgannwg's utterings—realised or fictitious—caused such an upswell of interest in the bards that they eventually refound themselves into something more coherent.

As a family, we take this last walking of the story around the orchard. Each tree is given cider for the roots and sung praise songs to make it blush, and then finally all spirits of bad influence are banished with a general roaring, a bashing of pans from the kids, and a blast from a double-barrelled shotgun into the night sky.

We gather around the youngest tree in the orchard. The chief wassailer—the gun man—all hair, height, and feathers, peers seriously at the jostling throng. He explains that this sapling is the most at risk in the orchard, its roots being shallow and hence prone to gusts of wind. Therefore the roar, the bashing of the pots, and most of all the gun shot, must be ferocious to scatter all denizens of doubt, disease, and general wickedness from its branches.

Amidst the guttural bellow that goes up, the almost frantic cracking and banging of the pots, the big man aims his heavy iron at the black sky and fires. Nothing happens. Whatever is dark in the tree's branches seem to curl with pleasure. He tries again. Nothing. This is very strange. The moment hovers between the energies of death and regeneration—which way will the coin spin? Suddenly our traversing of the rutted orchard seems more than entertainment. We lean in, willing hard for the upwards bellow. For the third time he hefts upwards and aims. Not a sound from anyone. Booom!! Face cracked by a grin, he rapidly reloads and aims two more devastating blasts into the scorched and trilling air.

The next time I look up I swear there are more stars in the sky, that the tree has grown a couple of inches and looks almost jaunty—like it's not planning to go anywhere anytime soon. With libation cider making the tree's roots gleam in the moonlight, we wassailers walk the story of the orchard together till every tree is suitably blessed. After several hours we are by the fire—kids illuminated with toast on sticks, extremely welcome glasses of the orchard's dark cider sloshed into the thirsty glasses of the adults. As I glance around at the lanterned faces, the kids, the bannocked moon, the illumined trees, tipsy vicar, and feathered dancers, suddenly the rebel spirit of England seems magically, wonderfully alive. It can't be YouTubed or downloaded (thank God), but it's out there. In the raw. Learn some strange dance; leap on your haunches through honey-cupped meadows; never be afraid to snuffle.

The quality of that young tree, growing its roots, supported by genial lunatics, blessed by the moon, offers us many clues as to the restoration of place and story in our own lives.

And what of our Scoriton tale? Is there not something in all of us peering out from the window on a Twelfth Night, asking to be told a story? It's a story of framed images—of the father and son, of a peering through the window at the ancient wassailing, of being lifted into the eternal cheer and goodwill of that midnight feast. The longing of the boy for the eerie is accomplished with a supernatural flourish at the window scene, and then that very awe is brought into the robustly village concerns of food, drink, music, and fellowship.

Is the father, the chief wassailer, not like one of those old oral myth-tellers, using the power of sound to barter relationship with the elemental powers of seed, root, and flower? Like the animal call words, the shepherds of the old speech, the bard in the blackened chamber gripping tight to his talking-rock, there is a world of arcane sympathies that are not entirely diminished. When we are so quick to damn animism right here in England, we lose sight of something unutterably important. It is easier to order some three-volume set of a distant culture's mythology than to entertain the oblique notion that a living mythos could be slipping like a pike through reeds under our very noses. To entertain that reality would require more personal work, more visioning, more buffeting by hard weather.

All through this book we have explored the shifting frontiers of what local could actually look like, even negotiated the arrival of a story from across the waters. We've seen that the figure of the nomad is crucial to the local, and that a degree of porosity is vital to any real culture. We've seen that some stories stay put, and some wander. Just like people. How can some be claimed by a place almost instantly on arrival, whereas others abide for generations with nary a drop of relationship? The difference is beholding—that the mythos of a land is a constant unfolding, not a hysteria for origination. Get underneath that endeavour and we witness activism aligned with beauty, a radical, robust, diligent stand in the detritus of our lives. Of course we're outgunned. But outnumbered? Not when you call in the myth world, not when you call to ancestors deserving of the name, not when you weft your life to the thinking of a hare or the open-shouldered stance of a midwinter beech. Make a stand for something small, specific, and precious. Do it today. Amen and let it be so.

In the end, we are all children now; we are all perched at a window, wondering at this great scene of the wassail. It is less about how we choose to craft a book, poem, or ritual about the wild and more about how the wild chooses to craft *us*. Without that submission to mightier powers, we hold the mythic but never the myth. We have a narrative but never a story.

So I wave the brandy of language in your direction. It's not the one big idea that will save us, no toxic hysteria of conquest or racial purity, not the New Age, but a tough, edifying return to bush soul. Then maybe we will come out of exile—get our last-minute, secretly longed for, long lost invitation to the great wedding; get scooped up into the warm laps of our wider, feathered, sleek-tailed, whiskered, hoofed and furry, scaled, and ancient horde; and maybe, just maybe, feel a glimpse of what could be called home. Dare to be a cultural historian of true things.

The land can smell if you're on the grab or not. It's that simple. If you can learn to bend your head, then anything is possible. Let the stories elegantly break you.

Get dreamt.

Epilogue

The car shuffles up the back lanes and onto the open moor. It's yet another fiercely cold day, with the touch of sleet on my cheek. I stride over flattened bracken and follow the sound of running water. Charcoal clouds billow from the far distant coast—for a moment I can see for miles, and then I am suddenly enveloped by the wintering wood. A red fleck of holly berry breaks up the mossy kingdom. I stop for a moment by the stream—deep enough now to bathe in—and gaze into its swirl of gray-gold foam galloping down from the high moor.

I look over the waters, and there it is. The shrine. Discreet, properly weathered, but there. It's in the old style: ancient timber forged like a lodge for a badger; glistening rocks guard the fire pit. I know this book is almost finished, so it's time for thanks—for the ten years that have held the writing of this trilogy. Within minutes of my speaking, that low sound comes from the beech trees, the ghost sound I first heard as a child, tucked behind the estate I grew up in. It's a lovely thing.

I produce my gifts. Those antlers, found so long ago at the beginning of my work, so cherished, so vital, must now be given back. I remember their finding and all the years since. I don't forget. I kneel on the cold January soil, place my coins, say my prayers, and hand them back. I get up and walk through the rain to the car.

They are for someone else to find now.

Appendix

REAVES, TRIBUTARIES, LIBATIONS

This is a succession of Devon folktales and moments from my wanders. They didn't require a chapter, but they have their power.

THE WOODCUTTER

Treeland Dan
was a steady man

you'd like him.

Bison broad,
big fists, gentle with
kids, a solid cut

He'd been working
a little north, an old
forest the other side
of Torrington

People said the
wood was wrong

Forest you went
into and never came
out. Got bent by
a magic sometime
back

Treeland Dan
just boomed out

his easy laugh
If trees
needed felling,
he'd be there

readies you see, the shillings

Sheepskins on the girl's
bed, cider in his belly,
something nice for Ruth
from Bovey market

cash in hand cash is king

He cracked on early
you should have seen him—
glistening by seven, mopping up
by midday

Down they went, old ones all,
crunch groan into the grasses
never hacked down a grove so quick

At his leaving he just picks off
an oak leaf from a felling
and sticks it jaunty-like in his hat

Sometime down the road
he stopped. His kit feels lighter
sure it is he's left an axe back
in the woods

Still, it's early
he turns the green lane
takes the sun on forehead
strolls back to the tree line

It's a different wood now.
Quilted with shadow
chill rank scent
He can't see straight

All church learnin' gone
like a snapped twig

Buckling leg,
felled like timber
like some Geordie ship
hitting the wave

His legs are gone utterly shot
face smeared and cut in the shingle
of a small stream gurgle

There are dreamtime sounds
around him, he remembers
their textures but doesn't know how

He can hear seventy languages
he should not know
and see fast low shadows
moving up and over his body

In the far distance world
outside the woods
he can hear the sound
of a chapel bells

An owl court
croons above
his head

It's late.

His wife places
a candle in the window

That slow night
he will crawl the lanes
haunch the crossroads
buckled like his oaks

Till at dawn
on knuckles
and stumps
the boom laughing man
arrives, ruined against
his cottage door

Reverent now for the hearth fire
and the bolt on the door

His wife nails a horseshoe
above the lintel

❁ ❁ ❁

The Ploughman

It was God's own morning
gulls on the breeze,
white winged
on blue sky

Emrys the Plough
was working the field
back and forth
like a sighing tide

Speaking the names
of each plough horse

gently and with love
A day gets spent
different with that
kind of disposition

In the centre of
the wine-red ridges
was a great boulder
larger than a man

Folks tried to get Emrys
to move it
said there'd be money
in it, a straighter furrow
for the heavy horses

Emrys liked it crooked
and that was that
there was no telling him

Big bloody rock
attaboy.

He'd always heard
sounds from it
under a summering moon
with the corn deliriously high
he'd heard music
other times speech
he couldn't quite place

And this morning,
belly rumbling from
his early start
he heard something
clear:

look out
the ovens hot!
The rock did have
a head of steam on it
and, reckless, as his
horses passed shouted:

bake me a cake then,
if you please!

Another half day's ploughing
it took before the field
was pretty
But Emrys
wouldn't rest

Another half day before
he'd break his fast

As he led his handsomes
off the field's rump,
something
caught his nose

Hot plum cake
nicely browned
settled on the rock
just right for one

Emrys the Plough
wouldn't hear a
word against the
Gentry of the Hill

Not a word.

He'd take to

the cobbles
for them
It was God's own morning
gulls on the breeze,
white winged
on blue sky

❀ ❀ ❀

CROCKERN TOR
Austere god come closer.

I am scrambled up, crunched up, bent up, salt licked by blue-skulled rocks against a north moor wind. At the heart. For the people, the heart of the moor is not the remoteness of Fur Tor, not the grandiose lump of Hay Tor—their hill of speech is Crockern Tor, just off the remote West Dart valley. This is where the tin diggers came for their parliament, to thrash it out, to instigate laws. This is where they roosted for hundreds of years. Devon men huddled in bleak moor—not the flirtations of some pub outside Widdecombe, but proper Baskerville bleak. This is the turf where working people spoke of what mattered: their living, their flourishing, their families.

I've come to give them good cheer, to lay the respects.

But not yet. There're layers to this ritual. Properness. The diggers strut on a God House. Crockern is a shape leaper; things walk clean out of it. All sorts. I have to attend to its layers before I speak to the people of the tin. So, I give first a story. North moor always wants a hard story first, wants you under its boot awhile.

❀ ❀ ❀

OLD CROCKERN

Every sorrowful wind
finds a nest at Crockern Tor

A north man, belly jut,
hands in pockets

surveys the scene, takes
the big views
A little drainage
iron-wheeled machines
some glowing fertiliser
money to be made money to be made

Pencil makes blunt sums
on fluttering scrap of paper

From a small hedge of trees
one starts to move separate itself
is not a tree at this particular moment
but an old time man
a traditional

Tattered red and white scarf,
britchescoat the shade of an olive
a brace of coneys long-ears
rabbits in his bundle

Bow legged thinker
he strolls his wandering
to the bluff scribbler

I be coming
from the wistmans wood sir
and I fell into dreaming
under the scrubby trees
till the trees dreamt me sir

And a man walked out
amongst them

it was Big Fella

Dartmoor

Old Crockern

He is all these rocks

Gray as granite,
eyebrows like sedge,
as deep as a
peat water pool

Tall not bent
No pity in him
None at all

Asked if I know you he did
said he wanted to give you words

Said you'd been witnessed
he's seen you now you marked
like the come-before-ones
that he'd touched
your thinking

That if you so much as
scratch his back with
a ploughshare

he will tear your pockets out
turn your balls to

lumps of coal

He'll show you his other face

Dyer

North man thought this
very funny

waved his pencil
at the old time man
Poacher turned away
with his bundle
back towards the woods
and bilberrys adders oaks
It was getting dark

Funny as it goes
as north man
tried to drain the bogs
it seemed the only
thing got drained
was his pockets

then his head

his heart

Soon he had
no taste
for his task

Woman long gone
and his kids

He is gone now

❊ ❊ ❊

As I tell the story of Crockern I glance up as the wind dips. Huge miles of freezing brown grasses and gray-blue hills. One thing stands out. Across the valley is one solitary, rust-conquered crane.

Maybe this all happened this morning.

For most of the telling I am assailed by wind. The shattering, freezing breath of Crockern. Crockern is great-grandfather of the moor. The big element. He is not a face to barter with, to plead with, to flatter unduly. If he wants you to dance like a monkey then you dance. He is the oldest one. He shows his style by riding a horse made entirely and only of bones. Anything that isn't the bone truth he grinds and cinders and mashes. You get his sacred message to fuck off only once. Then he really gets to work.

But he has a younger aspect. Not exactly sweet either. But even the great Saturn god of the moor wants to get loose occasionally. Cut a little rug. This is Dyer, the raw-gutting antlered god of humming, spasming, vegetative life. A grizzly amok in the estrogen. The one that, when he steps into the glade, leads the people of the caves to paint on their walls and piss a little. He duly honours the seasons, a-roar across the moor with his hounds of Yeth on Midsummer's Eve. Have you ever felt that little death wind in the middle of summer? That your dead uncle is standing alone under white birch in the moonlight? That's Dyer passing. Pushing you further into life.

Here is a story that charms him. The story of the one that got away. I grind beef and splash booze into the granite crevasses and begin speech.

HARE STORY (1)

A new moon in a mist
is worth gold in a kist

Moon woke the old woman
touched her bones, scuttled her up
from her dreams

Moon played a trick. Borrowed the
brightness of her lover,
the Sun

Had the woman filling her baskets
with good things to sell
down at Tavistock market

Down the west Dart valley

Having a start on the day
she took to the small hours
with her horse and goods
over the wet gorse

Hi hi and slow we go
Hi ho and slow we go

Moon kept up her end
as candle, a golden coin,
eradicating voodoo dark

Old woman sees things

A pounding streak
come towards her,
over tussocks
and wet grey slate
A witch moving
A swift paced hare

Jumps up and into her lap
all muscle twitch and wet fur
scent of bracken and smoke

Just time to push hare
down into a basket
and cover with a scarf

as thrum hoof announces

the incredible

the full arriving

the living field of wild

that is Dyer

Dyer:
A-thatch his darkling horse
and thigh deep in the swirling

of his darkling hounds
thrashing his whip
of sewn black tongues

Speaking is bone and boom
shuddering adders in the
glinting grass

Lady have you seen the hare?

An old woman's guile:
her guts broadened by
many years,
many husbands,
speaks up,

chin jutting like a
Spanish dancer

Take the bracken over Standon
towards Hare Tor
the old stronghold
the longhouse
the ale-hut
of those
march mad runners

you could still catch her sir

A nod

The black court shifts
are obsidian arrows
over the brow of Cudlipp Down

Old woman
she ambles off

Hi ho and slow we go
Hi ho and slow we go

Hare emerges from
the baskets
and is a young woman

Young woman
that is a dreaming
of the moors

I am of The Other People
and I will walk back
into the hill

singing I will go

I am fur smoke and moon

singing I will go

I am spring water moving

I gift you:

hens that lay two eggs for one
cows that twofold the milk
a tongue
that can never be bested

Young woman
that is a dreaming
walked into
dawn

walked into
dawn

walked into
dawn

and was gone

Now old woman's life is rich:
fried egg on the plate, cake risen
in the oven, wealth of speech

At the goose fair
the tellers' tent
shakes
with her language

Hi ho and slow we go
Hi ho and slow we go

❈ ❈ ❈

Three splints of antler bone slipped in the gray crevice of Crockern.

Old ones, do you see us here? Old woman is moor goddess, young woman is moor goddess, hare is moor goddess that is not so secretly the moon gliding over wet grass; Dyer is the love of the wild hunt, the erupting rumpus. The sun and the moon love to chase each other across the whole deck of cards.

❈ ❈ ❈

And now a blessing for the people of the tin.

I unravel good cheese, cider—the strong stuff, not the piss they had to drink. I send a blessing to the women of the tent and the peat fires and the smudge-black men they learnt to love. Scuffed people, deep inside themselves, here on their hill of occasional speech.

Tin men were hardly gentry—the gear is pick, shovel, and bucket. A small man's trade, at least for awhile. Before the landed names come, sweeping all before them. Cigar smoke names: *Edgecumbe, Prideaux, Copplestone.*

Step forward, you county darlings—waistcoat titles that roll for jollies into Ashburton twice a year to see their tin get stamped and pay the duty. Stand a round at the Exeter Inn, then back in the carriage.

Their people weren't even in the tavern as the cider passed. They are up in the immense silence of the moor, working the seam. They piss malnourished in the heather; when bread comes it is tough, cheese is hard, beer is thin. Their totem is the worm, or maybe the mole. Those who work for the lion-names of the county hazard the deep pits, whilst the small men content themselves with shallower depths of thirty or forty feet. Small men pump themselves up with titles, bang the iron pot with words: Wheal Fortune; Wheal Prosper; Wheal Lucky; *Wheal*, the old Celtic for "Mine."

Such bold names the moor pirates give their diggings. All they have. At night these rook-black men reach to their women by the peat fire. Time rambling their white hills is all the bounty they'll gain in this bent-back life. Some are nostalgic for old ways, when the tin was gathered by way of water, not the deep holes. Fast water would be passed over the tin gravel, separating it from the quartz and the feldspar. At least you could see the turn of day that way and not go banging on the door of the God house by digging too deep. It's grave work, digging that deep.

But these men had their powers. The Stannery Parliament with their intricate laws had some consequence to them. Here on Crockery Tor they held meet, here at the centre of the four quadrants: Ashburton, Chagford, Tavistock, and Plympton. Here in the unfurling winds they would have at it: petitions, penalties, registering mines, and setting laws.

So to the people of the wheals I end my praise. For the ecstatic ordinariness of it all. I throw money for the wealth that wasn't found. As I weave down through silvery rocks, keen to get back to the valleys shelter, Crockern speaks:

Tell them they dug enough.

THE BELLS
Ringer's Rules

IN THE BELFRY OF DREWSTREIGNTON CHURCH

Rule 1.
Whoever in this place shall swear,
Sixpence he shall pay therefore.

Rule 2.
He that rings in his hat,
Threepence he shall pay for that.

Rule 3.
He who overturns a bell be sure,
Threepence he shall pay therefore.

Rule 4.
Who leaves his rope under feet,
Threepence he shall pay for it.

Rule 5.
A good ringer and a true heart,
will never refuse to stand a quart.

The bells

To ring clear the land of spirits, they say. To extract ghoul from swamp, faerie from oak, to hoick the small brown people from under the hedges and up into that heavenly light. The bells as a four-square map, a grid of holy intent squashing the One over the many. But what if the ground was already holy? What if its tussocks and byres, beech and blackthorns already glittered with soulful power?

I say the bells *are* a spirit. I've been here long enough now that they've passed the audition. Their melodious clunks send news of births and deaths and marriages out across wintering fields and lively streams. Get village gossip into the badger's ear, up on that crust of oak above Manaton. I think the code is cracked by now. The swift charms the notes and the notes charm the swift. Crows budge their nests up in the graveyard to get an earful. I say the bells have gone rogue. The bells are allies to the land now. They're amongst us.

If the bells were about clearing, there'd be no moisture left in the bogs and no old women at the edge of the village, and you can be sure we've got plenty of both. Moors would be unthinkable without water; our moistness is our genius.

HARE STORY (2)

There is a hut with
an old woman and
her grandson Robin

Robin, an old
English magic name
hedgerow rustle, greenwood broad
flush of colour on snow
just when we need it

Grandmother

Rough knuckled from
digging her patch
between the reaves—more
bog and stone then soil

But she has the wyrd gift—
can turn her feet to paws,
fur backed, she can
become
a hare

Just like that

Just like her mother could

And witchiness runs with canniness

Sends the boy to the squire
with news of a hare
in his Longacre fields,

She knows he'll pay well
for that

And he does—
Six silver coins through the air

The old woman commits to changing,
takes to the fields, is a fetish for
the slobbering dogs

The grunt of man with a
saddle-bashed groin
the high whinge of the hounds
the sleek sweat bead of a horse too long in stable

Hare runs a thin moon crest
round the field then darts
under hedge and back
to the cottage

easy easy easy

At table the squire
is distracted, too much
black beer that evening,
when he mounts his wife
he sees a hare over grass
under moonlight

Needs no persuasions when the
boy brings news again

Six silver coins
Again the merry dance
and the sudden turn
into the invisible

Again and again she
slips away, and always
at the same moment

That boy has a jangling purse
now, has been seen buying
geese at the fair.

The squire dislikes that
kind of thing—a plump native

Final time boy arrives
this time they are waiting
the dogs, more men, a parson

They are swifter, and they've seen
the turn of these cards before
expect the sudden turn of the
animal

So they dog her back
to the cottage, keep step
she nips
through a hole on the kitchen wall
but is seen, as are heard the shrieks of
the boy

Run granny run

The last line is broken
a sweaty surge through the doors
hound, hunter, holy man
and up the stairs till the door is booted
A women in nightdress, combing
the sins of a culture out of her
thin
grey
hair
with a shard of whalebone

Like Sedna of the far north
But there is the truth of the thing.
A pitted range of snapping dog bites
on her shins and ankle

Consequence rains down

The parson girds himself
for a devil's confession

The squire recalls a choice
cell perfect for such a villain

The hounds slobber the timber

Then the bells start.

Across the grey waves of hate

the bells start.

Surroundingbeguiling
enchantingconfirming

Everything calms
slow dust in the sunlight
the parson lowers his cross

Could there still be a path
to the Door of Mercy?

HARE STORY (3)

Moll Stancombe
was a hut woman
from outside Chagford

She had the Hare-Lore
deep in her, and in her changing
she would be a big Puss
sturdy but swift, white gray

The people would
come for the powers
in her hands, how she
could make
a wound
glowthen heal

Made the proper doctor
over in Morton Hampstead
rage it did.

He knew about her leaping
and when he spotted her
in the furze stubble
he set his hounds

Not a chance, it's as if
they are standing still,
sniffing the turf

Made him
look a prize turkey
to the people
to the folk
So he went
the left hand way

Took up with
a witch in Widecombe
who didn't mind
flummoxing a rival

Silver bullet was needed
and under moonlight
not sunlight

The doctor got his
manservant on it
moulded silver
in his forge

Took to the hills
when the moon
was in full swagger

Giles saw Puss
straightaway
eating clover
bold as brass

Do not suffer a witch
to live

Gun blew up
in Giles' hand
took his fist off

Barely made it home alive

Hypocrite

Moll had warmed
his bed more than once
dragged her claws
down his hairy back

Taken his seed
Didn't complain then
did you?

The Widecombe witch
is consulted
this time a sprayed bitch
in pursuit would work

And she will stand by her door
tying knots in the wind
with her speech
to slow Moll's step

A mighty chase
closer than the other times
a bite on rump, but still
the hare's jagged run
lost the bitch

But a trail of blood
to a Chagford hut
is evidence enough
for the Bible thumpers

A wounded woman
left the people
left the hut
left the village
and in her
animal nature
walked right into
the moon

❋ ❋ ❋

And we should speak up for the younger ones too: Mary from Huccaby farm, just up from Hexworthy bridge, I passed you only yesterday. She waits for her Tom Redlake and his midnight stomp over from Postbridge. He's gone the way of the Benji, love. Spirits got him. Taken up at Bellaford Tor. He won't be coming. Consider Seth or Dan, or even Silas the postman—he's kept his powder dry for you.

Awake you pretty maids awake
refreshed from drowsy dream
and haste to the dairy house
for us a dish of cream

If not a dish of yellow cream
then give us kisses three
the woodland bower is white with flower

and green is every tree
The life of man is but a span
he blossoms as a flower
he makes no stay is here today
and vanished in an hour

My song is done, I must be gone
nor make a longer stay
God bless you all, both great and small
and send you gladsome May
TRADITIONAL WEST COUNTRY SONG

White Horse Hill

I'm a mud-spattered, primordial man, half crazed, wonky ankled, amidst 360 degrees of blue bog. I'm surrounded. Colder than a witches tit. Not again. There's a distant dry stone wall—if I can just get there, I'll never leave. I'll never try this again. Change my wandering ways. More ungainly lurches over bubbling black mud, thigh-deep crusts on my jeans. Already several hours of hot walking on me.

I slowly, slowly, slowly get to the confirming ridge of stone. Almost lost a boot, but I did it. From now on the pace is slow and precise, venturing out only a foot from the wall. God knows how I'll renegotiate this later. Finally the sludge rump firms into the slow lift of White Horse Hill. Galloping views of simmering purples and burgundy abound, the hills giving themselves to early winter.

I get to the place where a cairn has been discovered. Up here there is a little less swamp and a kind of snowy frost, as if every blade of grass has a rooster comb of hair or a little ivory flag.

So, here's to you, young woman. To the river hut of mystery that you are, buried here so close to the source of the Dart. Amber beads are the gift today, and just a few words for the crosswinds. May your story stay a secret for as long as you wish it.

They carry her ashes
carefully,
deliberately,
inside a basket.

Wrapped in bear fur,
with flakes of charcoal
from the burning:
of oak and hazel,
and floating strands
from her shroud.

The blue winds of

White Horse Hill
numb the jaws of
these far walkers,

So distant we can
barely see them.

The bairn's dust is
taken to the high hill,
haunt of bleak vastness.

A cairn is prepared,
the old sounds made.

Purple moor grass
stuffed about the bounty,
gathered in the
browning-hills-time.

Spindlewood ear studs,
from such trees that still grow
on the lower slopes, pelt,
a woven belt of nettles.

A necklace that
behooves a sovereign,
with precious amber beads,
from snowy east.

A place so far away
over there they whisper
that each bead is a word,
and a necklace a story.

Unfathomable wealth.

This crucible:
a basket wefted
from the inner bark
of a lime tree—the bast—
threaded with the
hair of cattle,
rendered and soaked
in Dartmoor water.
Innumerable hours
stitching your sorrow
to the Otherworld.

Thanks

To my family and friends, so terribly precious. To Schumacher College for the shepherd's hut—much of this was composed under its bowed tin roof and by its small fire. And thank you, Duncan Passmore, for your agile skill in creating such a thing.

To Stephan Harding's gleaming eye, wayward flamenco, and direct inspiration for the *deep time* rememberings of the introduction, I offer a glass of wine too fine to drink. Warm regards to David Abram. Respect as always to Steve Scholl and White Cloud Press.

To Tony Hoagland swimming across the lake in the dark, for Gavin Blench and the dignity of his art, thank you, always.

And thank you, dear reader by the lamp.

Bibliography

Abram, D. 1997. *The Spell of the Sensuous: Perception and Language in a More-than-Human World*. Vintage Books.

———. 2010. *Becoming Animal: An Earthly Cosmology*. Pantheon Books.

Anthony, D. W. 2007. *The Horse, the Wheel, and Language: How Bronze-Age Riders from the Eurasian Steppes Shaped the Modern World*. Princeton University Press.

Bachelard, G. 1958 *The Poetics of Space*. Beacon Press.

Barthes, R. 1972. *Mythologies*. Farrar, Straus and Giroux.

Belloc, H. 1948. *Selected Essays*. London.

Bogin, M. 1980. *The Women Troubadours*. W. W. Norton.

Bourriaud, Nicholas. 2009. *Manifesto of Altermodern*, Tate Britain Exhibition, Catalog.

Bringhurst, R. 2008. *Everywhere Being is Dancing: Twenty Pieces of Thinking*. Counterpoint Press.

Burton, R. 1621. *The Anatomy of Melancholy*. NYRB Classics.

Davis, O. 2003. *Popular Magic: Cunning Folk in English History*. Hambledon Continuum.

Deardorff, D. 2004. *The Other Within: The Genius of Deformity in Myth, Culture and Psyche*. North Atlantic Books.

Doty, W. G. 1986. *Mythography: The Study of Myths and Rituals*. University of Alabama Press.

Dudley, E., and M. E. Novak. 1972. *The Wild Man Within: An Image in Western Thought from the Renaissance to Romanticism*. University of Pittsburgh Press.

Dundes, A. 1984. *Sacred Narratives: Readings in the Theory of Myth*. University of California Press.

Eliade, M. 1963. *Myth and Reality*. Waveland Press.

Evans, G. E. 1966. *The Pattern Under the Plough*. Faber.

———. 1970. *Where Beards Wag All: The Relevance of the Oral Tradition*. Faber.

Evans, G. E., and D. Thomson. 1972. *The Leaping Hare*. Faber.

Falassi, A. 1980. *Folklore by the Fireside: Text and Context of the Tuscan Veglia*. University of Texas Press.

Foucault, M. 1988. *Madness and Civilization*. Vintage.

Fox, A., and D. Woolf. 2002. *The Spoken Word: Oral Culture in Britain, 1500–1850*. Manchester University Press.

Graves, R. 1948. *The White Goddess*. Farrar, Straus, and Giroux.

Griffiths, J. 2013. *Kith: The Riddle of the Childscape*. Penguin.

Harding, S. 2006. *Animate Earth: Science, Intuition and Gaia*. Green Books.

Harrison, R. P. 1992. *Forests: The Shadow of Civilization*. University of Chicago Press.

Havelock, E. A. 1986. *The Muse Learns to Write*. Yale University Press.

Heinrich, B. 1999. *Mind of the Raven: Investigations and Adventures with Wolf-Birds*. Harper Collins.

Hill, C. 1991. *The World Turned Upside Down*. Penguin Books.

Hiller, S. 1991. *The Myth of Primitivism: Perspectives on Art*. Rutledge.

Hillman, J. 1989. *A Blue Fire*. Harper Perennial.

Hughes, T. 1992. *Shakespeare and the Goddess of Complete Being*. Faber.

———. 1994. *Winter Pollen: Occasional Prose*. Faber.

Hyde, L. 2010. *Common as Air: Revolution, Art, and Ownership*. Farrar, Straus and Giroux.

Johnson, Samuel. 1755. *Dictionary*.

Illich, I. 1993. *In the Vineyard of the Text: A Commentary to Hugh's Didascalion*. University of Chicago Press.

Kingsnorth, P. 2008. *Real England: The Battle against the Bland*. Portobello Books.

Kingsnorth, P., and D. Hine. 2010. *Dark Mountain: Issue 1*. Dark Mountain Project.

———. 2011. *Dark Mountain: Issue 2*. Dark Mountain Project.

Levison, M., and A. Silk. 2007. *Dreams of the Road: Gypsy Life in the West Country*. Birlinn.

Levi-Strauss, C. 1955. *Tristes Tropiques*. Librairie Plon.

Lewis, C. S. 1964. *The Discarded Image: An Introduction to Medieval and Renaissance Literature*. Cambridge University Press.

Lewis, Franklin. 2000. *Rumi: Past and Present, East and West – The Life, Teaching and Poetry of Jalal al-Din Rumi*. OneWorld.

Littleton, C., and L. A. Malcor. 2000. *From Scythia to Camelot*. Routledge.

Marten, C. 1973. *The Devonshire Dialect*. Peninsula Press.

McCall, A. 2004. *The Medieval Underworld*. Book Club Associates.

McWhorter, J. 2008. *Our Magnificent Bastard Tongue*. Gotham Books.

Monbiot, G. 2005. "Gods of the Soil." Article in *The Guardian*, March 22.

Monmouth, G. 1973. *The History of the Kings of Britain*. Penguin.

Napier, A. D. 1986. *Masks, Transformation, and Paradox*. University of California Press.

Niles, J. D. 1999. *Homo Narrans: The Poetics and Anthropology of Oral Literature*. University of Pennsylvania Press.

Oelschlager, M. 1991. *The Idea of Wilderness*. Yale University Press.

Ong, W. J. 1982. *Orality and Literacy*. Routledge.

Rilke, R. M. 1934. *Choix de Lettres*. Stock.

Sager, K. 1994. *The Challenge of Ted Hughes*. Palgrave Press.

———. 2009. *Ted Hughes and Nature: Terror and Exultation*. Fastprint Publishing.

Shaw, M. 2011. *A Branch from the Lightning Tree: Ecstatic Myth and the Grace in Wildness*. White Cloud Press.

———. 2014. *Snowy Tower: Parzival and the Wet, Black Branch of Language*. White Cloud Press.

Skea, A. 1994. *Ted Hughes: The Poetic Quest*. New England Press.

Snyder, G. 1990. *The Practice of the Wild*. North Point Press.

Somé, M. S. 1995. *Of Water and the Spirit*. Arkana.

Spearing, A. C. 1976. *Medieval Dream-Poetry*. Cambridge University Press.

Stang, C. 2009. *A Walk to the River in Amazonia: Ordinary Reality for the Mehinaku Indians*. Berghahn Books.

Thomas, D. 1939. *Animal Call Words*. W. Spurrell.

Thomas, K. 1971. *Religion and the Decline of Magic*. Penguin Books.

Thoreau, H. D. 1992. *Walden and Resistance to Civil Government*. W. W. Norton.

Wehr, D. S. 1998. *Jung and Feminism*. Routledge.

Welwood, J. 2006. *Perfect Love, Imperfect Relationships*. Trumpeter.

Williams, J. 2015. *The Barddas*. Self published.

Winstanley, G. 1649. *The New Law of Righteousness*. Pamphlet.

Wood, R. 1767. *An Essay on the Original Genius and Writings of Homer*. London.

About the Author

Dr. Martin Shaw is widely regarded as one of the most gifted teachers of myth of his generation. Shaw lived in a black tent for four years on a succession of English hill sides exploring small remaining pockets of wilderness. He is the author of the Mythteller trilogy: *A Branch From The Lightning Tree*, *Snowy Tower*, and *Scatterlings*. A fellow of Schumacher College, Shaw has taught leadership on Desmond Tutu's programme at Templeton College Oxford, and founded and led the Oral Tradition course at Stanford University. Coleman Barks describes his work as "so very beautiful. A new animal. What will it do next?"

For more on his work visit:
www.drmartinshaw.com
www.schoolofmyth.com